Teaching Sports Economics and Using Sports to Teach Economics

ELGAR GUIDES TO TEACHING

The Elgar Guides to Teaching series provides a variety of resources for instructors looking for new ways to engage students. Each volume provides a unique set of materials and insights that will help both new and seasoned teachers expand their toolbox in order to teach more effectively. Titles include selections of methods, exercises, games and teaching philosophies suitable for the particular subject featured. Each volume is authored or edited by a seasoned professor. Edited volumes comprise contributions from both established instructors and newer faculty who offer fresh takes on their fields of study.

Titles in the series include:

Teaching Sports Economics and Using Sports to Teach Economics

Edited by

Victor A. Matheson

Professor of Economics, Department of Economics and Accounting, College of the Holy Cross, USA

Aju J. Fenn

Professor of Economics, Economics and Business Department, Colorado College, USA

ELGAR GUIDES TO TEACHING

 Edward Elgar
PUBLISHING

Cheltenham, UK • Northampton, MA, USA

Published by
Edward Elgar Publishing Limited
The Lypiatts
15 Lansdown Road
Cheltenham
Glos GL50 2JA
UK

Edward Elgar Publishing, Inc.
William Pratt House
9 Dewey Court
Northampton
Massachusetts 01060
USA

Paperback edition 2022

A catalogue record for this book
is available from the British Library

Library of Congress Control Number: 2022931716

This book is available electronically in the **Elgar**online
Economics subject collection
http://dx.doi.org/10.4337/9781800884182

ISBN 978 1 80088 417 5 (cased)
ISBN 978 1 80088 418 2 (eBook)
ISBN 978 1 0353 0817 0 (paperback)

Printed and bound by CPI Group (UK) Ltd, Croydon, CR0 4YY

This book is dedicated to all of the great teachers we have had in our lives who have inspired us to improve our teaching, including Joyce Hart, Gary McCourt, Stan Jozwiak, Gail Matheson, Rebecca Judge, Tony Becker, John Maakestad, Vi Haertling, Ed Foster, Rob Baade, P.C. Pathrose, George Galster, Barb Burnell, Fran Antonovitz, John Schroeter and all of our colleagues at the College of the Holy Cross, Colorado College, and the North American Association of Sports Economists.

Victor A. Matheson and Aju J. Fenn

Contents

Tables

Contributors

Abdullah Al-Bahrani, University of Northern Kentucky

David Berri, Southern Utah University

Stacey Brook, DePaul University

Amber Brown, University of Wyoming

Joshua Congdon-Hohman, College of the Holy Cross

Aju J. Fenn, Colorado College

Rodney Fort, University of Michigan

Jill S. Harris, United States Air Force Academy

Brad R. Humphreys, West Virginia University

Victor A. Matheson, College of the Holy Cross

Darshak Patel, University of Kentucky

Jane E. Ruseski, West Virginia University

Allen R. Sanderson, University of Chicago

John J. Siegfried, Vanderbilt University

Peter von Allmen, Skidmore College

Dustin White, University of Nebraska Omaha

Jadrian Wooten, The Pennsylvania State University

Introduction to *Teaching Sports Economics and Using Sports to Teach Economics*

Victor A. Matheson and Aju J. Fenn

One of the rewards of teaching well is to witness those "a-ha!" moments when students grasp a concept they have been struggling with. This book is a collection of teaching techniques that generate such moments. As economists we live with the stereotype among students, of economics being a dull and boring discipline. We have all had moments when we have bored our students to tears with "chalk and talk". The teaching methods outlined in the following chapters present interesting ways to engage one's students and to get them excited about Sports Economics, and Economics in general. These teaching methods may be easily adapted to most economics classes.

The pedagogy in this book covers a wide array of techniques. Chapters cover topics such as sports examples of principles of economic concepts, data driven exercises, discrimination, gender bias in sports economics, and film and case study based approaches to teaching sports economics. There is a chapter on field trip and guest speaker based classes, and another one on supervising undergraduate student research. The chapters are independent so instructors may pick whichever method they are interested in. Personally, we have had a lot of new ideas for teaching after reviewing the chapters.

In Chapter 1, John Siegfried and Allen Sanderson provide an overview of examples from sports that have been used to explain or illustrate principles of economics concepts, such as relative prices, marginal analysis, demand, surplus, efficiency, introductory game theory strategy, monopoly, monopsony, and cartels. It also includes a discussion of the role of government regarding public funds used to finance sports stadiums. The chapter concludes with a grab bag of economics concepts such as Opportunity Costs, Economic Profits, Comparative Advantage, Pareto Optimality, the backward bending labor supply curve and adverse selection, and the winner's curse. There is also a brief section on sports examples that relate to Behavioral Economics. Instructors will find plenty of food for thought in this chapter.

Chapter 2 fills a vital gap in the undergraduate research process. Peter von Allmen explains how one should go about educating students to read applied peer-reviewed journal articles and to understand how theory translates into testable hypotheses. The chapter presents a selection of sports economics journal articles that are used to reach this goal. The best time to teach students how to read about theory and testable hypotheses is when they are learning theory, rather than during a senior seminar, after they have taken their elective courses. The techniques and detailed assignments presented in this chapter may be easily extended to courses beyond sports economics to educate students on how to read the literature. This is a must read chapter for any undergraduate program with a thesis or capstone seminar.

In Chapter 3, Abdullah Al-Bahrani and Darshak Patel explain how to use Season 4 of the ESPN documentary series, *30 for 30* IX, to highlight economic principles. They cover concepts such as the production possibilities frontier, markets, preferences opportunity costs, the principal agent problem and much more. This chapter also contains references to previous work that covers earlier seasons of the *30 for 30* series.

In Chapter 4, Jill Harris shows how students may use sports economics data to study Gary Becker's concept of taste-based discrimination and Kenneth Arrow's concept of statistical discrimination. She offers four different lessons to make these connections. These include calculating Becker's discrimination coefficient for pitchers Satchel Paige vs Lefty Grove, using the value of a pitching win and earnings per game. Another exercise details how students may use NBA or WNBA statistics to study the hypothesized relationship between height and wins produced. A third exercise details how econometrics students can investigate the earnings gap between male and female elite swimmers. She also presents a useful lesson on interpreting regression results using an own-race bias study from the WNBA.

Of course, teaching isn't just about what goes on in the classroom. Teaching is also very much a part of mentoring relationships related to research. Sport-related research projects are common in undergraduate settings due to the availability of data and student interest in sports topics, and sport-related research is increasingly common at the graduate level as well. In Chapter 5, Brad Humphreys and Jane Ruseski provide suggestions about how to maximize the chance of successful research projects involving sports-related topics, focusing on creating clearly structured goals and intermediate steps along the way to a final product.

Chapter 6 written by Aju Fenn discusses the use of field trips and guest speakers to teach Sports Economics. He discusses the process of finding appropriate field trip venues and guest speakers and circumventing budget and time constraints. The chapter also explains how to prepare speakers and students to get the most out of the experience. He also discusses the logistics of setting up and executing a successful day trip to an offsite venue.

Victor Matheson explores how to incorporate written court rulings about sports into a sports economics class. Legal rulings, such as the one granting baseball an exemption to antitrust laws, have had a significant impact on the development of professional sports in the US, and these rulings often show how economics is used (or sometimes not used) in the creation of public policy. Delving into legal cases can also sharpen students' critical reading skills, and they also provide a source of supplemental readings that do not require students to have a background in statistics or quantitative analysis. Chapter 7 also includes an appendix of court cases that may be of interest to teachers of sports-related courses.

David Berri discusses the history of discrimination against women both in sports and in sports economics. His narrative in Chapter 8 is an eye opener for men who remain blissfully ignorant of how women have been treated as fans and as athletes. Indeed, the title of the chapter says it all – you aren't teaching sports economics if women are not part of your story. This chapter is a must read for every sports economics instructor.

In Chapter 9, Jadrian Wooten discusses productive ways to incorporate media into the sports economics classroom. He covers the use of television shows, documentaries, podcasts and news stories. He covers a variety of active learning techniques, such as using media to introduce a concept or generate discussion, recall a concept through a clip and a related poll question, problem sets, quizzes that ask students to summarize the story and the underlying economic concepts and writing op eds.

In Chapter 10, Victor Matheson explains the use of the Jigsaw Reading as it pertains to reading peer-reviewed journal articles. This chapter may be used to enhance the effectiveness of reading peer-reviewed work covered by Peter von Allmen in Chapter 2. Matheson describes the nuts and bolts of having students read, summarize, and present the findings of a journal article to others in class who have not read that article. The details laid out maximize student engagement, accountability, and retention of the material.

Chapter 11 is also written by Victor Matheson. Here he outlines the details of a simple classroom experiment that illustrates the concept of starting point bias. The data generated in class by the experiment demonstrate vividly to students that starting point bias does exist under certain conditions. He does this in the context of major league baseball. Victor specifically discusses the case of players that are eligible to negotiate with their teams in years 3 through 6 of their rookie contracts. He explains how final offer arbitration is able to prevent the strategic use of starting point bias that is prevalent in regular back and forth negotiations. He also presents empirical evidence from this experiment from his own classes. Instructors may wish to also read chapter 14 which discusses final offer arbitration in greater detail.

In Chapter 12, Joshua Congdon-Hohman and Victor Matheson present a simple in-class data-generating exercise to demonstrate the illustration of "the hot-hand fallacy" in sports. First, students generate made up data of the number of heads and tails counts of a coin flip and record these in a column without a heading. Next, they generate a second anonymous column with data from actual coin flips. The professor, using the principle of "the hot hand fallacy," will then tell each student which of their columns was made up and which one was generated by actual coin flips. This predictive power is enough to get the students' attention and one can then explain the details of "the hot hand fallacy" as laid out in the chapter.

Chapter 13 by Jadrian Wooten describes the use of a game-based online learning platform named Kahoot. This free platform can be used for quizzes used for summative or formative assessment. The format of Kahoot is like that of a trivia game played at a bar, with countdown times and a leader board. This social aspect generates enthusiasm among students, especially in large classes. The rest of the chapter walks users through the basics of setting up a Kahoot account and asking the right types of questions. Questions may be open-ended, simple calculations, recall of a reading etc. The author concludes with a discussion of the limitations of Kahoot.

In Chapter 14, Amber Brown presents a classroom experiment to simulate final offer arbitration in Major League Baseball. Students are assigned roles as owners or players or arbitrators. Each group is given a set of statistics to form their cases. The two sides then argue their cases in front of the student arbitrators. This is a powerful way to engage students as "doing" instead of lecturing helps them to retain the lessons about final offer arbitration. Then the rulings of arbitrators from the class are compared with the actual outcomes of major league baseball arbitration cases. The discussions that follow this in-class experiment highlight the topics of monopsony power, risk preferences, sabermetrics, and the determinants of marginal revenue product in baseball. Instructors may wish to explain why starting point bias explained by Matheson in Chapter 11 is prevented by final offer arbitration.

Chapter 15 maintains the theme of major league baseball. Stacey Brook discusses the details of calculating a batter's productivity in major league baseball. He presents two empirical calculation exercises based on the literature. Activity 1 assumes a working knowledge of basic regression and advanced computational skills in Excel. Activity 2 involves basic Excel computations and may serve as a computational lab to integrate Excel into any introductory or sports economics elective. In Activity 2, students are given basic statistics that they have to plug into an estimated regression equation to calculate the production of individual batters. Activity 1 is more involved and requires students to estimate the team's production function. These two exercises may be used as in-class exercises after the instructor has carefully gone over the detail, or as a take-home assignment.

In Chapter 16, Dustin White and Jadrian Wooten offer a Moneyball-based exercise to calculate the marginal revenue product of a player. Students download basic baseball statistics from given websites, fit trendlines to estimate regression equations and use some simple formulae to calculate the marginal product of a player and the marginal revenue of that product. They then compute marginal revenue product for each given player. They also present an online simulator which allows students to compute marginal revenue products of draft prospects. Chapter 16 and Chapter 15 are both meant for classes where instructors wish to emphasize the computational and quantitative aspects of the discipline.

Rodney Fort presents three in-class activities in Chapter 17. All three of these activities will work in small as well as large classes. If you are an instructor with a large class and wish to vary your presentations from slides or chalk and talk, you may wish to use one or more of these activities. Activity 1 involves the sale of a $5 bill, which serves to demonstrate the ruinous aspects of the college arms race or any escalation game. Activity 2 demonstrates the winner's curse by having students bid on a bag of quarters of unknown total value. Activity 3 is a version of "the hot hand fallacy" presented by Matheson in Chapter 12. Fort casts his activity in the form of a consecutive home run streak, with a nice backstory on hitters hitting a home run if they guess the next pitch correctly. The professor and students flip a coin simultaneously. The students whose outcome matches the professor's get to keep playing until there are none left after several rounds of coin flipping. The data generated from this exercise are used to motivate a discussion on skill versus luck in baseball and are connected to the game by data provided from various websites.

Both of us have taught sports economics (as well as other economics courses) for many years, but after reading these chapters from our colleagues, we both feel that we have a ton of new ideas that we can use in our own classrooms by incorporating the exercises and methods outlined in this book. We thank all of the contributors for their fine submissions, and we sincerely hope that you also find the material useful in your pedagogy of economics and sports economics courses.

PART I

Using sports to teach economics

1. Integrating sports into economics teaching[1]

John J. Siegfried and Allen R. Sanderson

The measurable impact of spectator sports on gross domestic product (GDP) is trivial. In 2018 the average gross revenue of a Major League Baseball (MLB) team was $330 million, just about the same as the Dippin' Dots company, which makes colorful small pellet-like ice cream dots sold primarily at theme parks and seashore kiosks.[2] The revenues of spectator sports as a whole constitute only a trivial 0.14 percent of GDP (Szymanski 2003). Such comparisons, however, fail to capture the important role of sports in American society.

A typical half-hour local evening television newscast contains about three or four minutes of sports news, roughly 20 percent of the substantive broadcast. The usual daily newspaper devotes one of only three or four sections exclusively to sports. Many more people discuss the challenges facing the local college football team with friends and family than ponder the fortunes of the neighborhood grocery store or ice cream dots. There is undoubtedly a lot of interest in sports by Americans in general, and by students in particular. In our opinion, students are more likely to engage in the deeper thinking that leads to retention if they are interested in the subject being discussed.

The advantages to using sports examples to teach college economics go beyond simply attracting students' interest. Economics is often taught by analogy (McCloskey 1990). Students are more likely to gain an understanding of a point if they can connect personal experience to the analogy, and a lot of young Americans have had substantial experience either playing and/or watching sporting events. Thus, students are more likely to grasp a lesson on marginal vs. average revenues or costs from an analogy about how the scoring average of a high school basketball player changes after a terrific game than from a rendition of the effect of an additional passenger on an airline's marginal and average cost per passenger mile.

Periodic changes in sports leagues' rules, like the shift in property rights over the future services of players from team owners to the players themselves when free agency was introduced in the latter decades of the twentieth century, or the use of a designated hitter or an additional referee, produce natural experiments that illustrate economics in action. The frequent occasions for decisions by owners, managers, and players offer a virtual experimental laboratory for analysis (and, some might say, even complete with rats).

The plethora of data available about the individual inputs and outputs of sporting teams (as well as the interest of professional economists in sports) has produced a substantial empirical literature that compares actual behavior to that predicted from economic models. Furthermore, many contemporary examples and data are easily accessible for classroom use because of the intense coverage of the "business of sports" by newspapers and magazines.

Both of us have regularly taught principles of economics courses and a specialized undergraduate course on the economics of sports. In this chapter, we relate some of the examples from sports that we use to illustrate important economics principles and some of the lessons we have learned from these experiences. We are certainly not the first to think of using sports as a vehicle to teach economics (Bruggink 1993; Merz 1996); there are now scores of specialized courses on the economics of sports being taught in America's colleges and universities, and almost all introductory economics textbooks use sports to illustrate some basic principles. The examples that follow vary in applicability and level of analysis from the introductory course to intermediate theory and applied field courses, but all should be within the grasp of motivated undergraduate students.

PRINCIPLES OF ECONOMICS IN SPORTS

Relative Prices

Press reports regularly claim that baseball ticket prices have soared beyond the reach of average fans, suggesting that it now costs a family of four well over $200 to attend a typical Major League Baseball (MLB) game.[3] Whether something is considered dear or inexpensive depends on several factors: (1) the rate of its price increase over some time period compared with a yardstick such as the Consumer Price Index (CPI); (2) its price relative to the price of available substitutes; and (3) its price relative to a measure of ability to pay, such as the wage rate or income. On each of these criteria, average baseball ticket prices, for example, are cheap and getting cheaper. An example such as this is an excellent way to introduce students to relative prices, changes in the price level, and changes in purchasing power. Ask them what the role of a price system would be if each individual price in the economy tracked the CPI perfectly.

Measured against inflation, the average admission price to a Major League Baseball game fell or remained constant for most years from 1950 to the early 1990s. Ticket prices have risen relative to the CPI in the last few years, but the inflation-adjusted price has only doubled over the last 70 years. In 2019, the average ticket price to a Major League Baseball game was still just $33. In 1950 the average ticket price was 0.047 of average annual income; by 2019 it had risen to 0.052 of average annual income, virtually no change.

Relative to the prices of many other forms of entertainment (i.e., substitutes), baseball ticket prices are lower and have risen less rapidly over time. Professional basketball, football, and ice hockey tickets are each at least three times more expensive[4] (but each of those sports either play many fewer games or play in indoor arenas that seat many fewer fans than baseball). Amusement parks, rock concerts, and theater tickets also cost considerably more than a baseball ticket. Museums, movies, and a walk in the park are exceptions (and a good topic for discussion).

Marginal Analysis

One of the core concepts in economics is decision making at the margin, and the distinction between marginal, average, and total values. Examples from the world of sports can help students understand and appreciate this concept. For example, Los Angeles Angels' slugger Mike Trout had been in Major League Baseball for ten years when he entered the 2021 season with a .304 lifetime batting average. If he hits .347 in 2021 with the same number of at-bats as he averaged over the previous ten years, how does this (marginal) year change his lifetime batting average?[5]

Many athletic contests are decided "at the margin." Just one missed tackle in the National Football League (NFL) or one missed free throw in a Women's National Basketball Association (WNBA) game can cost a team a win. A second baseman signaling to the shortstop whether the next pitch is a fastball seldom makes a difference, but the one time it does during a season can put a team into the playoffs. For example, in 2018, the Houston Astros successfully stole opponents' catchers' signs to the pitcher and occasionally transmitted the information to their teammate in the batter's box by banging on the lid of a garbage can a certain number of times. That helped the batter anticipate the kind of pitch to expect. It apparently worked enough to give the Astros a significant advantage, for which the team and some of the participants eventually were penalized heavily by the Commissioner of MLB. Swimmers, skiers and runners try to save precious seconds by the aerodynamic design of their clothing or equipment because the difference between winning a race and finishing second is often measured in hundredths of a second, as Lindsay Vonn illustrated when finishing third by 0.47 of a second behind the gold medal winner in the 2018 women's Olympic downhill skiing race in South Korea.[6]

The public often questions values in a culture that rewards young athletes with multi-million-dollar contracts yet balks at paying elementary and secondary school teachers – to whom we entrust society's best hope for the future – a relative pittance. This issue is perfect for the transition from the traditional water–diamond paradox, which most students grasp and appreciate, to a contemporary sports illustration. It is relative scarcity at the margin, not total value that determines price. It is simply easier – and less expensive – to find one more person who can teach fourth grade or high school history well than it is to find someone who consistently can hit .300 (or snowboard like Shaun White). The fact that we spend about $60 billion a year on sporting events but $700 billion annually (in 2017) on public elementary and secondary education suggests that our values are reasonably respectable.

Fans and commentators often criticize athletes who exhibit anti-social, and/or even illegal behavior on or off the court or field of play. Quarterback Michael Vick's staging of illegal dog fights while playing in the NFL in 2007, Pete Rose's gambling while he was a manager in baseball (that led to a lifetime ban from participating in MLB in any way and has so far kept him out of the Baseball Hall of Fame), Tonya Harding's role in orchestrating an attempt to kneecap her figure skating rival, Nancy Kerrigan, in 1994, which eventually led to Harding being banned from figure skating for life, and the allegations in 2020 and 2021 against Deshaun Watson, the Houston Oilers' quarterback, and Trevor Bauer, a Los Angeles Dodgers starting pitcher for sexual abuse of women are but a few examples. Employers would fire most of us for similar stunts. Apart from the fact that some of this behavior may increase the demand for tickets (there is evidence, for example, that fighting in the National Hockey League (NHL) attracts fans (Jones et al. 1993; Rockerbie and Easton 2019)), the point to emphasize is that these individuals receive large economic rents in spite of their anti-social behavior because there are few perceived substitutes for them. In contrast, because there are close substitutes for the typical worker (including school teachers), he or she earns little economic rent. Thus, behavior that the boss perceives as inappropriate can be met with immediate dismissal in schools or universities. In sports, however, termination likely means the destruction of considerable economic rent that is accruing to the franchise owner, which is one reason why the unexpected dismissal of volatile basketball player Latrell Sprewell by the Golden State Warriors for choking his coach in November 1997 was so surprising and attracted so much attention at the time.

Demand

Basic microeconomic models posit that the quantity demanded of a particular good or service is inversely related to its price, *ceteris paribus*. Factors held constant include the price and availability of substitute and complementary goods, income, tastes, expectations, and population. Sports offer a convenient way to get students to think about *ceteris paribus* issues.

For example, the quantity demanded for baseball is a function of the admission price. Other considerations that must be held constant to properly estimate the effect of price on attendance include: the quality of the home team and opponent; how closely the teams are matched; the time the game is played; weather conditions; promotions (such as pre-game souvenirs or post-game fireworks); the location; convenience of travel to and quality of the venue; competing events or entertainment alternatives; whether the game is televised; per capita income and the local unemployment rate; and the population with public transit access or within driving distance of the game.

In addition to the concept of holding other things constant, an instructor can also explore elasticities: how sensitive are fans to ticket prices; does this sensitivity vary with the price level; how income elastic is the demand for baseball, bowling, tennis or cricket? A related demand concept that we find more difficult for students to grasp is the derived demand for a factor of production. Players' salaries are determined by demand derived from the demand to watch particular sports and by the employment alternatives available to players. The profit-maximizing price is what the market will bear, based on the anticipated demand for the sport. Players' salaries do not determine ticket prices, no matter how often owners allude to their rising payrolls in order to justify ticket price hikes. The demand for players, and the level of their salaries, is derived from the overall demand to watch the sport in person or on television and to purchase logo merchandise.[7]

Efficiency

Many resource allocation decisions in sports affect efficiency. We focus on just one of them, the allocation of playing talent across teams, in order to illustrate the importance of matching the quantity supplied to the quantity demanded for maximizing social welfare.

Professional team sports leagues take steps allegedly designed to balance the level of playing skills among competitors. They allocate players new to the league on the basis of a "reverse-order draft" that awards the most promising players to those teams that have recently enjoyed the least success on the playing field.[8] Currently the National Football League, the National Hockey League and the National Basketball Association (NBA) limit the total player payroll of teams in an effort ostensibly to prevent "wealthy" teams (those located in more densely populated areas or in areas with more avid fans) from securing a disproportionate share of the most talented freeagent players. Major League Baseball sets a payroll threshold. If a team exceeds the threshold, it must pay a "luxury tax" to the league, apparently for the "luxury" of spending excessive (of the threshold) money on payroll, so reducing the incentive for teams playing in large markets from accumulating so many talented players as to injure reasonable competitive balance.

Economists have long recognized (Rottenberg 1956) the futility of efforts to balance team playing talent when the teams play in different localities that vary in population and in front of fans that vary in their willingness to pay for a winning local team, and when contracts of players can be transferred among teams. As the Coase theorem reminds us, in the absence of significant transactions costs, resources move to their most valuable use regardless of initial ownership. If a talented baseball player is valued more highly in New York than in Kansas City because there are more New Yorkers willing to pay to see the Yankees win than there are Kansas City residents willing to pay to see the Royals win (or, even with similar populations, if the average New York resident values winning more than does the average resident of Kansas City) the player's contract will be transferred from Kansas City to New York for a price between his value at the two locales. Transfers like this would occur regardless of whether the property rights over the player's services reside with his original team (as in the days when a "reserve clause" granted perpetual ownership rights to the team that first signed a player unless it transferred those rights to another team) or with the player himself, as is the case for those veteran players who qualify for "free agency" today.[9]

Because of player trades and sales, player drafts do not tend to promote a balance of playing skills among teams. Player drafts may subsidize weak teams by granting them initial property rights over players whom they can subsequently sell to other teams. The extent of the subsidy depends on the elapsed time before a player can become a free agent. Free agency for players does not promote a balance of playing skills among teams either. Wealth-maximizing players will sell their services personally to the team willing and able to pay the most for those services, a demand derived from the player's expected contribution to the team's performance and the willingness and ability of local residents to pay for better performance. Occasionally a good veteran player will accept a contract below his estimated market value in order to play on a talented team with a chance to win the league championship or because he and/or his partner prefers its location (e.g. San Diego), further exacerbating competitive imbalance.

For the sake of economic efficiency, this failure to balance competition may be fortunate. The argument that balanced competition is desirable rests on the false belief that fans value only one characteristic of games, namely uncertainty of outcome. Fans are clearly not indifferent to the level of uncertainty of outcome (Knowles, Sherony, and Haupert 1992), but they also value winning, and the response varies by geographic area (Porter 1992). Although a large imbalance in team playing-skills reduces the uncertainty of games and thereby the demand for those games, the greater willingness to pay for winning by fans of certain teams than by fans of other teams can mean that the efficient level of competitive balance is far from perfectly even (Fort 2011, Chapter 6). Imbalance leads to more winning by teams situated where people get more satisfaction from winning, and less winning by teams whose fans in the aggregate care less about it. Whenever the difference in the value of winning to the fans in two locations exceeds the loss in value associated with less evenly matched games, efficiency is promoted by moving playing skill from the team located where winning is valued less to the team located where winning is valued more.[10] It is also unlikely that severe imbalance of playing talent would be efficient. As playing-skills become more unequally distributed, the uncertainty of games diminishes, the marginal utility of winning more games to the fans of the more successful teams diminishes, and the marginal utility of winning more games to the fans of the less successful teams grows, both acting to slow the payoff from further unequal allocations of playing skill. Another disadvantage of equally balanced competition is the increased likelihood that the outcome of a contest will be determined by chance – an unusual bounce of a ball or an official's error.

Surplus

Efficiency is achieved when economic resources are devoted to those activities that create the greatest value for consumers. This basic economic concept is often difficult for students to comprehend. Getting the allocation right is relatively more important if the value of resources when they are devoted to their best use substantially exceeds the value that could be created if they were allocated to their second-best use. This difference is surplus.[11] It is large when the demand for the output is high and the opportunity cost of the resources (their value in their next best use) is low, as is common in sports. Although there are a few, the number of potential actors, surgeons, lawyers, and Wall Street bankers among professional athletes is limited. The essence of resource allocation is maximizing consumers' plus producers' surplus.

Many people confuse aggregate revenues with surplus, the net value created by getting the allocation decision correct. The 1994–95 Major League Baseball players' strike provides an opportunity to illustrate this difference. Some television news programs reported the "economic loss" from the strike as the amount of ticket and television revenue that would have been received by teams if the cancelled games had been played, plus an estimate of how much fans would have spent on hotels, restaurants, parking, etc. while attending games. Ask students if this is a good estimate of the social welfare loss of the strike.

There are at least two (potentially offsetting) errors in using foregone revenues as a measure of social welfare. Each emphasizes an important economic concept. First, revenues fail to include the consumers' surplus lost to the strike. Thus the "economic loss" due to the strike may exceed forgone revenues. To the extent that sports consumers are *fan*atics, and have inelastic demands, unless the teams can perfectly price discriminate, this forgone consumers' surplus could be quite large.

Second, the use of foregone revenue to measure economic loss ignores the possibility that the striking players and/or their families may value their newly created leisure time above zero. This value is the area under the (short-run) marginal cost curve. It should be subtracted from total revenue to obtain an accurate estimate of the net economic loss caused by the strike. The value of leisure time created by the strike might have been quite high because it is rare for players to have much time with their families during the summer.[12]

What is really needed to estimate the economic cost of the strike is a measure including all benefits, both those accruing to the consumers as surplus and those captured by the teams and excluding the alternative value of the released resources (of which the players are the largest component, but could include the value of alternative uses of the stadium, for example, as voting locations during the 2020 election). Taking these considerations into account, Chris Douglas (1996) estimated the contemporaneous economic cost of the 1994–95 baseball strike at $813 million dollars, about $10 million per day, while forgone revenues were only $8 million per day. Forgone spending on hotels, food, souvenirs and parking contributed almost nothing to the social welfare loss of the strike because for the most part those services are provided in competitive markets with quite elastic supply and demand. Fans simply drank their beer elsewhere in late summer of 1994. Little surplus was lost by their relocation. However, the inelastic demand for baseball created a substantial loss in consumer surplus. Zipp (1996) provides a good empirical account of these issues.

Strategy

Game theory now appears as a separate chapter in many introductory economics texts and is being infused throughout other courses in the economics curriculum. Basic concepts of game theory – think ahead, put yourself in your rival's shoes, backward induction, indirect effects, dominant and dominated strategies – are enormously useful in everyday life.

Most sporting events are zero-sum games. As Coco Gauff gains a point, Serena Williams loses one. As the Green Bay Packers gain four yards, the Dallas Cowboys lose four yards. The concepts of game theory are usually introduced with zero-sum games. Their symmetry simplifies the analysis of pure strategy games, allowing more attention to the fundamental ideas. In addition, the concept of preventing your rival from being able to take advantage of your own strategy by making her indifferent among her alternative strategies is an intuitively appealing basis for teaching mixed strategies that evaporates for variable-sum games.

Although the existence of multiple equilibria is probably the most discon-certing characteristic of games for veteran economists, the appearance of counterintuitive results often creates a mental obstacle for the rookie student. Because of their experience with sports, many students believe they "know how to play the game." Producing counterintuitive results in this context is persuasive evidence that there is something useful to learn from serious study of economics. A simple exercise with a mixed strategy equilibrium game demonstrates the importance of taking indirect effects into account, which is a key element of "thinking like an economist."

The payoff matrix in Figure 1.1 reports the success of a baseball batter against a pitcher. For simplicity, the pitcher has only two pitches, a fastball and a curve, and the batter knows that is the pitcher's complete repertoire. The batter is relatively more successful against fastballs. When he guesses the pitcher will throw a fastball and the pitcher does throw a fastball, he bats .600. When he guesses correctly that the pitcher will throw a curve, however, he hits only .400. When he guesses incorrectly what will be thrown, he always bats just .200. The goal of the pitcher is to minimize the batter's average and the goal of the batter is to maximize it.

		Batter	
		Guess Fastball	Guess Curveball
Pitcher	Throw Fastball	.600	.200
	Throw Curveball	.200	.400

Figure 1.1   *Baseball game payoff matrix (hitter's batting average reported in cells)*

The pitcher knows that if he is predictable, the batter has a substantial edge. If the pitcher were to throw only one type of pitch, it would be a curve, but the batter still would be successful 40 percent of the time. There is no *dominant* strategy for either the pitcher or batter because the best pure strategy of each depends on the pure strategy undertaken by the other. There is no pure strategy Nash equilibrium in this game.

There is a mixed-strategy Nash equilibrium, however. If the pitcher throws fastballs p percent of the time so as to ensure that the batter cannot take advantage of the pitcher's mix between fastballs and curves, then the batter must be indifferent between guessing fastball, guessing curve, guessing 50 percent fastballs and 50 percent curves, or guessing any other combination available to him. Thus, the batter's expected payoff when guessing any combination of fastballs and curves must be the same. If it is not, he will select the strategy that gives him the higher expected batting average and thus take advantage of the pitcher. The calculations are easiest with the batter's pure strategy alternatives. The expected payoff to him from guessing fastball is $\{.600p + .200(1 - p)\}$; his expected payoff from guessing curve is $\{.200p + .400(1 - p)\}$. The value of p, the percentage of fastballs thrown, that equalizes the two expected payoffs is 1/3.[13] The expected batting average of the batter is .333. Students need to be reminded that while the pitcher's optimal strategy is to throw 1/3 fastballs and 2/3 curves, the actual delivery of the pitches must be unpredictable.

Now comes the fun. Suggest to the students that you have a tip for the batter: "choke up" on the bat. The effect of this is to raise the batter's success when he is expecting a curve, but the pitcher delivers a fastball. Fewer of these pitches now "blow by" the batter. The batting average in the upper right cell of Figure 1.1 rises to .300. Ask students what the pitcher should do now that the batter is better at hitting fastballs (when he was expecting a curve). The majority will respond that the pitcher should throw more curves. Then solve for the mixed strategy equilibrium.

The new equilibrium mix for the pitcher is 40 percent fastballs, an increase from 33.3 percent prior to the batter "choking up" on the bat, and opposite the usual student prediction. The new expected batting average is .360, a rise of .027, as would be expected when the only change was a batting improvement. Throwing more fastballs after the batter improved his hitting against fastballs will puzzle some students because they will fail to take into account how the batter will change his optimal strategy with his newly discovered skill. The batter's original optimal guessing mix was one-third fastballs. After the tip to "choke up" on the bat, his optimal mix is to guess fastball only one-fifth of the time. He guesses curve more frequently after the tip because the tip has helped his batting when he guesses curve. So, he guesses curve more frequently, 80 percent rather than 67 percent of the time. The pitcher, in turn, adjusts his optimal mix by favoring fastballs because now the batter is guessing curve more frequently, and the pitcher always does worse when actually pitching what the batter is expecting. So, the pitcher throws 40 percent fastballs rather than 33 percent fastballs. This exercise helps students appreciate the importance of thinking about how their rival might react to a change in circumstances as well as how they should adjust their own behavior.[14]

Moving from the theoretical world of game theory and analytics to actual experiences on the field, court or ice, can engage students. For example, in soccer, where should a team position its goalie for a penalty kick, and do they employ a mixed strategy? Should a team "sit on a lead" and choose ball control over the risks associated with trying to score again? In basketball when does it make sense to foul an opponent on purpose near the end of a game? After scoring a touchdown, should a football team attempt a two-point conversion with about a 50–50 probability or settle for the virtually certain 1-point kick?

The structure of sports leagues locks teams into a classic prisoner's dilemma. Winning is a zero-sum game. Attendance rises with winning, and so revenue depends on a team's success on the playing field. Thus, each team faces an incentive to sign high-quality free-agent players, even though, when all teams sign comparable free agents, nothing different happens to collective win–loss records. Indeed, the aggregate "output" of the league in terms of games won cannot increase as long as the schedule remains fixed. As a result of competition for free agent players, each team's expenses rise, revenues remain constant, and profits decline. In order to escape this prisoners' dilemma, over the years leagues have devised various schemes such as reserve clauses and reverse-order player drafts, the latest of which are aggregate player payroll ceilings (inappropriately called "*salary* caps").

Levi Leipheimer, former road racing cyclist, Olympic medalist, and Lance Armstrong's teammate, admitted to doping and using performance-enhancing products because he felt everyone else in cycling was doing it, so he figured it was either go along or be satisfied with not being a contender. He was trapped in a prisoner's dilemma. After the pervasive cycling scandals became public knowledge, racing officials tried various techniques to alter the game payoffs so as to eliminate performance enhancing drugs as a dominant strategy (Eber, 2008; Cartwright, 2019).

In the 2015 Super Bowl between the Seattle Seahawks and the New England Patriots, it all came down to the last 26 seconds. Seattle, down 28–24, had the ball on the Pats' one-yard line, and they had their powerful running back, Marshawn Lynch, ready to dive into the end zone. Six points, the extra point, and they own the Lombardi trophy. But Seahawks' coach Pete Carroll – think mixed strategy here – chose to pass instead, figuring Pats' coach, Bill Belichick, would stack the line in anticipation of Lynch's plunge. But maybe Belichick was thinking that Carroll would think this way. The Patriots intercepted the supposedly unexpected pass, and the rest is legend.

Monopoly

There are numerous examples of monopoly power in sports. Most professional sports teams have market power over local ticket sales because their geographic distance from other teams in the same league creates substantial costs to a consumer who would try to substitute live performances of another team in the face of a price increase.[15] Teams don't have to worry about other suppliers moving into their territory because all of the professional sports leagues have restrictions on team movements, especially those that would place a relocating team near another franchise. In addition, the entry of new teams is strictly limited by the existing teams, who have authority to grant or refuse entry into their league. In a business where new entrants must rely on the cooperation of existing firms to produce their product (who will they play if the incumbents refuse?) there is not likely to be entry from hostile new competitors.[16]

Although expenditures on sports obviously come at the expense of expenditures by consumers on other goods and services, and most likely at the expense of other entertainment options, evidence also suggests that consumers do not even view different sports as particularly good substitutes.[17] Studies of the demand for tickets to professional team sporting events find elasticities of demand at the average price generally less than −1.0 (Fort, 2006) which at first glance suggests that team owners set prices too low to maximize profits. Students can be shown how a profit-maximizing team with very low marginal costs would maximize profits by setting ticket price so that the elasticity of demand is close to (minus) one. If marginal costs are higher, the profit-maximizing price is in the elastic region of demand. Marginal costs are certainly minuscule for additional patrons to an individual sporting event that is not sold out, and also quite low for additional games during a season. But if a team owner is more interested in maximizing attendance, or if a team earns profits from the sale of parking and concessions that increase if attendance is larger, then the profit-maximizing price easily could be in the inelastic region of demand (Fort, 2006).[18] Newspapers and magazines similarly price in the inelastic region of demand in order to boost circulation and therefore advertising rates.

Perhaps the most interesting application of monopoly to sports involves league decisions to expand. Absent the contrived scarcity of teams that evolves from limitations on expansion, the price of franchises would be modest. Who would be willing to pay almost a billion dollars for an existing franchise when one could get a new one for free? Whereas existing franchises might have some goodwill value, new franchises do not. Yet recent prices for expansion franchises in football, baseball, and ice hockey have been close to prices at which the ownership of average incumbent teams (not the most valuable franchises, which are now in the billions of dollars)[19] has been transferred, suggesting that the lion's share of the franchise price represents the scarcity value of a franchise rather than established goodwill.

How, then, would leagues determine the optimal rate of expansion to maximize the net present value of the entry fees they collect from expansion franchises? The entry fees are distributed among the incumbent members of the league. No expansion generates no fees. Rapid expansion reduces the willingness of prospective owners to offer high fees for an expansion franchise, because the availability of more expansion franchises is then anticipated to be just over the horizon. Between these extremes is an expansion rate that maximizes the net present value of league entry fees. Leagues must expand slowly enough to keep some franchise-hungry cities and potential owners chomping at the bit, in effect creating the artificial scarcity symptomatic of all monopolies. This scarcity scares bidders into inflating their offers for fear of otherwise being rationed out of the market. But leagues also must expand fast enough to ensure that the number of vacant cities that could support a team does not approach a number that could support an entire new league (perhaps eight teams). Although an incumbent league can prevent the hostile entry of individual teams by refusing to play them, it cannot similarly block the entry of an entire independent league. Indeed, in 1960 the American Football League (AFL) initiated operations that were so successful that it eventually successfully challenged the incumbent NFL. Of course, once both leagues recognized the effects of competition on owners' profits (via salary competition for new and free-agent players), they merged, with the legal blessing of Congress.

Franchise owners often plead their case for monopoly power to Congress. Both the NFL and the NBA secured legislation that allowed them to merge with competing leagues in the 1960s and 1970s without incurring antitrust liability. The NFL also persuaded Congress to pass the Sports Broadcasting Act of 1961, permitting teams in professional sports leagues to sell their broadcast rights collectively. (Universities are not covered by the Sports Broadcasting Act. Thus, in 1984, they were ruled to be in violation of the Sherman Antitrust Act for engaging in similar behavior.)

Congressional pleadings invariably include owners' claims of poverty. Most professional sports teams are privately owned, and not required to disclose financial information publicly. For the most part, the teams have asked the public to take it on faith that owning a professional sports team is not profitable. Economists find these claims disingenuous in light of the rapid rate of increase of franchise values, averaging from 11 to 18 percent annually over the 1990s (Fort 2011, p. 7) and from 11 to 16 percent annually from 2008 to 2016 (DeSantis 2018) for the four major team sports (Scully 1995, p. 132). Why, we might ask, would smart businesspeople, who have earned fortunes in other industries, pay ever-increasing prices for an asset that is expected to generate only losses for their poor owners into the foreseeable future? This conundrum provides an opportunity to discuss with students the source of asset values and the possibility of nonpecuniary returns, as well as the honesty of professional sports franchise owners.

Monopsony

For many years professional sports franchises were able to buy (players' services) low and sell (tickets and broadcast rights) high. They enjoyed monopsony power in the purchase of their primary input – players – through an agreement among the teams in a league not to hire a player from another team unless the owner of that team voluntarily relinquished rights to him (usually by selling or trading him to the team that most desires the player's services). They sold their tickets in markets insulated from competition with other teams in the same sport by agreement with the other teams in their league and sold national broadcast rights collectively as monopolists, a practice sanctioned by Congress in 1961.

The linchpin of the professional leagues' financial success was their monopsony power over players. Beginning with the emergence of players' unions in the 1960s and exacerbated by strikes, union contract settlements, and periodic legal skirmishes, the monopsony power of professional sports teams over veteran players has been drastically curtailed. Each of the leagues still drafts new players, who may play only for the team that selects them (or the team to which the draft rights are sold or traded). This continues to depress the earnings of relatively new players below competitive market rates. It is perpetuated through the complicity of veteran players who agree to incorporate the draft rules limiting salaries of young players into their union contract with the leagues, thus exempting the draft from the antitrust laws. Veteran players gain by the exploitation of rookies to the extent that funds that would otherwise go toward meeting competitive market salaries for new players are available for negotiations between teams and their veterans (White 1986).

Rookie professional players are also disadvantaged by rules adopted by the NFL and NBA that do not allow teams to draft players until people in their high school graduating class have completed either three years (NFL) or one year (NBA) of college, respectively. These rules allow the professional leagues to keep the players on lower salary "rookie contracts" later through their careers, when they often are approaching the peak of their playing skills. It also helps college and university teams to maintain a high quality of play while paying no salaries to players, and to attract sufficient revenues to pay coaches well (if not exorbitantly) and build superb playing facilities.

The dissipation of market power over veteran players has produced a natural experiment to test the predictions of the monopsony model. Statistical studies of salaries show convincingly that when draft and player-retention schemes were relaxed in the 1970s, large increases in player compensation resulted (Raimondo 1983; Scully 1989; Quirk and Fort 1992; Kahn 1993). In the 2020s, apprentice baseball players' salaries remain under the control of the teams through an agreement with veteran players to include such restrictions in the Collective Bargaining Agreement. As a result, players in their first three years in the league make about 30 percent of their estimated free market value (Krautman 2019). Compensation has grown most rapidly when either courts or collective bargaining weakened the draft and retention schemes and has grown faster as players have won more relief from these constraints. Over the past two decades professional basketball players' salaries have risen fastest, baseball players' second fastest, football players' third fastest and ice hockey players' slowest. The rapid increase in football player salaries in the 1990s, following the introduction of true free agency for veteran NFL players in 1993, further corroborates the connection between salary levels and competition in the labor market for players.

As monopsony power over their labor inputs has eroded, professional sports teams have turned increased attention to their second most costly input – a facility in which to stage their games. Each of the four major professional team sports leagues operates under a provision similar to the NFL's Rule 4.3, which requires approval of a supermajority (75 percent in the NFL) of the owners for franchise relocation. This voting requirement provides a strategic advantage to both incumbent teams negotiating a stadium contract extension with their existing landlord (often the city or county in which they are located), and teams negotiating with a stadium owner in a location to which they propose to relocate. An incumbent tenant can threaten to relocate and also to form a coalition to block any other franchise from replacing it, thus creating monopsony power for the team in renegotiating its facility lease. A relocating team can credibly threaten to block the relocation of any other team that competes with it for a stadium lease because it needs to form only a sub-majority coalition (of at least 25 percent of teams) to do so, thus deterring competitive bidding for the facility with which it is negotiating.

The result of franchise relocation restrictions in professional sports leagues is a balance of bargaining power tilted toward tenants – that is, team owners. The exploitation of this monopsony power in the stadium and arena market in recent decades is illustrated by the shift in stadium and arena financing. In the 1950s, a majority of professional sports facilities was privately owned and financed. Today, almost all stadiums and arenas are constructed with public funds and leased to teams at trivial rents because the landlords expect to receive external (to the team) rents in the form of marketing and enhanced prestige for their city. As the leagues' monopsony power over players has declined, professional sports teams have taken advantage of the country's obsession with sports by demanding free, or at least heavily subsidized, facilities from communities that believe a professional sports franchise is needed to acquire the image of a "major league" city and see building a stadium as the best way to get one (Noll and Zimbalist 1997; Coates 2019).

Collusion and Cartels

Both professional and intercollegiate sports are replete with collusive agreements that illustrate the fundamental principles of cartels. Here we focus on activities of the National Collegiate Athletic Association (NCAA) (Tollison 2012). Featuring the NCAA to teach about cartels has two advantages. First, many students are enrolled at institutions that are members of the NCAA and take delight in evaluating and criticizing their college or university. Second, the NCAA is not exempt from the antitrust laws prohibiting collusive conduct as are Major League Baseball, national television broadcasting contracts of all professional sports leagues, and the league mergers in basketball and football.

The case for collective behavior in the organization of sporting contests among colleges and universities originated with two private market failures – a public good problem and an externality. The first was the necessity to develop standard rules for football, and the second was the need to control player violence that helped individual teams win games but was destroying public interest in college football in the late nineteenth century. Individual colleges were caught in a prisoner's dilemma. They all agreed that college football would be better off with less violence, but any team that unilaterally cleaned up its act would suffer on the scoreboard and financially. Collective action was required.

The NCAA was founded in 1905.[20] Once it succeeded in controlling violence, the organization expanded into economic regulation. Its most important market restrictions were developed after World War II, when members agreed to limit player compensation to tuition, room and board (initially called a "Sanity Code," as if paying players were insane) and to centralize the sales of rights to televise live college football games.

In the 1950s, the NCAA developed a system to detect and punish cheating on the agreements and extended its control of output by limiting the annual number of games in football and men's basketball. Punishment for cheating (e.g., broadcasting a game in competition with the collectively negotiated exclusive NCAA broadcast, or compensating a player beyond the agreed-upon limit of tuition, room and board) could be severe, because the NCAA controlled all college sports and a violation in one sport could spawn sanctions in all.

NCAA sports are ripe for a cartel. There appears to be quite inelastic demand, and entry is difficult.[21] These characteristics ensure substantial rewards to a successful cartel. It is relatively easy to police the behavior affecting some parts of the cartel agreement (e.g., agreement not to televise live football games in competition with the game sold collectively), and institutional arrangements have been devised to limit cheating on other aspects of the cartel agreement (e.g., investigations of and sanctions for exceeding the agreed limit on payments to players).

The restriction of output by limiting the number of games played and televised and limitations on the price of the most important input – the players – enhance net revenues sufficiently that institutions face strong incentives to field successful sports programs. The natural outcome has been a costly expansion of competition in unregulated areas, for example, recruiting, which erodes the net revenues derived from the programs. The NCAA reacted by imposing limitations on some forms of non-price competition, such as limiting the number of coaches, the number of scholarship players, and player recruitment activities. In addition to direct efforts to control costs, the NCAA also enjoys external support for its efforts to protect the revenues produced by cartel restrictions from being squandered via rent-seeking competition (e.g., amateurism is "good" [for players, but apparently not for coaches] on moral grounds). But not all outlets for competitive pressure have been capped. Universities still compete for players by building bigger and better (than the competition) facilities to impress potential recruits.

In contrast to professional sports teams, which historically monopsonized player markets by means of an agreement not to hire players who were allocated to other teams, there is no "draft" of players into college sports. The NCAA controls the player market not by creating market power for individual teams through a draft that limits player mobility, but rather by establishing a maximum wage below the competitive equilibrium wage for the entire market. This provides a pedagogical opportunity to analyze price controls without resorting to the usual examples of New York City rent controls, or usury laws. The gap between a player's marginal revenue product and the cost of tuition, room and board illustrates the incentive facing coaches, athletic directors and boosters to offer clandestine payments to college athletes and to overindulge in complementary factors of production such as coaches, stadiums, or training facilities as a means of competing for the best athletes.

The NCAA should be recognized as a cartel of colleges and universities, whose behavior is more closely parallel to OPEC (Organization of Petroleum Exporting Countries) than Mr. Chips (Sanderson and Siegfried 2019). The fact that the members are not-for-profit institutions does not dampen their incentive to maximize revenues, for those revenues can be put to uses that enrich the individuals in control. The frequent claims that athletic departments are in poverty are difficult to accept when so few major programs are terminated and so many coaches and athletic directors appear to be paid many times their value in their next best use.[22] Apparently, many of the benefits do not show up on athletic department financial statements, providing an opportunity to discuss rent seeking and external benefits with your students (and why head football coaches often are paid many multiples of what professors of economics are paid).

The Role of Government

Sports examples can be used to explain the role of government in a market economy. For example, under public-interest rationales for government we consider market imperfections – using antitrust laws to create or maintain competition; dealing with natural monopolies; improving efficiency when there are capital-market imperfections; internalizing externalities; providing public goods; correcting for information asymmetries; and equity issues. The empirical record of government involvement in sports has been far from favorable to competition – baseball's antitrust exemption, the Sports Broadcasting Act (permitting the collective sale of television rights to broadcast games), condoning the NCAA cartel, sanctioning mergers between competitive leagues, constraining labor mobility, and so forth; instructors can invite students to come up with examples – positive or negative – that fall under one or more of the usual public-interest rationales for government intervention. In addition, one need not look far to find illustrations of the use of government to promote private interests in sports.

The recent controversies surrounding public financing of stadiums and arenas provide an excellent context for discussing the role of government. Why do cities offer teams "free" or highly subsidized places to play more frequently than similar assistance to fellowship clubs, bowling alleys, bookstores, or movie theaters? Do the grounds for public participation fall under public interest or private interest criteria? What are the redistribution consequences, given the average wealth levels of owners, players and fans vs. taxpayers in general (or, depending on how the stadium is financed, the incidence of sales taxes or property taxes or of lottery revenues)? Is a stadium or arena a public good? Would free riding occur? Does a major league sports team create positive (e.g., favorable image, entertainment options) or negative (e.g., congestion, bad role models) externalities? Are sports leagues natural monopolies? Finally, is league control of entry, relocation, labor relations, etc., a good substitute for direct government control if there is, indeed, a public interest reason to forego reliance on competitive markets (Siegfried and Zimbalist, 2000)?

In recent years the NCAA has tussled with federal antitrust law and state laws involving compensation of athletes. These disputes offer good classroom illustrations of the economic role of government, monopsony, monopoly and the law.

The conflict began in 2009 when former UCLA (and NBA) basketball player Ed O'Bannon sued the NCAA for the unauthorized use of his likeness in Electronic Arts video games, for which he received no compensation. On August 8, 2014, District Court Judge Claudia Wilken found in O'Bannon v. NCAA that the NCAA's rules and policies prohibiting players from receiving compensation for the use of their images and likenesses were an unreasonable restraint of trade, violating antitrust law. The case challenged the NCAA's member colleges' and universities' collective agreement to refrain from compensating athletes for the use of their names, images and likenesses. The ruling was affirmed on appeal in 2016. Subsequently, many separate but similar related laws were crafted and approved in individual states, starting in California. The "Fair Pay to Play Act," passed in California's legislature in 2019, allowed college athletes to acquire their own endorsements and sponsorships without losing NCAA eligibility. Popularly known as "NIL" laws – Name, Image, Likeness – were then enacted in states across the nation and began to take effect in July 2021.

On June 21, 2021, the United States Supreme Court ruled 9–0 in favor of college athletes in NCAA v. Alston. In its decision the Court held that NCAA restrictions about how much education-related compensation players could receive, based on the collective agreement among colleges, universities and conferences and implemented through the NCAA, violated federal antitrust laws by preventing players from receiving fair-market compensation for their labor. Justice Gorsuch wrote the opinion; Justice Kavanaugh wrote a strongly-worded concurring opinion about agreements among colleges and universities (a cartel) limiting player compensation more generally (to tuition, room and board and some other educationally related benefits) that foresees greater trouble for the NCAA in the inevitable future judicial disputes about college athlete compensation.

ADDITIONAL ILLUSTRATIONS

Space prevents us from including detailed descriptions of the many various applications of economic principles to sports. In this section we briefly identify a limited grab bag of possibilities.

Sports is a fertile field for examples of *comparative advantage*. Babe Ruth was a superb pitcher for the Boston Red Sox before he was converted to a right fielder in order to keep his bat in the daily lineup. (In his last three years as a pitcher for the Red Sox he was a combined 46–25). Although he had an absolute advantage in pitching over many other players, his comparative advantage was in hitting (Scahill 1990). So, after he was sold to the Yankees for $125,000 in 1920, he remained a right fielder.

Just two years short of a century after Babe Ruth was converted exclusively to an outfielder (Ruth pitched in only four games after the Yankees acquired him in 1920). MLB welcomed former Japanese baseball star Shohei Ohtani, who has an absolute advantage in both pitching and hitting. Ohtani was leading the American League in home runs when he appeared as the starting pitcher for the American League in the 2021 All-Star Game, and then was the lead-off batter as the designated hitter. Because the designated hitter rule allows him to rest his arm between pitching starts, he has become the first star pitcher to also bat regularly in games between his pitching starts.

After some thought, most students accept the notion that *free exchange* can benefit both traders, though when it comes to US trade with China almost everyone seems to believe that only China benefits. Politicians are easily duped into believing that most other countries (China, Mexico, Canada, Japan) benefit from trade at the expense of the United States. The sports counterpart is that some commentators and fans believe that if two teams engage in a player trade, only one benefits. They find it hard to believe that, at least *ex ante*, both teams *expected* to gain from the transaction. Every city and every sport have lists of famous "bad trades," where the home team's general manager exposed his incompetence. Thus, we got a summer 2016 newspaper headline: "Atlanta Hawks get Dwight Howard in move that will benefit both parties" – as if this were something that only happens on rare occasions (Golliver, 2016). It was surely not written by someone schooled in economics.

Trade opens up related applications of exchange, including *Pareto optimality* (when we've exhausted all opportunities for mutually beneficial gains), the fact that trade value depends upon the marginal values and opportunity costs (such as, what do I have already, in terms of point guards or outfielders, and what do I have to give up?), and diminishing marginal returns or gains. The advantage of agents as negotiators whose broader reputation is at stake and who can insulate the player they represent from creating animosity with a general manager is also relevant. In spite of the loathing they receive from owners and the media, agents' comparative advantage presumably is to perform functions that lower transaction costs. The agent market is characterized by relatively free entry and price-taking behavior, not unlike real estate agents.

Instructors can employ a simple sports example to illustrate many concepts associated with *production* (Scully, 1974; Jamil, 2019). A discussion might ensue about what constitutes the objective function or output for a team owner – is it victories, the margin of victory (i.e., point spread), championships, attendance, revenues, or television shots of the owner basking in glory in his or her private booth with celebrity friends? Traditional inputs in the production process are players, owners, and managers/coaches, but there are others such as training, grounds keepers, computers and technology, the stadium, promotions and gustatory amenities. As a team employs higher quality inputs – that is, acquires better players – its expected number of wins and attendance rise, but after some point the rate of increase begins to diminish, and it is conceivable that total attendance and/or revenues could even decrease if a team were so dominant that its contests became predictable and boring.

It is difficult to come up with examples of a *backward-bending labor supply curve* for individuals. Annika Sorenstam provides an option. In 2002, at age 32, Sorenstam won 12 tournaments on the LPGA tour (in that single year) – total dominance for a golfer. That year she announced that she planned to cut back on her 2003 schedule and retire well before she was 40, thereby reducing her supply of labor. The implication was that she planned to start a family and had plenty of money to live on for the rest of her life (her net worth of approximately $40 million in 2020 will allow Annika, her husband and their two children to live comfortably for the rest of their lives).

Sports offer convincing examples of the principle of *specialization and division of labor*, and it has become more evident over time. The "olden days" often saw more multi-sport players, both in college and in the professional ranks, than exist today. To excel at the highest level of performance, athletes (and musicians and other performing artists) simply must start earlier and practice longer. Time split between two major activities entails a large opportunity cost for each. Even within a sport, say football, one used to see one athlete play more than one position – in the 1950s both on offense and defense, for example, or as a position player and a punter or field goal kicker. Football rosters now contain many more specialty players – pooch punters, nickel backs, long snappers, etc. Baseball relies more and more on specific role positions – a designated hitter (in the American League), long and short relievers, closers, and even base-stealing specialists, which is one reason the versatile Shohei Ohtani is such a sensation for the Los Angeles Angels. Young girls must now choose between gymnastics and figure skating even if they exhibit considerable talent in both sports. Roger Bannister, who broke the four-minute mile barrier in 1954 while he was a full-time medical student, and other earlier track stars, were really amateurs. They trained part-time, whereas now track is a full-time occupation for world class runners.

The economics of ticket resale ("scalping") provides another refreshing alternative to New York rent control as an example of the effects of a *price ceiling*. In locations where scalping is illegal, the price ceiling is zero, preventing tickets from getting to those who value them the most. Arizona added an interesting twist to scalping a few decades ago, legalizing it within a specially marked area outside the event arena or stadium at a specified time. With all the scalpers together in one place along with all the buyers, the area looked like the floor of the Chicago Board of Trade (before everything went electronic), and the market power of scalpers who preyed on buyers ignorant of lower prices on the other side of the venue was dissipated (Happel and Jennings 1995).

The market for used baseball players illustrates problems caused by *asymmetric information*, *adverse selection*, and the "*winner's curse.*" Pitchers who are signed as free agents spend more time on the disabled list than those who re-sign with their original team (Lehn, 1982). This can be explained by asymmetric information (Lehn, 1984). Healthy pitchers are re-signed by the incumbent teams, leaving only "lemons" for the "used pitcher" market because of asymmetric information. Further exacerbating the problem of disappointing free-agent signings is the winner's curse, caused by a player signing with the team bidding for his services that makes the most overly optimistic estimate of his future productivity (Cassing and Douglas, 1980). Teams try to protect themselves against these possibilities by scouting, requiring physical examinations and adding performance incentives to player contracts, but it doesn't always work. The winner's curse also affects bidding among cities for hosting the Olympic Games or FIFA World Cup, causing most of them to end up in the red after the event (Andreff, 2014).

For most young students, a wise investment decision is to remain in school through college or even completion of a graduate or professional degree. The forgone income for a four- to eight-year period is rewarded by higher earnings (almost double for a four-year college degree vs. a high school diploma) over a 40- or 50-year horizon. Many textbooks discuss and display these earnings streams and suggest how one would calculate an *internal rate of return*.

For someone contemplating a career as a professional athlete, the age–earnings profile looks much different – earnings could start before high school (for a figure skater or tennis star) or as late as one's mid-20s (for a baseball player) and may virtually truncate around age 30 (as the average length of a professional career in the four premier team sports leagues in the United States is four to six years). A good question for students to ponder is the rate of return at which it makes sense for a young person with reasonably attractive educational and nonathletic career options to devote herself or himself to athletic training. Given such a short earnings period, one can understand why a talented athlete would choose to forgo some or all of college, especially if there is an opportunity to return later. If Tiger Woods had remained at Stanford after his sophomore year until his class graduated, the Stanford golf team would have been much better, but Tiger would have missed out on the winner's trophy for seven PGA tournaments (including the 1997 Masters Tournament) and almost $4 million in tournament earnings.

An example of *opportunity cost* is the case of Jeff Fosnes, the star forward on Vanderbilt's 1974 Southeastern Conference champion basketball team. Fosnes was drafted in an early round of the NBA draft. He opted for medical school, however, comparing the expected earnings of a 50-year-old physician with those of a 50-year-old NBA player. For him, the opportunity cost of a professional basketball career was too high because, at the time, medical schools did not admit "older" students. If Fosnes had "gone pro," he would not be a physician today.[23] In light of the relative growth of NBA salaries, and the willingness of medical schools now to accept older entering students, a graduating star forward with an opportunity to play in the NBA today might make a different decision.

The quality of play and the athletic quality of players in professional sports today is better than ever, and economics has a lot to do with it. Why? Because more opportunities for fame and fortune have lured a higher percentage of a growing (domestic, and international, and, since Jackie Robinson, racially integrated) population into sports. Today's athletes are bigger, stronger, faster; they are in better physical condition; they start training earlier in life and put in more hours of practice. Thanks to free agency, they also get to keep a higher percentage of the revenues they generate. Salary levels attainable by these top performers produce strong incentives for them to stay in shape and to play better. When one could lose his job as a major league shortstop 60 years ago and return to his local community at a wage roughly comparable to what he earned scooping up ground balls, the financial inducements to stay in shape were not overwhelming; today, however, when even a mediocre professional baseball player's sports income easily exceeds $1 million a year, the sacrifice from returning to an ordinary job is enormous.

In a market economy, *economic profits* arise from several factors – hard work, chance, ownership of a specialized resource, entrepreneurship and business acumen, imperfect information, collusion with rivals, barriers to entry, or government protection. Many of these sources reflect a short-run imbalance that eventually is competed away, but some endure. Students can speculate about which factors apply to professional sports. For professional sports leagues and team owners, continued public protection from rivals, allowed collective action in selling broadcast rights and limiting expansion and team relocation, financial entry barriers[24] and infusions of taxpayer dollars for new facilities, may produce an expectation of continued profitability despite owners' protests that they are losing money. Finally, the direct financial rate of return from owning a sports franchise might be lower than for alternative investments because of the nonpecuniary benefits of ownership – it's fun and it bestows instant celebrity status on the owner (presumably a positive attribute).

Sports also can be used to illustrate the principle of *discounting* or *present value*. An obvious application is to players' multi-year contracts. The media invariably reports the undiscounted sum of the annual salaries over the life of the contract. So, a four-year contract that pays a good third line NHL defenseman $2 million, $2.5 million, $3.0 million, and $3.5 million annually for 2020, 2021, 2022, and 2023 is reported as an $11 million contract, when its initial net present value at an 8 percent annual investment opportunity cost is only

$9.7 million (if the salaries are paid at the beginning of each respective year, and before taxes and his agent's cut).

Moral hazard can be illustrated by the difference in hit batsmen in the American and National Baseball Leagues. Since the American League uses a "designated hitter" for the pitcher, who never appears at the plate, a pitcher in the American League has less risk of direct retaliation if he were to hit a batter on the opposing team. Early empirical evidence supported this supposition (Goff, Shughart, and Tollison 1997). However, subsequent research argued that retaliation is more efficiently directed at sluggers than at weak hitting pitchers, and showed that American League designated hitters are plunked more frequently than are National League pitchers. Revised estimates showed that the designated hitter effect on hit batsmen is not statistically significant (Trandel, White, and Klein 1998). And one wonders what the wearing of a modern helmet, and foot, shin, and elbow pads by batters has on a pitcher's propensity to throw closer to a batter and/or the batter's inclination to crowd the plate to avoid being struck out with a fastball on the outside edge of the plate?

Adverse selection can be illustrated by a *Chicago Tribune* June 18, 2002, report that "The White Sox don't fare well before big crowds." The White Sox were only 7–16 when attendance exceeded 27,000. But larger crowds likely meant the White Sox were playing a better opponent, and so they would be expected to perform worse. Although the *Tribune* article doesn't say, the White Sox poor record could also be because the larger crowds were at away games, since the White Sox were a notoriously poor team and drew few fans to home games that year.

Economists also have useful insights pertaining to *distributional issues*. We can unmask the winners and losers from particular policies, especially when many of the effects are indirect and the distributional impacts are obscured. For example, in a study of the income levels of consumers of different products based on the 1994 Consumer Expenditure Survey (CES), Timothy Peterson (1997) discovered that the weighted mean income of consumers of tickets to sporting events was 78 percent above the average consumer's income. Such information can help people assess the distributional consequences of proposals to subsidize sporting facilities from tax revenues collected via regressive state and local sales taxes. Although it is not clear who benefits most from such subsidies – team owners, players, or fans – none of them is eligible for food stamps.

A further distribution issue that can foster a good (and often heated) discussion is differences in compensation between men and women. Should men's and women's national soccer teams be compensated similarly because they play with the same rules and expend comparable energy? Or should men be paid more because they attract larger crowds that are willing to pay more for admission to the games? Should prize money be the same on the PGA and LPGA golf tours? Currently it is not.

Finally, we offer a few examples from the most recent sub-field emerging within economics – *behavioral economics*. David Romer's (2006) analysis of the decision of a football coach to go for a first down rather than punting on fourth down has attracted a lot of attention. Based on the probability of making the first down, and the chance of subsequently scoring vs. getting the ball back after punting and holding the opponent's offense, or kicking a field goal, he discovered that coaches punt or try field goals (i.e., kick) far too often. Why? Perhaps coaches value the decrease in chances of winning because of failed gambles that are immediately evident and increases from successful gambles that pay off further in the future asymmetrically, called "present bias." Maybe the instant humiliation if the team does not succeed in making the first down when it does not kick outweighs the eventual scoring benefits of the times when they do make it.

Devin Pope and Maurice Schweitzer (2011) examined putting by professional golfers who seldom leave putts short, because few putts that are left short go into the hole! They discovered that professional golfers leave putts short more frequently when attempting a putt for a birdie than when attempting a similar putt just to save par. Apparently, the thought of turning a possible birdie into a bogey by launching the initial birdie putt far enough beyond the hole that they would subsequently face a difficult par putt coming back induces them to play it safe and leave the putt short more often, insuring the par, but sacrificing a chance at a birdie. The behavior suggests they don't want to give up an almost guaranteed par when they face a birdie putt and are willing to pay for it by sacrificing some of their chance at a birdie. In behavioral economics it is called "loss aversion." Baker Mayfield, the Cleveland Browns quarterback, also illustrated it when he stated: "I hate losing more than I love winning" while describing his resolve to lead the Browns to the Super Bowl (Canova 2021).

DOs AND DON'Ts

This list of guidelines should help instructors who use sports to illustrate basic principles of economics.

- Do remember that not all students are sports fans. Students come with different levels of understanding of league and team names, star players, and knowledge of the histories and strategies of various games. Sometimes background details are required.

- Do bear in mind the instructor–student age gap when selecting examples and illustrations; think Rory McElroy, Naomi Osaka, and Simone Biles rather than Jack Nicklaus, Chris Evert, and Mary Lou Retton, respectively.
- Do use current media accounts and data for both illustrations and measurement purposes.
- Do encourage students to be creative in the application of economic theory to the "wide world of sports."
- Do let students shine when they know more than you do about a particular game or its rules or history.
- Don't rely exclusively on North American sports examples and US male sports figures; instead diversify.
- Don't get caught up in the facts, personalities, or the rules of particular sports.[25]
- Don't overdo it on sports jargon.
- Don't forget it's an economics course, not a sports course.
- Don't rely too heavily on sports examples; choose your sports carefully, and tie them into economic theory.

CONCLUSION

In this chapter we have tried both to convey the usefulness of using sports in teaching economic theory to undergraduates and to illustrate some of the ways this can be done. Our coverage is not exhaustive in depth or breadth, but it should give instructors a start. Other economics topics that can be dealt with through sports examples include risk and uncertainty; union behavior; income and substitution effects as they apply to the supply of labor; racial discrimination; the structure of the competition and expected outcomes, such as more likely repeat champions in tennis than golf; and externalities.[26]

One could teach an entire introductory (or intermediate level) price theory course using nothing but sports examples. Although we do not advocate such specialization, it is nevertheless our contention that a dose of sports illustrations can contribute toward making an economics course more enjoyable and productive for both instructors and students.

ACKNOWLEDGMENT

The authors thank the late T. Aldrich Finegan for comments and Amara Haider and Madelaine Ryan for research assistance that improved the chapter.

NOTES

1. This chapter is an updated and revised version of Chapter 8, "Using Sports to Teach Economics," in William E. Becker and Michael Watts, eds., *Teaching Economics to Undergraduates: Alternatives to Chalk and Talk*. Edward Elgar Publishing, 1999. Used with permission of the publisher.
2. https://entrepreneurshandbook.co/how-dippin-dots-went-from-bankruptcy-to-330m-in-annual-revenue-in-6-years-ae65a18bd59d.
3. A 2019 study by *Team Marketing Report* in Chicago found that it costs a family of four an average of $234 to attend an MLB game. The usual tally of a family's outlay for a game includes tickets, soft drinks and beer, hot dogs and desserts, parking, and souvenirs. Although a family may indeed purchase all of these items on a given evening, (a) they are not required to buy anything beyond the admission tickets, (b) the food substitutes for the cost of what would have been eaten at a restaurant or prepared at home, and (c) the souvenirs are not likely to be purchased on repeat trips to the ballpark. Similar 2019 costs for the NHL, NBA, and NFL were $424, $430, and $540, respectively.
4. 2019 average ticket prices were $33 for MLB, $89 for the NBA, $102 for the NFL, and $135 for the NHL.
5. In historian Doris Kearns Goodwin's book, *Wait Till Next Year*, her memoir of a young girl growing up in Brooklyn in the 1950s, she often listened to Dodgers games during the day and then retold the story of the game to her father in the evening. According to Goodwin,
    When I had finished describing the game, it was time to go to bed, unless I could convince my father to tally each player's batting average, reconfiguring his statistics to reflect the developments of that day's game. If Reese went 3 for 5 and had started the day at .303, my father showed me, by adding and multiplying all the numbers in his head, that his average would rise to .305. If Snider went 0 for 4 and had started the day at .301, then his average would dip four points below the .300 mark. (Goodwin 1997, 17)
6. Fans and commentators frequently complain that a particular baseball player "can't hit," when in fact the difference between an average hitter – someone with a .260 average – and a player on the verge of stardom and a multimillion dollar contract – someone who can hit .300 – is only one hit a week.
7. In 2019, each NFL team received $255 million annually from the league's television contracts, up 150 percent from $100 million in 2010. Under the 2020 television contracts, which began during the 2014 season, regular season games are broadcast on five networks: CBS, Fox, NBC, ESPN, and the NFL Network. The 150 percent increase in television revenues obtained by the NFL from 2010 to 2019 did not lower ticket prices just because owners and leagues now had more money from non-ticket sources. Ticket prices remained high as a reflection of strong demand to watch live football. NFL player salaries increased, both because of revenue-sharing arrangements and because salaries are derived from the overall demand for football viewing. This is an excellent example of the order of causality.
8. The reverse-order draft provides an opportunity to discuss the frequent conflict between strong *incentives*, arguably one of the most important ideas in all of economics, and equality of either opportunities or outcomes. For example, why reward a team that performs badly with the best player in the subsequent draft? Why not make it draft last, or demote it to minor league status and replace it with the best minor league team for the next season, as is done in European professional

soccer? What are the pros and cons of such a promotion and relegation approach that rewards success and punishes failure (vis-à-vis a reverse-order-draft that rewards failure and punishes success) and why might different leagues in different circumstances choose different incentives? The reverse-order draft also offers an opportunity to discuss unintended consequences. When some teams realized they were out of contention for the annual championship, they would sit star players under contract to reduce the risk of injury to them and also to increase their chances of losing (called "tanking") and thereby increase the probability of drafting one of the most talented among the new young players entering the league. Once fans realized some teams were tanking, attendance waned. To combat this unintended consequence, the leagues put a group of teams with the worst records together into a group and choose the order of drafting by lottery among them. Thus, finishing last rather than fourth to last in the league standings no longer was valued as highly.

9. In the 1960s, The Kansas City Athletics (now the Oakland Athletics) sold so many good players (including the home run king Roger Maris) to the New York Yankees that commentators sometimes referred to the Athletics as a "Yankees' farm team." But the receipts received by the Athletics for the players kept the team out of financial trouble.

10. A slightly different competitive balance issue concerns not whether a team from a home territory that values winning highly wins a larger proportion of its games, but rather whether it tends to win relatively more games played in front of its home crowd. In the NBA, for example, where the home team retains virtually all of the gate receipts, scheduling (e.g., arduous road trips) appears to give more of an edge to home teams. It is not surprising, then, that the NBA has the highest home court winning advantage among the four major professional sports in North America.

11. Be sure to distinguish for students the two different meanings of the word "surplus" in economics. We label an excess of quantity supplied over quantity demanded as "surplus" and also call the area between the demand curve and opportunity cost "surplus." The latter is the more pervasive use by economists, but students are likely to think the former is the only important use.

12. Players on strike are not unemployed. In US labor statistics they are counted both as in the labor force and employed. However, if the players are locked out by the owners, then they are considered unemployed.

13. Set the two expressions equal to each other and solve for p.

14. For another application of game theory to baseball see Merz (1996), who discredits Roy Blount Jr.'s (1993, 68) allegation that the great Giants' centerfielder Willie Mays, who never led the league in doubles, often retreated to first base when he realized he could get to second (but not all the way to third) after a hit into the gap. Blount contends that Mays returned to first because left-handed pull-hitter Willie McCovey followed him in the Giants' batting order for 13 years. With Mays on first base, the first baseman had to move to the bag to hold Mays close, opening a bigger hole for McCovey on the right side of the infield, while if Mays had gone on to second rather than retreating to first the opposing team would have walked McCovey intentionally. If McCovey got a hit, Mays could then easily make it from first to third with the Giants ending up with men on first and third rather than first and second bases. Merz explains how this alleged strategy of Mays is dominated by going to second no matter what the opposing pitcher does when McCovey comes to bat. Furthermore, why is the first baseman holding Mays on the bag to reduce the probability of a steal of second when Mays just returned from second

to first voluntarily? This is an example of how to infer intentions from observable behavior, the economist's stock-in-trade.

15. In the few instances where there are two professional franchises in the same sport in the same city, it turns out that ticket prices exceed the league average, a surprising result when competition is considered. This result occurs because even just one half of the population in these few cities (Los Angeles, San Francisco, New York, Chicago) vastly exceeds the average population of the cities in which franchises are monopolists.

16. The prospects for entry in professional team sports also differ substantially from other franchise industries because of the monopoly nature of the four major team sports in North America. If, for example, McDonald's, Pizza Hut, Chevron, or Verizon determines not to place a franchise in St. Louis, Burger King, Papa John's, Exxon, or AT&T may enter the St. Louis market. But if the NFL decides not to locate a franchise in St. Louis, there is no comparable professional football league whose entry into the St. Louis market can satisfy that demand.

17. See, for example, Noll (1974) for a series of studies of different sports in which the presence of another sport in the same community does not appear to affect attendance. More recent studies on basketball and MLB in the 1990s find a negative effect of the presence of another sport on attendance, but similar research on Australian Rules Football, Rugby League, and Rugby Union in Australia finds, like Noll, no effect (Borland and MacDonald 2003, p. 490).

18. If the price of attendance is more than just the ticket price that is used in calculating the elasticity of demand, which it is if travel to the game is required, then the true elasticity of demand exceeds that estimated using the ticket price alone.

19. In October 2020, billionaire Steve Cohen paid $2.4 billion to purchase the New York Mets baseball team.

20. Portions of this section are from Siegfried (1994) and are used with permission of the copyright holder, Federal Legal Publications, Inc. for an extensive analysis of the NCAA as a cartel see Fleisher et al. (1992) and Sanderson and Siegfried (2018, 2019).

21. Entry may be difficult into NCAA sports, but it is easier than entry into professional sports leagues. College teams that wish to upgrade to Division I status (the highest level of competition, and the only level that generates substantial revenues) have numerous teams they can approach as prospective opponents. In contrast to professional sports, collegiate teams attempting to join a major conference also have alternatives, as there are more than a half dozen major college athletic conferences.

22. In October 2020, national champion Louisiana State University head football coach Ed Orgeron voluntarily took a $300,000 per year (5 percent) reduction in his salary to match the 5 percent pay cut imposed on all non-coaching employees of the LSU athletic department. A $300,000 pay cut would reduce most people to zero; it left Orgeron with $5.7 million.

23. The first Heisman Trophy winner, Jay Berwanger of the University of Chicago, faced similar salary offers from the NFL and business entities when he graduated in 1936. He selected business.

24. Because individual teams can't enter the industry, to be a credible threat requires sufficient capital to form an entire new league with a minimum of probably eight teams.

25. Some years ago, a student attempted to enroll in The Economics of Sports course taught by one of us. That course requires intermediate microeconomic theory as

a prerequisite. The student did not meet the prerequisite, but insisted he would have no difficulty because he "knew more about sports than anyone else." When he was denied admission to the course (a review of his record in principles confirmed that he surely did not "know more than anyone else about economics") he muttered that there must be something seriously wrong with a course on The Economics of Sports if a thorough knowledge of sports was not sufficient background to take it. If he had realized the power of the core of economics principles and understood the way in which economists apply those few powerful ideas to myriad issues, he might have recognized that a discipline founded on the idea of "have tools, will travel" relies mostly on the tools, not the travel.

26. One could also tie in Peltzman's well-known 1975 study of offsetting driver behavior with regard to seatbelt usage with a sport's proposition that better and more protective equipment for NFL players doesn't reduce injuries – they just run at each other harder and attempt riskier behavior until their injury rate reaches the prior equilibrium they are willing to tolerate.

REFERENCES

Andreff, W. 2014. The winner's curse in sports economics. In O. Budzinski and A. Fedderson, eds., *Contemporary Research in Sports Economics*. Frankfurt: Peter Lang Academic Research.

Blount, R. Jr. 1993. Plink-fumba-baraumba-boom. *Sports Illustrated* 79 (August 9): 64–74.

Borland, J. and R. MacDonald. 2003. Demand for sport. *Oxford Review of Economic Policy* 19(4): 478–502

Bruggink, T.H. 1993. National pastime to dismal science: using baseball to illustrate economic principles. *Eastern Economic Journal* 19 (Summer): 275–294.

Canova, D. 2021. Baker Mayfield talks Super Bowl Drive: I hate losing more than I love winning. FoxNews (April 29).

Cartwright, E. 2019. Guilt aversion and reciprocity in the performance-enhancing drug game. *Journal of Sports Economics* 20(4): 535–555.

Cassing, J., and R.W. Douglas. 1980. Implications of the auction mechanism in baseball's free agent draft. *Southern Economic Journal* 47 (July): 110–121.

Coates, D. 2019. Franchise relocation and stadium subsidies. Chapter 24 in P. Downward, B. Frick, B. Humphreys, T. Pawlowski, J. Ruseski, and B. Soebbing, eds., *The Sage Handbook of Sports Economics*. London: Sage.

DeSantis, A.A. 2018. An economic analysis of the rise in franchise values in the four major North American sports leagues from 2008–2016. Honors Theses. Union College Digital Works. 1703.

Douglas, C. 1996. The economic cost of the baseball strike. Senior Honors Thesis, Vanderbilt University (April).

Eber, N. 2008. The performance-enhancing drug game reconsidered. *Journal of Sports Economics* 9: 318–327.

Fleisher, A., B. Goff, and R. Tollison. 1992. *The National Collegiate Athletic Association: A Study in Cartel Behavior*. Chicago: University of Chicago Press.

Fort R. 2006. Inelastic sports pricing at the gate: a survey. Chapter 77 in W. Andreff and S. Szymanski, eds., *Handbook on the Economics of Sport*. Cheltenham, UK: Edward Elgar Publishing.

Fort, R. 2011. *Sports Economics*, 3rd edition. Upper Saddle River, NJ: Pearson.

Goff, B., W.F. Shughart, and R. Tollison. 1997. Batter up! Moral hazard and the effects of the designated hitter rule on hit batsmen. *Economic Inquiry* 35(3): 555–561.

Golliver, B. 2016. Hawks get Dwight Howard in move that will benefit both parties. *Sports Illustrated* (July 1).

Goodwin, D.K. 1997. *Wait Till Next Year*. New York: Simon & Schuster.

Happel, S.K., and M.M. Jennings. 1995. Herd them together and scalp them. *The Wall Street Journal* (February 23): A-14.

Jamil, M. 2019. Team production and efficiency in sports. In P. Downward, B. Frick, B. Humphreys, T. Pawlowski, J. Ruseski, and B. Soebbing, eds., *The Sage Handbook of Sports Economics*. London: Sage.

Jones, J.C.H., D.G. Ferguson, and K.G. Stewart. 1993. Blood sports and cherry pie: some economics of violence in the National Hockey League. *American Journal of Economics and Sociology* 52 (January): 63–78.

Kahn, L.M. 1993. Free agency, long-term contracts and compensation in major league baseball: estimates from panel data. *Review of Economics and Statistics* 75 (February): 157–164.

Knowles, G., K. Sherony, and M. Haupert. 1992. The demand for major league baseball: a test of the uncertainty of outcome hypothesis. *The American Economist* 36 (Fall): 72–80.

Krautman, A. 2019. The baseball players' labor market. In P. Downward, B. Frick, B. Humphreys, T. Pawlowski, J. Ruseski, and B. Soebbing, eds., *The Sage Handbook of Sports Economics*. London: Sage.

Lehn, K. 1982. Property rights, risk sharing, and player disability in Major League Baseball. *Journal of Law & Economics* 25 (2): 343–366.

Lehn, K. 1984. Information asymmetries in baseball's free agent market. *Economic Inquiry* 22 (1): 76–89.

McCloskey, D.N. 1990. *If You're So Smart*. Chicago: The University of Chicago Press.

Merz, T.E. 1996. Willie Mays: meet John Nash. *Journal of Economic Education* 27 (Winter): 45–48.

Noll, R.G. 1974. Attendance and price setting. In R.G. Noll, ed., *Government and the Sports Business*. Washington, DC: The Brookings Institution.

Noll, R.G. and A. Zimbalist, eds. 1997. *Sports, Jobs, and Taxes*. Washington, DC: The Brookings Institution.

Peltzman, S. 1975. The effects of automobile safety regulations. *Journal of Political Economy* 83 (August): 677–726.

Peterson, T. 1997. Public subsidies for professional sports events are a subsidy for the wealthy. Senior Honors Thesis. Vanderbilt University (December).

Pope, D. and M. Schweitzer. 2011. Is Tiger Woods loss averse? Persistent bias in the face of experience, competition, and high stakes. *American Economic Review* 101 (1): 129–157.

Porter, P.K. 1992. The role of the fan in professional baseball. In *Diamonds are Forever: The Business of Baseball*. Washington, DC: The Brookings Institution.

Quirk, J. and R.D. Fort. 1992. *Pay Dirt: The Business of Professional Team Sports*. Princeton, NJ: Princeton University Press.

Raimondo, H.J. 1983. Free agents' impact on the labor market for baseball players. *Journal of Labor Research* 4 (Spring): 183–193.

Rockerbie, D. and S. Easton. 2019. Economic issues of the National Hockey League: a survey of the literature. Chapter 31 in P. Downward, B. Frick, B. Humphreys, T. Pawlowski, J. Ruseski, and B. Soebbing, eds., *The Sage Handbook of Sports Economics*. London: Sage.

Romer, D. 2006. Do firms maximize? Evidence from professional football. *Journal of Political Economy* 114 (2): 340–365.

Rottenberg, S. 1956. The baseball players' labor market. *Journal of Political Economy* 64 (June): 242–258.

Sanderson, A. and J. Siegfried. 2018. The National Collegiate Athletic Association cartel: why it exists, how it works, and what it does. *Review of Industrial Organization* (March) 52 (2): 185–209.

Sanderson, A. and J. Siegfried. 2019. The economics of the National Collegiate Athletic Association. Chapter 12 in P. Downward, B. Frick, B. Humphreys, T. Pawlowski, J. Ruseski, and B. Soebbing, eds., *The Sage Handbook of Sports Economics*. London: Sage.

Scahill, E. 1990. Did Babe Ruth have a comparative advantage as a pitcher? *Journal of Economic Education* 21 (Fall): 402–410.

Scully, G. 1974. Pay and performance in major league baseball. *American Economic Review* 64 (6): 915–930.

Scully, G.W. 1989. *The Business of Major League Baseball*. Chicago: The University of Chicago Press.

Scully, G. 1995. *The Market Structure of Sports*. Chicago: The University of Chicago Press.

Siegfried, J. 1994. Review of *The National Collegiate Athletic Association: a study in cartel behavior*, by Fleisher, A.A., B.L. Goff, and R.D. Tollison, in *The Antitrust Bulletin* 39 (Summer): 599–609.

Siegfried, J. and A. Zimbalist. 2000. The economics of sports facilities and their communities. *Journal of Economic Perspectives* 14 (2): 115–134.

Szymanski, S. 2003. The economic design of sporting contests. *Journal of Economic Literature* 41 (4): 1137–1187.

Tollison, R. 2012. To be or not to be: the NCAA as a cartel. Chapter 18 in L. Kahane and S. Shmanske, eds., *The Oxford Handbook of Sports Economics: Vol. 1, The Economics of Sports*. Oxford: Oxford University Press.

Trandel, G., Lawrence H.W., and Peter K. 1998. The effect of the designated hitter rule on hit batsmen: pitcher's moral hazard or the team's cost-benefit calculation? A comment. *Economic Inquiry* 36 (4): 679–684.

White, M.D. 1986. Self-interest redistribution and the National Football League Players Association. *Economic Inquiry* 24 (October): 669–680.

Zipp, J.F. 1996. The economic impact of the baseball strike of 1994. *Urban Affairs Review* 32 (November): 157–158.

2. Using sports-related empirical research to teach critical reading skills in intermediate microeconomics

Peter von Allmen

INTRODUCTION

A typical presentation of microeconomic theory is mostly silent on how one would translate a theoretical principle into a testable hypothesis. At the introductory level, this can lead to students wondering if economic models are anything more than lines on a graph. At the intermediate level, when we expect students to engage with the fundamentals of modeling as presented using the algebra and calculus of comparative statics, students can easily get lost in the computational challenges of Lagrangian multipliers, cost functions and reaction curves. As a result, they may leave with no sense of how economists actually "do" empirical economics. Anyone who has taught intermediate microeconomics for any length of time has likely had a student, after weeks of poring over production and cost graphs, ask how a firm could actually determine its cost function. As the level of mathematical sophistication that appears and is expected in a typical undergraduate theory course has marched steadily forward over time (paralleling that at the graduate level), students necessarily devote increasing effort in learning how to solve models and less on how to actually employ them. High scores on exams made up largely of calculus problems couched in economic terms can give students the false impression that they understand the power of the models to answer questions. The question of the balance of content in an intermediate theory course and "right" amount of calculus is not new (for example, see von Allmen and Brower, 1998). My argument is not the level at which it is pitched, but the extent to which it is applied that makes the difference in what students take away from the course.

The goal of this chapter is to describe a pedagogical approach that improves students' ability to create a meaningful understanding of how theoretical concepts are applied to research questions. The underlying goal of the change is for students to see micro theory as more than whiteboards filled with derivatives and graphs couched in shallow examples with little staying power. In what follows, I describe a mechanism instructors can use to bring theory to life and at the same time teach students the process of reading professional literature.

Context

Skidmore College is a highly selective liberal arts college that, until 2013, offered a typical intermediate microeconomic theory (hereafter micro theory) course with the typical prerequisites of intro micro, intro macro and calculus I. Following this course and intermediate macro, majors are required to take four advanced electives and write a senior thesis. In both electives and the thesis course, students are frequently required to read journal articles and book chapters from the professional literature. Prior to 2013, the in-class component of the theory courses was typical of our peer institutions, having three contact hours per week with significant emphasis on technical skills.[1]

Under this curriculum, students found it very challenging to effectively read journal articles in advanced electives. With no formal introduction to the literature, students are likely to struggle to appreciate the central arguments in a typical journal article or see how empirical models represent applications or tests of theoretical constructs. The problem in such cases is not with the students *per se*, but instead rooted in a failure to teach them how to read such work. While reading journal articles is second nature to professional economists, the genre of writing is completely unfamiliar to even the strongest undergraduate students. The purpose of this chapter is to describe our effort to change this outcome for the better through systematic pedagogical strategies designed to teach the process of reading professional scholarship.

THE PRESENTING PROBLEMS

Our decision to explicitly teach the process of reading professional literature in economics stems from two interrelated problems. First, despite our best efforts to make the course applied, the relatively heavy sledding of a calculus-based theory course resulted in our devoting much of class time, and so also student attention, on how to solve models rather than apply them to real-world problems in a research setting. As a result, students learned less about both the strengths and weaknesses of the models than they otherwise might. More troublesome was that they often missed the importance of the assumptions that make a specific model (in)appropriate for a particular application. In the abstract, even a concept as simple as a demand elasticity can prove difficult to translate from formula to a sound policy recommendation. This dimension of the challenge was clearly aggravated by our need to teach calculus methods such as partial derivatives and Lagrangian multipliers "on the fly" to students with no prior knowledge of them.[2] At times, even good students may focus so intently on how to solve the models that they write answers that violate basic theoretical assumptions or are clearly impossible as a result of simple arithmetic errors.

Second, as a department faculty, we had the strong sense that in our advanced electives (all of which require either micro theory, macro theory, or both) students were struggling to read the professional literature. This slowed the pace of our advanced courses as it reduced what we could expect students to learn on their own. It also exacerbated heterogeneity among the students. In a typical group of students in a 300-level elective such as labor economics, at least some will have already had several electives. As a result, they have gained meaningful facility in reading empirical research. For others, labor is their first elective and they have never read a journal article. For such a student, their experiences with academic reading may be limited almost exclusively to textbooks.

The combination of these structural weaknesses in the curriculum meant that when students enrolled in our senior seminar, they had mixed and uneven experience in how to engage with the literature in a way that would allow them to write a strong thesis paper. Nor were they well positioned to apply their knowledge in the job market.

A WAY FORWARD

The most important element of crafting a way forward was to not blame the students or an instructor, or even a course. The problem lay in the structure of the curriculum. What we needed was a new approach to teaching micro theory that led to better outcomes both in that course and all subsequent courses. A presenting problem in finding a workable solution was that micro theory is already a very dense course in which more can lead to less (this is arguably where we already stood). To make the space for more direct student engagement in quantitative problem solving as well as making significant space for teaching the process of reading the professional literature, we added an additional hour of in-class contact time for both macro and micro theory beginning in the Fall of 2014. As a department faculty, we agreed that this additional contact hour carried no expectation that we would use that time to cover additional chapters. While in practice it may have made it marginally easier to bolster some presentations or make it to those last chapters on the syllabus, we wanted to explicitly set aside the notion of more textbook-based content. Instead, the hour would be used to (1) explore more examples, special cases, and applications of existing chapters; (2) do more in-class ungraded work on quantitative methods; and (3) most importantly, add approximately six journal articles to the syllabus, chosen specifically to teach both how theory is applied in a research context and how to do close, critical reading of such work.

A typical class size for micro theory at Skidmore is in the low twenties. The process of implementing the readings is straightforward. For each major unit – consumer theory, cost and production, market outcomes, labor – students read at least one journal article. These articles include an empirical estimation of demand, a behavioral paper, a cost paper, and several empirical papers on monopoly or monopsony power, including strategic pricing under conditions of market power. Later in the chapter, I provide examples of several of these.

The best papers for this process have two defining characteristics: they are applications that most students can relate to and will find interesting, and they require minimal time spent explaining minutiae or industry-specific terminology. Using this as guide, papers are typically drawn from either highly descriptive pieces typically found in the *Journal of Economic Perspectives*, in which students can see the authors' either implicit or explicit use of models to frame questions and discuss outcomes, or examples from field journals in which high quality data are readily available and empirical tests are relatively straightforward. The data issue is important as it reduces the proportion of the papers spent describing workarounds and esoteric econometrics. In this latter category, research on the economics of sports leagues, contracts, and facilities are among the most approachable and inherently interesting to students. While it sometimes requires a bit of class time to explain details such as the need to recognize heterogeneous groups of labor (skill sets), or the structure of an open league with promotion and relegation, it also represents a nice opportunity for students who already understand the distinction to explain it to others.

The Process

The goal is to get students to see how theory is applied in a research setting and to be able to independently read primary empirical research scholarship in economics. To be sure, the details of the econometric methodology in many papers is beyond the grasp of undergraduates. But with carefully chosen papers, directed by prompts or reading questions, students can reach the point where they have a solid understanding of what the authors hoped to learn, how they proceeded, what they found, and why it matters. As described in the examples below, reading questions are typically tailored to the individual assignment, but are derived from a generic set of questions that essentially form the goals for students' comprehension when they read.

For each assigned article, students are assigned to read the paper and prepare notes on the reading questions. These notes are not collected or graded. Students first meet in small groups of three or four to discuss their understanding of the paper and their responses to the reading questions, after

Table 2.1   *Generic reading questions*

1. What is the research question?
2. Why does it matter? That is, does it test a theory from the larger economics literature? Does it investigate a particular phenomenon in one industry or market? Is it meant to drive policy?
3. What was the authors' methodology? That is, what data did they use? How did they construct the key hypothesis test(s)?
4. What are the results? Which coefficients are significant? Which are not? What does that tell us about the hypotheses? Do they conform to expectations based on theory?
5. What can economists and/or practitioners learn from this paper?

which we move to a plenary discussion with the same goal. Having the small group conversations in advance of the plenary discussion has two advantages: it creates a bit of peer pressure to come to class having done the assignment, and it increases students' confidence such that they participate more readily in the plenary discussion. As a way of scaffolding student skills, the reading questions for the first several papers are specific to the assigned article but in the latter part of the semester, I sometimes give students the generic reading questions shown in Table 2.1.

Students' understanding of the papers – which focuses explicitly on their ability to explain how and why any given paper is relevant for our study of the-oretical models and what the results tell us about the hypotheses being tested (i.e., why they matter) – is included on all exams and comprises a significant proportion of the totals points (typically 20–25 percent). I return to the subject of assessment in the next section.

Examples

The most important part of creating these assignments is choosing the papers. Especially at the start of the semester, papers with long theoretical derivations or extensive use of esoteric econometrics can result in frustration as students lose track of the research questions and get lost in notation that is beyond their grasp. The most effective papers are those in which the authors are clear about their goal and clearly articulate how the empirical model allows the authors to state what they have learned.[3] More generally, it is useful to put oneself in the place of the student, reading questions in hand, and have a good sense that the answers are there to discover.

Another important characteristic is topic. At Skidmore, topics that have been best received are those related to sports, the environment, health and behavioral aspects of consumer theory. Below, I briefly explain three examples from the sports literature. Beyond their inherent interest to students, research related to professional sports has a number of advantages. First, many students in the room have a working knowledge of the sport and so some familiarity with the data. More importantly, because the papers often test general theoretical predictions (as in Example 1 below on attendance demand) students need not know anything about the sport. Second, there is a good supply of papers that test basic theoretical constructs, such as whether two goods are substitutes or complements or whether an employee receives a wage that is consistent with what theory would predict. Finally, because high quality data are readily available, there is less time spent constructing and defending proxies that students may find troublesome.

A vital caveat to the choice of papers, and in particular the use of sports-related research, is the need to be inclusive. Despite recent improvements in the gender balance of faculty, the broader discipline is predominantly male and much of the sports-related research is written by white men.[4] This can be discouraging to students of other affinity groups and run counter to efforts to diversify the field. Experience in our department indicates that students are quite attentive to not just what the papers are about, but also who wrote them. As the broader discipline struggles to diversify the ranks of PhDs, allowing all students to see themselves in this role can be a meaningful motivator (see for example, Porter and Serra, 2020).

Example 1: Stadium attendance and television audience in English league football (Babatunde Buraimo, 2008).

In this paper, Buraimo (2008) tests the relationship between live attendance and television ratings for English soccer. We read this paper following the unit on consumer theory. There are several elements of this work that make it both popular and effective. The first is the topic. As a football (soccer) paper, it appeals to students interested in sports. Because it is non-US centric, it also appeals to many international students. Importantly, because the paper is about demand rather than the game itself, it requires no knowledge of soccer whatsoever. One only need accept that it is an enormously popular spectator sport in Europe and consumers can either watch the games in person (live attendance) or on television. Finally, it requires little motivation to get students to grasp why firm (team) owners would find the relationship between these two demand functions important. The paper estimates two separate demand functions, each with a number of potentially important explanatory variables. The only challenge specific to this paper is that the television equation is estimated using two-stage least squares with both stages reported, requiring some advance prepping of students regarding where to focus their attention as they look for tests of the key hypotheses.

Buraimo's goal is to determine whether television demand and live attendance are substitutes or complements. The prior expectation, of course, is that they are substitutes. Buraimo reviews a number of papers which find that televising matches in other sports and in other countries does indeed reduce attendance. He extends this work by testing this relationship in both directions – whether live attendance is a substitute for television and whether televising a match creates a substitute for attendance. Importantly, in the data and models sections, he includes demand equations for both models that look much like those we might specify in an abstract model in class. He also includes a nice description of how he chose the league (few sell out games that cause econometric problems) and his list of explanatory variables (essentially operationalizing tastes and preferences).

It makes for interesting discussion that he finds the results to be asymmetric. That is, television does appear to be a substitute for live attendance (though the results vary based on the network), but the reverse is not true. Instead, live attendance serves as a complement to television demand. Because of this asymmetry, students see that the coefficient on the "televised" variables in the live attendance model are generally negative while the coefficient of the attendance variable in the television ratings model is positive. Thus, the model shows that having fans at the games is an important product characteristic.[5] It's more fun to watch a game on TV with a stadium full of cheering fans than an empty house. While it would be ideal if the author had price variables instead of quantities such that the signs were reversed and matched cross-elasticity signs, students are still able to see that it is a test of a well-established element of consumer theory and that the results make intuitive sense. Specific discussion questions for this paper appear in Table 2.2. The extensive list of explanatory variables includes product (game) characteristics such as: day of the week, indicators for rivalries, competing programming, match quality and others. In Questions 4 through 7, students have the opportunity to discuss the author's choice of what to include and the results of the estimation process. Finally, in Question 8, the students are asked to consider how the results should influence team strategy.

Example 2: Take me out to the Yakyushiai (Leeds and Sakata, 2012).

Another excellent example of estimating consumer demand is Michael Leeds and Sumi Sakata's (2012) study of baseball attendance in Japan. This paper uses data from the Nippon Professional Baseball league to investigate the determinants of live attendance. This paper is more straightforward than that of Buraimo in that it tests only live attendance. Like the Buraimo paper, it requires no baseball knowledge and the authors do an excellent job of explaining the market specific variables. It is particularly well-suited to the task of showing how a theoretical model is operationalized as the authors present the model in a series of equations that mirror those that students have already seen

Table 2.2   *Reading questions for "Stadium attendance and television audience in English league football"*

1. What is the author's goal in this paper? That is, what is the research question?
2. What are the previous findings regarding this relationship?
3. What league and time period did the author study?
4. What factors did the author consider in his model of *attendance* demand?
5. In addition to access to a broadcast of the game itself, what other substitutes did the author consider? Can you think of others that might be relevant?
6. What factors does the author consider in the model of *television* demand?
7. Based on the results of the attendance and televised demand models, what factors *do* matter? a. What is the relationship between attendance and televised games?
8. Given the author's conclusion, what challenge does this present league organizers?

in the text and lectures. Their equations (2) and (3) are shown below (Leeds and Sakata, 2012, 39). In their equation (2), P_i is a measure of price, Y_i represents income, N_i is the number of consumers in the market and T_{ijt} are tastes and preferences.

$$Q_{ijt} = f(P_i | Y_i, N_i, T_{ijt}) \tag{2}$$

$$Q_{ijt} = \beta + \gamma' X_F + \delta' X_S + \mu' X_A + \theta' X_w + \varepsilon_{ijt} \tag{3}$$

Each equation is fully explained, including how the authors use the various vectors of X to measure specific components of the independent variables in their equation (2).

There are several aspects of the results that students should find both illuminating and interesting. The first is that teams tend to price in the inelastic range of demand. While this result is more the norm than the exception in sports demand modeling, it appears to fly in the face of rational profit-maximizing behavior. The authors discuss this point extensively at a level that is entirely accessible to students. Moreover, the table of results (their Table 3) groups explanatory variables by subgroup, facilitating discussion of the various aspects of demand. Students can easily see that most of the results are consistent with expectations based on consumer theory, such as the greater popularity of weekend games, that baseball is a normal good, and preference for the chance to see better quality games. It also gives the students a chance to think about and discuss the authors' explanation for the unexpected finding that all else being equal, higher population areas have lower attendance: an increase in the number of available substitutes.

Example 3: Pay and performance in Major League Baseball (Gerald Scully, 1974).

A principal argument in this chapter is that the tidy elegance of undergraduate microeconomic theory can lead students to master derivations without having any idea as to how one would operationalize them to answer a question. Perhaps nowhere is this more evident than the derivation of labor demand. With just a few equations (production and revenue functions) and a few quick derivatives, we can get the result that marginal revenue product should equal the wage in a competitive market. This is reassuring because it also passes our commonsense test that in a competitive market, workers will be paid a wage equal to the value of their marginal product. With a few more equations and accompanying graphs, we can see that when markets are not competitive, they will likely receive less.

But does this actually happen? And if it did, how would we know? How would one even go about testing such a claim? In most industries, we do not have data on individual salaries such that we have accurate wage data. And while we might be able to determine the contribution of output to revenue to approximate marginal revenue, we do not have data on individual contributions to output to create marginal product. To resolve this problem, economists need better data. In Scully's paper, we see how an economist employs the incredibly rich, individual level data from professional sports to create the empirical model. Prior to the mid-1970s, all Major League Baseball players in the United States were subject to a labor market restriction known as the reserve clause. The reserve clause effectively bestowed complete monopsony power on teams in that all players signed contracts that effectively bound their services to one team for the entirety of their career. Even if a student is completely unfamiliar with baseball as a game, it should make sense to them that this would put workers at an enormous disadvantage. With no such thing as free agency, players could either play baseball for the team that held their rights, or not play professional baseball and work in some other industry for what amounts to a reservation wage.

In a landmark paper published in the *American Economic Review (AER)*, Gerald Scully (1974) constructed an empirical test of monopsonistic exploitation that stands as perhaps the most widely cited empirical study in all of sports economics.[6] Scully's hypothesis, based directly on theory was the following: *Because professional baseball players are subject to monopsony power, they will be paid a wage lower than their marginal revenue product (MRP).* Thanks to the wealth of individual-level data at his disposal, he was able to carefully construct a revenue and production function from which he could, in step-by-step fashion, build an estimate of *MRP* for each player and then compare that with their wage. Because each function is shown and described in the paper, students can see in just a few equations how he constructed the estimates of *MRP*.

Scully's paper can be readily assigned in a wide variety of programs. For those programs in which instructors can be confident that all students have a significant calculus background, he includes a step-by-step derivation of the relationship between wins, and revenue and cost, using first-order conditions of the profit function to show that "teams maximize profits by selecting a level of player skills and nonplayer inputs such that players receive a wage equal to their marginal revenue products less monopsony rents" (Scully, 1974, p. 917). For classes in which students do not have the tools to work through the theoretical model, he explains its predictions in simple terms, allowing students to follow the empirical specification. One can easily construct the logic of marginal revenue product for hitters in three simple equations:

Output = Wins = f(hitting, pitching, non-player inputs)

Revenue = g(Wins, other inputs)

$MRP_H = (\Delta Wins/\Delta hitting)(\Delta Revenue/\Delta Wins) = (MP)(MR) = MRP_H$

While some baseball knowledge is helpful, even students with no knowledge of baseball can easily follow along. Scully defines output as winning percentage (PCTWIN). The results of his empirical estimation of the production function (his equation (9)), are:

PCTWIN = 37.24 +.92TSA +.90TSW − 38.57NL + 43.78CONT − 75.64OUT

The two variables of interest are TSA (team slugging average), which represents the productivity of hitters, and TSW (team strikeout walk ratio), which represents the productivity of pitchers. Thus, the coefficients are the marginal products. A one-point increase in TSA increases PCTWIN by .92 points. Similarly, a one-point increase in TSW increases PCTWIN by .90 points.

His estimated revenue function (equation (10)) is:

REVENUE = −1,735,890 +10,330PCTWIN + .494SMSA + 512MARGA + 580913NL − 762,248STD − 58,523BBPCT.

Students can readily see that the coefficient on PCTWIN represents marginal revenue, as each one-point increase in PCTWIN (output) increases revenue by $10,330. Multiplying the marginal products of hitters (.92) and pitchers (.90)

by the marginal revenue of a win (10,330) results in the estimated marginal revenue products for each type of player.

MRP hitters = .92 × $10,330 = $9,504 per point TSA

MRP pitchers = .90 × $10,330 = $9,297 per 1/100 point TSW

After adjusting these figures to reflect the fact that TSA and TSW are produced by an entire roster of players rather than a single player and further adjusting MRPs downward to reflect player training costs (creating what he calls *net MRP*), he arrives at annual *MRP* estimates that can be compared with salaries. Scully shows the comparison of gross and net marginal revenue product to wages across a wide range of hitter and pitcher quality. Students see the result that players suffer an extraordinary level of monopsonistic exploitation, typically receiving about 20 percent of their marginal revenue product, and that the best players suffer the greatest exploitation, precisely what the theory of monopsony would predict.

What makes this example so powerful is that it is set in an industry familiar to most students and easily grasped by others; he explicitly shows how one can take a seemingly abstract theoretical concept (*MRP*) and put it into terms that are easy to make sense of; there is a clear prediction to be made based on theory regarding monopsonistic exploitation; and, finally, Scully's results show precisely what one would expect to find based on those predictions.

Other Examples

Obviously, not all empirical papers are appropriate for undergraduates. As noted above, those that contain advanced econometric models or techniques such as quantile regression can cause students to lose the forest among the trees. Similarly, papers that have extensive derivations with densely written proofs and/or use advanced mathematical notation are likely to cause students more confusion than clarity, especially in courses that make minimal use of calculus. Because some students may not have taken statistics and only in rare cases would have taken econometrics before enrolling in intermediate theory courses, it may be necessary to provide an overview of how to read results and what is implied by statistical significance of coefficients. To give a sense of the possibilities, Table 2.3 lists examples of some of the papers previously assigned along with the theoretical concepts they are designed to reinforce.

Table 2.3   *Other examples*

Title and author(s)	Topic
The market for charitable giving (List, 2011)	Behavioral. Overview of charitable giving markets; helps students to understand how giving coexists with self-interest.
Prospects for Nuclear Power (Davis, 2012)	Production and cost. Explains the rise and fall for the demand for power as well as detailed explanation as to why it is not economically viable with direct links to cost concepts familiar to students.
Variable ticket pricing in Major League Baseball (Rascher et al., 2007)	Advanced pricing in imperfectly competitive markets. Shows how advanced pricing increases profits.
Management practices, relational contracts and the decline of General Motors (Helper and Henderson, 2014)	Transaction costs; production and cost. Good discussion of labor input and management influence on labor productivity.
Pricing and patents of HIV/AIDs drugs in developing countries (Borrell, 2007)	Monopoly or advanced pricing in imperfectly competitive markets. Multi-market price discrimination.
Uber and the persistence of market power (Gabel, 2016) Disruptive change in the taxi business: the case of Uber (Cramer and Krueger, 2016)	Two short papers, assigned as a pair. Differing perspectives on the influence of Uber on the taxicab industry.
Do health insurers possess monopsony power in the hospital services industry? (Bates and Santerre, 2008)	Imperfect competition. Bilateral monopoly in the context of hospitals and health insurers.
The causes and consequences of Walmart's growth (Basker, 2007)	Production and cost. Monopoly and monopsony power. Non-empirical. The retail production function, scale and scope economies, pricing in concentrated markets.

ASSESSMENT

Assessing the benefits of this curricular change is challenging in part because it accompanied the additional hour of contact time each week. That said, there are a number of dimensions along which meaningful change is evident. It is clear that students read the papers and spend significant time considering the reading questions. This is no doubt in part due to their knowledge that exams will contain required questions about the substance of the papers and how they relate to the course. But evidence from informal class surveys and course evaluations indicates that students also find this to be an enjoyable part of the course (and likely a welcome break from the calculus of optimization). It is also likely that the small group discussions add an element of peer pressure to come prepared.

Examples of essay questions from midterm exams are below for the papers by Buraimo, Leeds and Sakata, and List. Students are expected to provide detailed information on each component of the question, supported by graphs and/or model specifications. The goal is to press students to make direct links between the models presented in class and those employed in the paper. Scores on student essays provide clear evidence that they are successful in doing so.

(a)   Explain the author's research question(s) in Babatunde Buraimo's paper on stadium attendance and television demand. That is, specifically, what did he want to know about English League Football? Explain the author's theoretical model in terms of the material we have studied in this class – what relationships was he investigating? How did the author operationalize the theoretical model in the empirical model? That is, what variables were used to test the expected relationships? What did he find about the relationship between demand for televised matches and live attendance? Beyond this relationship, discuss the key determinants of live attendance demand. If you were a team owner, which games would you televise?

(b)   In the paper "Take me out to the Yakyushiai…" by Michael Leeds and Sumi Sakata, the authors study the demand for attendance in the Nippon Professional Baseball League (NPB). What is the authors' central research question? How do they go about answering it (outline their methodology)? Briefly summarize the authors' research findings (results). That is, based on their results, what brings Japanese fans out to the ballgame? Assuming that team owners want to increase attendance, what strategies might they pursue?

(c)   In the paper "The market for Charitable Giving," by J.A. List, the author describes how it is that we can reconcile charitable giving with the standard utility maximizing model in which consumers derive utility from consumption. Explain his argument and show using a graph (or graphs) how an individual's indifference curves would change based on his explanation such that the quantity of giving goes from zero to a positive value. He goes on to discuss ways in which the government creates incentives for giving. How do these incentives alter the consumer budget constraint and what is the likely impact on the level of giving (show and explain)? What types of institutions are the most frequent recipients of gifts? Finally, briefly explain what List means when he says that gifts are "sticky downwards" and why this might be so.

Finally, anecdotal evidence suggests that students in advanced electives benefit from the experience of reading journal articles in intermediate theory courses. The same is true for students in the senior thesis course.

CONCLUSION

While students in advanced electives and capstone courses are often required to read articles from the professional literature, there is no obvious place in the curriculum where they are introduced to the skills needed to do so. In addition, students in theory courses that focus on quantitative tools at the expense of applications may leave students with little idea as to why theory is important or how empirical work can be used to validate predictions.

By explicitly teaching the process of critical reading of peer-reviewed scholarship at the intermediate level, students benefit in many ways. They learn about how professional economists employ data and statistical modeling to test theory, they learn the process of critical reading in a highly specialized form of writing, and they arrive in upper-level electives more prepared to read the professional literature. Last but certainly not least, students almost universally report that they enjoy doing so.

ACKNOWLEDGMENT

I am indebted to Marketa Wolfe for her insightful comments on an earlier draft.

NOTES

1. In this previous model, both theory courses had a fourth credit hour, but it was not traditional class time, was frequently used for problem-solving sessions and did not incorporate journal reading assignments.
2. Typical of many intermediate theory courses, Skidmore's intermediate micro and macro require one semester of calculus (univariate). While additional calculus is recommended and many students do take additional courses, they are not required prerequisites.
3. A surprising number of published papers contain no clear statement of purpose or goal.
4. Despite a 67 percent increase in the number of bachelor's degrees awarded to women between 1995 and 2014, women earn the lowest share of degrees in economics of all the social sciences at every level. As of 2014, only about 30 percent of bachelor's degrees in economics are awarded to women. (https://www.nsf.gov/statistics/2017/nsf17310/digest/fod-women/economics.cfm)
5. This product characteristic became abundantly clear when television ratings of sports broadcasts plummeted during the 2020 COVID pandemic, a problem that leagues often attempted to mitigate with fake fan sounds, including booing.
6. As of March 18, 2020, Google Scholar reports nearly 1000 citations.

REFERENCES

Basker, E. (2007). The causes and consequences of Wal-Mart's growth. *Journal of Economic Perspectives*, 21(3), 177–198.

Bates, L.J. and Santerre, R.E. (2008). Do health insurers possess monopsony power in the hospital services industry? *International Journal of Healthcare Finance and Economics*, 8(1), 1–11.

Borrell, J-R. (2007). Pricing and patents of HIV/AIDs drugs in developing countries. *Applied Economics*, 39(4), 505–518.

Buraimo, B. (2008). Stadium attendance and television audience demand in English football. *Managerial and Decision Economics*, 29(6), 513–523.

Cramer, J. and Krueger, A.B. (2016). Disruptive change in the taxi business: the case of Uber. *American Economic Review: Papers & Proceedings*, 106(5), 177–182.

Davis, L.W. (2012). Prospects for nuclear power. *Journal of Economic Perspectives*, 26(1), 49–66.

Gabel, D. (2016). Uber and the persistence of market power. *Journal of Economic Issues*, L(2) (June), 527–534.

Helper, S. and Henderson, R. (2014). Managerial practices, relational contracts, and the decline of General Motors. *Journal of Economic Perspectives*, 28(1), 49–72.

Leeds, M.A and Sakata, S. (2012). Take me out to the Yakyushiai. *Journal of Sports Economics*, 13(1), 34–52.

List, J.A. (2011). The market for charitable giving. *Journal of Economic Perspectives*, 25(2), 157–180.

Porter, C. and Serra, D. (2020). Gender differences in the choice of major: The importance of female role models. *American Economic Journal: Applied Economics*, 12(3), 226–254.

Rascher, D.A., McEvoy, C.D., Nagel, M., and Brown, M.T. (2007). Variable ticket pricing in Major League Baseball. *Journal of Sport Management*, 21(3), 407–437.

Scully, G. (1974). Pay and performance in Major League Baseball. *American Economic Review*, 64(6), 915–930.

von Allmen, P. and Brower, G. (1998). Calculus and the teaching of intermediate microeconomics: Results from a survey. *Journal of Economic Education*, 29(3), 277–84.

3.   Using ESPN *30 for 30* to teach economics – revisited

Abdullah Al-Bahrani and Darshak Patel

INTRODUCTION

The role of educators at the introductory economics course level is to develop students' interest in economics and to lay the foundations of economic knowledge for students to build on in higher level courses. Lecture format remains the most common method of instruction at the introductory level (Asarta, Chambers and Harter 2020). While lecturing may be an effective method of teaching, using active learning and discussion-based methods can also engage students with the content and provide different learning opportunities. Over the last decade, there has been an increased effort by economic educators to incorporate active learning in their classroom. However, Sheridan and Smith (2020) find that most educators overestimate the amount of time they engage their students in active learning or discussion.

In 2015, we encouraged educators to harness the power of documentaries and sports to elicit student interest in economics (Al-Bahrani and Patel 2015). Educators, especially at the introductory levels, can serve as facilitators and connect economic concepts to students' lives and interests. Recently, the economics profession has come under attack for its lack of diversity. While many resources have been devoted to increasing diversity of representation, the role of introductory level educators has not received much attention (Al-Bahrani 2020). If the economics profession is to increase diversity, it will have to diversify its examples and increase efforts to create a more inclusive curriculum.

We revisit the use of ESPN *30 for 30* documentaries in the economics classroom. These documentaries provide students with examples of economic principles drawn from real world situations. They also provide a diverse and global perspective of world events that are useful to elicit discussion and help students bridge connections between what they are learning and the world they see. This chapter revisits examples from volumes I and II of the ESPN *30 for 30* series provided in Al-Bahrani and Patel (2015) and provides newer documentaries from a recent season released since our initial article. These films assist in expanding learning beyond the four walls of a classroom. Other than using the videos to make the learning process for students more active, they can also be used to engage reading/book clubs and economic clubs. With the shift to virtual education due to the Covid-19 pandemic, educators can use these documentaries to spur discussion board posts and reflection pieces.

This chapter provides a valuable resource to educators looking to diversify the type of media content they share with their students to teach economics, or to individuals interested in historic sports events and their relevance to economics. The ESPN *30 for 30* series is an engaging and well-produced program that helps bring economics to life through storytelling. The videos are pleasing to watch and use a historical and emotional connection to connect to its audience. ESPN's *30 for 30* series provides a unique opportunity to take advantage of full episodes and apply "big picture" topics to demonstrate economic lessons.

THE USE OF POPULAR MEDIA TO TEACH ECONOMICS

The use of alternative teaching methods in economics has gained interest because of the decline in the number of students taking economic courses (Simkins, 1999). According to Becker (2004), roughly 1.5% of all under-graduate degrees were awarded to economic majors in 2000. This is a decline from its height in 1988 when economics accounted for 2.3% of all degrees. Recently, there has been increased interest in diversifying the content covered in economic courses to increase the representation in the economics profession.

Ziegert (2000) finds that student personalities play a major role in student success in economics due to the subject's analytical structure. Changing the instruction methods to incorporate active learning may increase interest in the major by attracting other personality types (Stowe, 2010). However, the main reason for the increase in use of active learning in economics has been due to the method's effectiveness in developing student knowledge and the retention of complex concepts. Students actively involved in trying to understand and acquire information will have a more meaningful learning experience (Shuell 1986).

In the 2010s there was an explosion of resources to help educators incor-porate media into economics classrooms. To be relevant in the classroom, instructors can choose from music, TV shows, movies, social media, to even Broadway musicals (Wooten et al. 2020). The number of options can be overwhelming for new instructors. Wooten (2018) – as well as his chapter else-where in this book (Wooten 2022) – provides educators with a media library that can be sorted by topic, concept, courses, or media source. This chapter provides specific examples for educators interested in a theme that revolves around major historical moments in sports.

ESPN *30 for 30*

To celebrate and recognize ESPN's 30th anniversary, ESPN created a "*30 for 30*" series. ESPN produced 30 films by 30 different directors that cover events from the past 30 years. Each producer provides their own personal insights into the events that led to changes in the sport or social views. These events range from political issues, rivalries, the spirit of the game, to music. ESPN has extended beyond the 30 films in response to the popularity of the original documentary series. ESPN and Gartland.com joined together to develop *ESPN 30 for 30 Shorts*, which are shorter versions of selected films. Additionally, in the summer of 2013, ESPN introduced *Nine for IX* to celebrate the 40th anniversary of Title IX. Title IX is a federal law established to make discrimination on the basis of sex at institutions that receive federal financial assistance illegal. *Nine for IX* are nine documentary films about women in sports. ESPN also released their first *30 for 30* podcasts in 2017. To date, seven seasons have been produced. In this chapter, we focus on the initial *30 for 30* films as shown in Table 3.1. Table 1 of Al-Bahrani and Patel (2015), provides a complete list of the films aired in the original series and descriptions of each film. The clips and timings (Table 3.2) from Al-Bahrani and Patel (2015) were extracted from ESPN Films *30 for 30: Complete Season 1* DVD boxset. Currently, the *30 for 30* series can be found on Amazon prime and ESPN+. The timings of the clips will vary based on the source.

Pedagogical Approach

The use of media in the classroom involves additional work. There are many things to consider, such as copyright issues, when to introduce the movie clip and how to successfully play the movie during class. Mateer and Stephenson (2011) provide advice for faculty members new to the use of media in the classroom. For more detailed information on copyright-protected work and the "fair use" exemption, see Sexton (2006). Sexton provides a good summary concerning the legal issues of using copyrighted work. In this chapter, we suggest the best way to use ESPN's *30 for 30* films and how to incorporate them for lecture enhancement and active learning. We discuss an approach that we have implemented in class that we feel is best in generating an active and engaged discussion with the *30 for 30* films.

We find that complementing class lectures with selected clips from *30 for 30* videos helps to promote active learning by encouraging students to participate in classroom discussions and apply the economic principles they are learning

Table 3.1   *The title and description of each of the 30 for 30 films and the economic topics covered in Season 1*

No.	Length (min)	Movie title	Topics Covered
1	53	*King's Ransom*	Demand, Trade, Market share
2	56	*The Band That Wouldn't Die*	Game theory, Invisible handshake, Marginal/rational thinking, Monopsony, Opportunity cost, Production possibility frontier, Risk, Signaling, Tradeoffs
3	54	*Small Potatoes: Who Killed the USFL?*	Competition, Diseconomies of scale, Economic systems, Markets, Monopoly, Production/expansion, Self-interest
4	54	*Muhammad and Larry*	Incentives, Marginal thinking, Secondary effects, Utility
5	53	*Without Bias*	Marginal thinking, Opportunity costs, Political barriers, Secondary effects, Substitutes
6	51	*The Legend of Jimmy the Greek*	Comparative advantage, Correlation, Cost, Current/real prices, Discrimination/Prejudice, Economic systems, Invisible handshake, Monopoly, Opportunity cost, Political foot, Preferences, Risk, Substitutes, Sunk cost
7	104	*The U*	Competition, Demand, Externalities, Incentives, Marginal/Rational thinking, Opportunity cost, Political foot, Promotion, Secondary effects, Self-interest, Substitutes, Sunk cost, Invisible handshake, Preferences
8	71	*Winning Time: Reggie Miller vs. The New York Knicks*	Markets, Price, Repeated interaction, Strategy
9	54	*Guru of Go*	Innovation, Production, Strategy, Resources
10	83	*No Crossover: The Trial of Allen Iverson*	Crime, Demographics, Income, Rationality, Externalities, Negative shocks
11	53	*Silly Little Game*	Economic growth, Economic systems, Innovation, Private property rights, Strategies, Substitutes, Technology, Trade
12	54	*Run Ricky Run*	Rationality, Utility, Production, Productivity, Externalities
13	54	*The 16th Man*	Discrimination, Invisible foot, Economic systems
14	51	*Straight Outta L.A.*	Brand, Demand, Market, Innovation, Complements, Crime
15	53	*June 17 1994*	Rationality
16	106	*The Two Escobars*	Investment, Human capital, Economics of crime, Development, Tradeoffs (soccer or drugs), Poverty, Trade, Invisible hand, Incentives matter

No.	Length (min)	Movie title	Topics Covered
17	51	*The Birth of Big Air*	Innovation, Property rights, Entrepreneurship, Risk, Uncertainty, Production methods (making the half pipe), Investment in industry, shifts in demand (taste measures ESPN making it more popular), Comparative advantage
18	51	*Jordan Rides the Bus*	Rationality, Decision making, Information asymmetry, Externalities, Shifts in demand, Unions, Contracts, Negotiations, Gambling (risk aversion)
19	51	*Little Big Men*	Unobservable, Uncertainty, Asymmetric information, Prediction, Game theory
20	53	*One Night in Vegas*	Uncertainty Decision making, Rationality, Crime, Slavery/civil rights movement, Human capital, Short run production
21	52	*Unmatched*	Economic system, Capitalism, Socialism, Strategy, Information, Repeated interactions
22	52	*The House of Steinbrenner*	Short-run costs, Long run planning, Production, Possibility frontiers, Shifts in demand, Principle-agent problems, Monopsony, Monopoly, Elasticity, Prices
23	52	*Into the Wind*	Investment on research and development, Public good, Private goods, Externalities, Market failure, Maximization of objectives, Information asymmetries, Rationality
24	52	*Four Days in October*	Strategy, Repeated interaction, Game theory, Brand loyalty
25	82	*Once Brothers*	Economic systems, Trade, Production, Wages, Immigration, Investment, Human capital, Resources, Command, Capitalism
26	52	*Tim Richmond: To the Limit*	Health economic topics, Information cost, Epidemics, Market failure
27	52	*Fernando Nation*	Minimum wage, Income inequality, Demand shifts, Demographic change, Immigration, Labor laws, Property rights, Unions
28	54	*Marion Jones: Press Pause*	Rationality, Production, Resources, Comparative advantage, Maximization, Utility
29	102	*The Best that Never Was*	Cartel, Oligopoly, Monoposny
30	105	*Pony Excess*	Cartel, Market structure, Rationality, Profits, Unions, Wages, Economic systems

Note: Summaries of each documentary can be found at ESPN 30 for 30 website. http://espn.go
.com/30for30/volume1

Table 3.2   A list of clips from the 30 for 30 *series that discuss specific economic concepts from Season 1*

Concepts	Film	Start	End
Allocation of Resources	*Unmatched*	8.00	8.40
Antitrust Laws	*Straight Outta LA*	8.55	10.05
Brand	*Straight Outta LA*	24.45	31.00
Causation vs. Correlation	*The Two Escobars*	20.00	22.00
Comparative Advantage	*The Legend of Jimmy the Creek*	10.36	11.11
Comparative Advantage	*Guru of GO*	13.16	13.59
Competition	*Who Killed The USFL*	3.59	6.11
Competition	*Who Killed The USFL*	8.00	8.51
Competition	*Who Killed The USFL*	23.13	24.14
Competition	*Who Killed The USFL*	42.09	47.05
Competition	*Who Killed The USFL*	49.32	50.15
Competition	*The U*	2.20	4.05
Competition	*Unmatched*	23.30	24.20
Complements	*Straight Outta LA*	14.15	14.50
Complements	*One Night in Vegas*	3.10	3.30
Correlation	*The Legend of Jimmy the Creek*	9.03	8.18
Cost	*The Legend of Jimmy the Creek*	37.46	40.10
Current/Real Prices	*The Legend of Jimmy the Creek*	18.50	19.50
Demand	*King Ransom*	6.40	8.13
Demand	*King Ransom*	11.00	11.20
Demand	*King Ransom*	31.50	32.40
Demand	*King Ransom*	40.00	42.10
Demand	*King Ransom*	43.20	43.40
Demand	*The U*	2.20	4.05
Demand	*The U*	6.00	7.00
Demand	*Winning Time: Reggie Miller vs. The New York Knicks*	13.00	15.00
Demand	*No Crossover: The Trial of Allen Iverson*	6.45	7.20
Demand	*Straight Outta LA*	8.57	10.03
Demand	*Straight Outta LA*	24.45	31.00
Demand	*House of Steinbrenner*	6.00	7.10
Demand	*Unmatched*	46.35	47.00
Demand	*Jordan Rides the Bus*	25.00	27.00
Demand	*Fernando Nation*	11	15
Discrimination/Prejudice	*The Legend of Jimmy the Creek*	16.21	17.00

Concepts	Film	Start	End
Diseconomies of Scale	*Who Killed The USFL*	21.10	21.48
Economic Growth	*Silly Little Game*	38.28	40.47
Economic Growth	*Silly Little Game*	42.04	44.04
Economic Systems	*Who Killed The USFL*	3.10	3.26
Economic Systems	*The Legend of Jimmy the Creek*	15.00	16.15
Economic Systems	*Guru of GO*	45.39	47.25
Economic Systems	*Silly Little Game*	38.28	40.47
Economic Systems	*Unmatched*	5.25	6.05
Economic Systems	*Unmatched*	17.20	19.20
Elasticity	*House of Steinbrenner*	41.30	44.00
Externalities	*The U*	92.00	95.00
Externalities	*The U*	96.00	99.00
Externalities	*Straight Outta LA*	17.36	20.30
Externalities	*Jordan Rides the Bus*	31.00	37.20
Game Theory	*King Ransom*	44.10	45.00
Game Theory	*The Band That Wouldn't Die*	17.40	19.18
Human Capital	*One Night in Vegas*	26.40	28.00
Human Capital	*One Night in Vegas*	27.00	29.00
Incentives	*Muhammad & Larry*	7.05	7.35
Incentives	*Muhammad & Larry*	13.00	13.40
Incentives	*Muhammad & Larry*	30.05	30.24
Incentives	*The U*	23.25	25.30
Incentives	*Run Ricky Run*	7.09	8.01
Incentives	*Straight Outta LA*	8.57	10.03
Income Mobility	*Tim Richmond: To the Limit*	7.00	12.00
Inequality	*The Two Escobars*	20.50	23.40
Information Asymmetry	*Into the Wind*	6.00	7.45
Information Asymmetry	*Into the Wind*	21.00	23.00
Information Asymmetry	*Tim Richmond: To the Limit*	24	27
Innovation	*Silly Little Game*	38.25	40.50
Innovation	*The Birth of Big Air*	13.00	15.00
Invisible Handshake	*The Band That Wouldn't Die*	37.55	39.15
Invisible Handshake	*The Legend of Jimmy the Creek*	11.12	12.02
Invisible Handshake	*The U*	34.24	45.55
Invisible Handshake	*The U*	50.51	55.02
Labor laws	*Fernando Nation*	17	18
Marginal/Rational Thinking	*Muhammad & Larry*	7.05	7.35

Concepts	Film	Start	End
Marginal/Rational Thinking	*Muhammad & Larry*	13.00	13.40
Marginal/Rational Thinking	*Muhammad & Larry*	30.05	30.24
Marginal/Rational Thinking	*The Band That Wouldn't Die*	7.30	9.30
Marginal/Rational Thinking	*The U*	23.25	25.30
Marginal/Rational Thinking	*Without Bias*	34.18	35.33
Marginal/Rational Thinking	*Guru of GO*	25.56	29.29
Marginal/Rational Thinking	*Into the Wind*	32.00	33.15
Marginal/Rational Thinking	*One Night in Vegas*	1.00	2.22
Marginal/Rational Thinking	*Four Days in October*	27.00	31.00
Market	*Who Killed The USFL*	1.18	1.44
Market	*House of Steinbrenner*	38.00	41.00
Market	*Little Big Men*	7.30	9.00
Market	*Jordan Rides the Bus*	27.00	28.30
Market	*The Birth of Big Air*	16.00	17.00
Monopoly	*Who Killed The USFL*	3.59	6.11
Monopoly	*Who Killed The USFL*	42.09	47.05
Monopoly	*Who Killed The USFL*	49.32	50.15
Monopoly	*The Legend of Jimmy the Creek*	6.40	7.38
Monopsony	*The Band That Wouldn't Die*	17.40	19.18
Monopsony	*The Band That Wouldn't Die*	49.30	50.15
Monopsony	*Straight Outta LA*	8.57	10.03
Monopsony	*Jordan Rides the Bus*	48.00	49.00
Opportunity Cost	*King Ransom*	5.38	6.15
Opportunity Cost	*King Ransom*	29.00	31.30
Opportunity Cost	*Without Bias*	34.30	34.48
Opportunity Cost	*The Legend of Jimmy the Creek*	12.31	13.30
Opportunity Cost	*The U*	96.00	99.00
Opportunity Cost	*The Band That Wouldn't Die*	41.00	41.37
Opportunity Cost	*Run Ricky Run*	0.10	1.45
Opportunity Cost	*Jordan Rides the Bus*	42.10	42.50
Political Foot	*Without Bias*	44.06	45.57
Political Foot	*The Legend of Jimmy the Creek*	11.12	12.02
Political Foot	*The Legend of Jimmy the Creek*	24.05	25.00
Political Foot	*The U*	78.00	85.00
Political Foot	*The U*	89.00	94.00
Political Foot	*The U*	94.00	96.00
Political Foot	*The Two Escobars*	6.10	8.20

Concepts	Film	Start	End
Political Foot	*The Two Escobars*	10.00	12.10
Political Foot	*The Two Escobars*	27.00	29.00
Preferences	*The Legend of Jimmy the Creek*	20.35	22.00
Preferences	*The Legend of Jimmy the Creek*	37.45	40.10
Preferences	*The U*	34.20	45.55
Preferences	*The U*	50.50	55.05
Preferences	*The Two Escobars*	20.00	23.40
Private Property Rights	*Silly Little Game*	38.28	40.47
Private Property Rights	*Fernando Nation*	7.45	9
Production	*House of Steinbrenner*	16.20	20.25
Production	*House of Steinbrenner*	18.00	19.00
Production/Expansion	*Who Killed The USFL*	21.10	21.48
Production/Expansion	*The Band That Wouldn't Die*	41.00	41.37
Production/Expansion	*House of Steinbrenner*	34.40	36.00
Promotion	*The U*	2.20	4.05
Risk	*The Band That Wouldn't Die*	7.30	9.30
Risk	*The Legend of Jimmy the Creek*	20.35	21.59
Rivalry	*Winning Time: Reggie Miller vs. The New York Knicks*	0.00	2.43
Scalping	*King Ransom*	11.00	11.20
Scarcity	*Into the Wind*	30.00	31.30
Scarcity	*One Night in Vegas*	31.00	33.15
Secondary Effects	*Muhammad & Larry*	41.50	44.02
Secondary Effects	*Without Bias*	44.06	45.57
Secondary Effects	*The U*	96.00	100.00
Self-Interest	*Who Killed The USFL*	30.33	34.24
Self-Interest	*The U*	23.25	25.30
Signaling	*The Band That Wouldn't Die*	31.10	34.31
Signaling	*The Band That Wouldn't Die*	35.20	36.47
Strategies	*Winning Time: Reggie Miller vs. The New York Knicks*	2.44	9.44
Strategies	*Guru of GO*	16.51	21.35
Strategies	*Guru of GO*	36.51	40.52
Strategies	*Silly Little Game*	13.00	14.16
Strategies	*Unmatched*	16.00	16.50
Strategies	*Little Big Men*	9.30	11.00
Strategies	*Four Days in October*	7.10	10.10

Concepts	Film	Start	End
Substitution	*Without Bias*	36.15	36.50
Substitution	*The Legend of Jimmy the Creek*	7.46	8.02
Substitution	*The U*	2.20	4.05
Substitution	*The U*	96.00	100.00
Substitution	*Silly Little Game*	32.47	33.09
Sunk Cost	*The Legend of Jimmy the Creek*	14.51	15.05
Sunk Cost	*The U*	23.25	25.30
Surplus	*King Random*	25.00	26.00
Technology	*Silly Little Game*	42.00	44.45
Trade	*King Random*	25.00	25.20
Trade	*Silly Little Game*	22.58	25.08
Trade Off	*The Band That Wouldn't Die*	41.00	41.37
Trade Off	*Into the Wind*	27.00	27.40
Trade Off	*Into the Wind*	31.00	32.30
Unions	*Fernando Nation*	28	32
Utility	*Muhammad & Larry*	14.00	16.00

in that class period. We typically introduce concepts and follow up with a clip that reinforces the economic idea. This will allow students to make the connection themselves and also assist in keeping the discussion focused. We find that there is a tradeoff between how controlled the discussion is, and the active learning environment. Therefore, we suggest that the instructor introduces the topic, opens discussion, allows students to veer off, and then regroups and shows the specific clip of interest. In our experience, we find students often extend the discussions after the video. For this approach, students may need some background about the issue covered in the film from which the clip will be shown. At the same time, instructors should approach sensitive topics with caution. To avoid a melee in the learning environment, instructors should set clearly identifiable goals (restating the goals if necessary), set ground rules (respect, interruptions, focusing on idea criticism and not each other, language), and facilitate by bringing students safely in and safely out.

The shift to online education due to the pandemic has increased interest in how to engage students in a virtual setting. The ESPN *30 for 30* documentaries provide educators with the opportunity to leverage entertainment content to elicit discussion. Instructors can use them as part of a discussion board in asynchronous or synchronous format. The documentaries can also be used to engage student clubs or survey courses. They can be designed to supplement any course or engage student organizations.

In this chapter we provide a few examples from the most recent season (Season 4) that educators can use in the classroom. In the original paper we detail more examples from Season 1 for use in the economics classroom. We have found these clips to be useful in generating "an economic way of thinking" among students. In the original paper we provide specific clips that can be used. In this chapter, we include an introduction to some of the newer documentaries and the major concepts that can be covered using that documentary. One major limitation of Season 4 compared with other seasons of *30 for 30* is that the length of the films has increased drastically. Showing an entire documentary in class is no longer possible. We recommend assigning the documentaries for out of class viewing and reflection.

THE FILMS AND CONCEPTS FROM SEASON 4

Long Gone Summer

Instructors interested in teaching about Production Possibility Frontiers (PPF) or production functions can use the documentary *Long Gone Summer*. The documentary looks back at the 1998 Major League Baseball season and the home run race between Mark McGwire and Sammy Sosa. Both players managed to break the 61 home runs record set by Roger Maris. Mark McGwire would end up with 70 and Sammy Sosa hit 66 home runs that year.

The documentary discusses several decisions that the players made in their career to help set the stage for the 1998 record-breaking season. Both players discuss their early decisions to specialize as hitters, although both could play other positions well. This lends itself to a discussion about specialization and the difference between absolute and comparative advantage. The documentary also provides an opportunity to discuss competition and its impact on market outcomes. A question that arises while watching the film is whether Mark McGwire would have broken the record had he not had competition from Sammy Sosa. The threat of competition and push to innovate and increase quality of output is a great way to introduce how market economies with competitive markets lead to better outcomes. On the other hand, the film also discusses how both Mark McGuire and Sammy Sosa were later found to have used performance enhancing drugs, which led to a violation of their player agreements. This provides an opportunity to discuss the merits of regulation and market oversight when market participants have an incentive to cheat and consequently harm other participants.

This can motivate a discussion on the Prisoner's Dilemma. Students can be asked to explain the most likely outcome to occur in a prisoner's dilemma and then be asked to solve the McGuire–Sosa problem on whether to dope or stay clean. What is the Nash equilibrium? Do you think the prisoner's dilemma is effective at getting suspects to testify, allowing for an indictment to be reached? Why or why not? Professors may choose to summarize and discuss the simple prisoner's dilemma presented by Shermer (2008) of the decision to dope or stay clean. It shows how effective detection of performance-enhancing drugs and sanctions can change the Nash equilibrium from both players doping to neither doping.

The Infinite Race

The film "*The Infinite Race*" explores the lives of Tarahumaras, an Indigenous community who live in Chihuahua, Mexico. The Tarahumaras, who also call themselves the Rarámuri, received lots of publicity due to the release of Christopher McDougall's 2009 book, *Born to Run: A Hidden Tribe, Superathletes, and the Greatest Race the World Has Never Seen.* The book describes the Tarahumaras tribe and their ability to run distances of over 100 miles regularly, often while barefoot or in flimsy sandals. From this exposure and increased interest from the West, Ultra Marathon Caballo Blanco races were formed. These are challenging races of various lengths: 31 miles, 62 miles or even 100 miles. The film explores the ultramarathon and barefoot running fad, cartel influence, the push for authority from the West on championing a community and profiting from the indigenous culture.

This film provides an opportunity to discuss concepts covered in the first couple of classes, on the principles of microeconomics. Instructors can ask students to watch the documentary and identify as many principles of economics concepts as possible as part of a discussion board to facilitate communication among students. Concepts covered include markets, preferences, comparative advantage, property rights, opportunity costs, incentives, investments, rational thinking, demand, discrimination, and externalities. The film starts off with a good description of who the Tarahumaras (which means "foot runners") are, their geographical location by the mountains, and their knowledge of how to make running sandals using tire treads. Rarámuri communities were separated by miles of challenging terrain. Running was both a necessity for connection and a deep part of their heritage. All economic activities require the locals to walk or run several miles, unintentionally providing them with training and hence a comparative advantage in long distance running.

Discussion on externalities and discrimination should be approached carefully. The following clips can be used to introduce discrimination (Amazon Prime TV: 17:34–19:32 and 59:59–1:03:22). A good start here would be creating small groups and asking students to provide responses to the following: Have you ever experienced discrimination? Where, when and what happened? How did you feel? Responses to these questions would bring light to the different kinds of discrimination that exist. Instructors should then show the clips and look for responses in terms of whether they observe any discrimination that might have occurred. The first clip talks about Christopher McDougall's 2009 book and its movement in running and running footwear. This clips also connects the popularity/fad of Vibram's FiveFingers ("barefoot shoes") to the culture of the Tarahumaras. It was hereon assumed that running barefoot could reduce foot injuries and strengthen foot muscles. The second clip focuses on the idea that the tribe's comparative advantage is nothing to do with running barefoot and when foreigners do that, it's a mockery to the Tarahumaras culture. They run barefoot owing to their lack of resources. This is a great opportunity to insert and discuss the lawsuits many "barefoot shoe" companies settled. The clip also emphasizes how Western culture discriminates against indigenous tribes on the basis of their culture and clothing, but always looks to profit from this discrimination. Another way to approach this topic is by soliciting responses on questions such as what is the first thing you notice when you look at people? Do people have an opinion on the language, clothing, or origin of other people? This provides a strong link to understanding that discrimination exists in various ways.

Another important topic that we cover in economics is externalities (Amazon Prime TV: 21:44–26:05). Instructors should introduce the definition of externalities and then share the clip with the classroom. After students watch the clip, students should work in groups to jot down any examples of externalities shown on the clip. The clip helps spur discussions on the externalities of cartels. The clip sets the scene of a massive drought and the hunger experienced by the Chihuahua area. Reasons mentioned include climate change, which has impacted the agriculture lands. The cause of climate change is linked to deforestation from legal and illegal logging by the two large cartels who use the mountain for their drug trade. Other negative externalities mentioned include people being forced out of their ancestral homes and death threats for those who counter the cartel. Instructors can poll students on their beliefs of climate change and discuss other potential harmful effects of climate change. It is important to ensure that students understand why markets fail. A common practice is to poll students on whether we want more or less: cartels, deforestation, crime, climate change. The most common response would be that the society would prefer less of the aforementioned. Instructors can show a graph where market equilibrium indicates that society is overproducing these activities and the ideal consumption is lower. These discussions can be further progressed after the instructor covers solutions to externalities. Students should work in groups to provide solutions to the externalities mentioned on the clip and then sort them based on the different types of textbook solutions. The clip suggests some solutions to these externalities: education and government support.

The film also provides a good background on how a market for ultramarathons was formed, how it became a fad, and its impact on the running footwear industry. This is an excellent opportunity for instructors to introduce the popularity/fad of Vibram's FiveFingers ("barefoot shoes") and tie it to the culture of the Tarahumaras. People presumed running barefoot could reduce foot injuries and strengthen foot muscles. Students will be able to articulate that the tribe's comparative advantage has nothing to do with running barefoot and when foreigners do that it's a mockery to the culture of the Tarahumaras. The locals run barefoot owing to their lack of resources. This is again a great opportunity to discuss the lawsuit many "barefoot shoe" companies settled due to their false claims. This sets the scene for discussions on the incentives needed to participate in ultramarathons. The races are challenging and both physically and mentally draining. However, the community struggles from droughts and shortages of food and clean water, so this lack of resources creates high importance with regard to the race prizes. The locals only participated in these races due to high poverty. Completing the race qualified a person for food vouchers, and some races come with a winning prize of $1,800. The clip discusses how it would take a local five months to a year to make that quantity of money. Students will be able to discuss the opportunity cost of time and the benefits of participating. The recipient of the race prize was able to bring access to clean water to the community through using the winnings (positive externality). These long-distance races come at a high cost, but the community and the participants value the benefits to be much higher.

One and Not Done

The episode *One and Not Done* covers the career of college basketball coach John Calipari. The discussion of Coach Calipari's career provides an opportunity to discuss principal–agent problems and how organizational rules can create perverse incentives. The behavior of economic agents can be legal and also raise ethical and moral concerns. John Calipari made a career by recruiting college basketball players who are eager to transition to the professional ranks. His ability to recruit these players was only possible due to the National Basketball Association (NBA) rules that require players to be 19 years old or be one year removed from high school. This rule creates a market for talented basketball players that need to spend one year in college to meet the requirement set by the NBA.

The John Calipari documentary can also be used to teach expected values, risk and returns, or marginal analysis. At the end of the college basketball season, college athletes must decide on whether to return for another season or enter the draft. For each player, this calculation is a function of the marginal benefit of another season versus the marginal cost, which includes a probability of injury and never being able to play again. The documentary discusses the career of Dajuan Wagner, who was drafted after one year of college basketball and was picked sixth overall in the 2002 draft. Wagner's career was cut short due to an ulcerative colitis, a medical condition he was never aware of. Luckily, he managed to play one year before his diagnosis.

Instructors can use this episode to engage their students in an active learning exercise. Provide students with a "real-life" decision that requires them to consider differences in returns. If presented with two options, which of the following would you pick? Option 1: drop out of college today (age 19) to take a job that pays $53,000 and is expected to increase by 3% until you are 65 years old. Option 2: complete college (22 years old), your first-year salary will be $55,000 and will increase by 4% until you are 65 years old. Which option do you pick and why?

This active learning exercise provides the context to discuss growth rates, compound interest, and net present value in the context that might be more familiar to students. The assignment can be modified by increasing the time differences between first salary, the starting salaries, and the growth rates, or instructors can add uncertainty by making one of the options dependent on market outcomes. The level of complexity will depend on instructor choice and student ability.

Instructors can also use this documentary to discuss how regulations in one market can impact related markets. The NBA's decision to make recruitment directly from high school illegal, created an incentive for players to enroll in college for one year only. The impact of this rule on the culture of college basketball is a debate that most students are eager to participate in. Students are quick to identify the tradeoff between having talented basketball players play in college rather than go directly to the NBA and the cost of having less consistent and transient players that impact team culture. This discussion provides instructors with the opportunity to discuss cost benefits, regulation, and market interdependence.

CONCLUSION

Many instructors have adopted the use of different media to increase student engagement in undergraduate Economics courses. These different pedagogic approaches have further linked economics to the real world. These teaching supplements have enabled instructors to create lasting impacts by showing the relevance to the real world which they hope will improve content retention and increase student interest.

We revisit the use of ESPN *30 for 30* films to help increase interest in economics. These films help spark discussions and allow a more enjoyable learning experience for students. The novelty of these films is that they aren't all sports related. A wide variety of social issues can be discussed, which increases interest among many rather than just a narrow group of students. Overall, the storytelling nature of the documentaries helps students engage, discuss or critically think about the media and economic lessons. The depth of the *30 for 30* films provides instructors with a valuable complementary tool to their teaching.

REFERENCES

Al-Bahrani, A.A. (2020). Classroom Management and Student Interaction Interventions: Fostering Diversity, Inclusion, and Belonging in Undergraduate Economics (July 7, 2020). Available at SSRN: https://ssrn.com/abstract=3644803 or http://dx.doi.org/10.2139/ssrn.3644803

Al-Bahrani, A. and Patel, D. (2015). Using *ESPN 30 For 30* to Teach Economics. *Southern Economics Journal* 81(3), 829–842.

Asarta, C.J., Chambers, R.G. and Harter, C. (2020). Teaching Methods in Undergraduate Introductory Economics Courses: Results from a Sixth National Quinquennial Survey. *The American Economist*, November.

Becker, W.E. (2004). Good-Bye Old, Hello New in Teaching Economics. *Australasian Journal of Economic Education* 1(1), 5–17.

Mateer, D.G. and Stephenson, E.F. (2011). Using Film Clips to Teach Public Choice Economics. *Journal of Economics and Finance Education* 10(1), 28–36.

McDougall, C. (2009). *Born to Run: A Hidden Tribe, Superathletes, and the Greatest Race the World Has Never Seen*. New York: Alfred A. Knopf.

Sexton, R.L. (2006). Using Short Movie and Television Clips in the Economics Principles Class. *Journal of Economic Education* 37, 406–417.

Sheridan, B.J. and Smith, B. (2020). How Often Does Active Learning Actually Occur? Perception versus Reality. *AEA Papers and Proceedings* 110, 304–308.

Shermer, M. (2008). The Doping Dilemma. *Scientific American* 298(4), 82–89.

Shuell, T.J. (1986). Cognitive Conceptions in Learning. *Review of Educational Research* 56(4), 411–436.

Simkins, S.P. (1999). Promoting Active-Student Learning Using the World Wide Web in Economics Courses. *The Journal of Economic Education* 30(3), 278–287.

Stowe, K. (2010). A Quick Argument for Active Learning: The Effectiveness of One-Minute Papers. *Journal for Economic Educators* 10(1), 33–39.

Wooten, J. (2018). Economics Media Library. *The Journal of Economic Education* 49(4), 364–365.

Wooten, J. (2022). Incorporating Media into the Sports Economics Curriculum. In V.A. Matheson and A.J. Fenn (eds), *Teaching Sports Economics and Using Sports to Teach Economics*. Edward Elgar Publishing.

Wooten, J., Al-Bahrani, A.A., Holder, K. and Patel, D. (2020). The Role of Relevance in Economics Education: A Survey (May 20, 2020). Available at SSRN: https://ssrn.com/abstract=3606301 or http://dx.doi.org/10.2139/ssrn.3606301

Ziegert, A.L. (2000). The Role of Personality Temperament and Student Learning in Principle of Economics: Further Evidence. *The Journal of Economic Education* 31(4), 307–322.

4. Uncovering bias: using sports to teach about the economics of discrimination

Jill S. Harris

INTRODUCTION

Sporting competitions have been around for thousands of years; by that measure the discipline of sports economics is in its infancy, with a mere seven decades under its belt.[1] In that relatively short amount of time, sports economists have been busy. Scores of papers on baseball covering everything from the player's labor markets to the evaluation of Major League Baseball umpires (see Mills, 2017, for example) fill volumes of academic journals. Dozens more on the nature and evaluation of competitive balance (see Humphreys, 2002, for starters) flooded editors' inboxes. Just about the time that Rottenberg (1956) was ruminating on the nature of the reserve clause in baseball, Becker (1957) was writing about the economics of discrimination. In what was to become a familiar intersection, economists from labor, industrial organization, applied microeconomics and other fields found themselves knee-deep in the realm of sports. Many of these scholars remain in this familiar intersection. One of the reasons for this is the comparative advantage of plentiful data. But, if you asked some of the veteran scholars—as well as the newcomers—why they choose to invest their research time in sports, you will likely hear a common reply: it's fun and it's great for teaching economics.

Our culture is sports obsessed. To be sure, one of the first laments after the COVID-19 virus evolved into a global pandemic was that sports were cancelled. Stadiums were empty. Courts were silent. Fields were green but no cleats were in sight. College students play sports, enjoy sports, and in some states even bet on sports. They put the "fanatic" in fandom at big D1 programs and they pour money into the multi-billion-dollar online gaming industry. This means that a sophomore or junior who would rather eat a worm than take an elective economics class ends up in your economics of sport course. You have their undivided attention for these contact hours. You can teach them anything about economic theory that you want. They come for the sports, but they leave with a renewed appreciation for the economic way of thinking. What will you do with this power and influence?

Using sports to teach about the economics of discrimination is a rich and rewarding curricular opportunity. It allows us to engage students in meaningful learning experiences around a challenging and sensitive topic while at the same time improving their analytic and critical thinking skills. It illustrates how much of the behavior that interests, intrigues, or perplexes us in "real-life" is also on display in the life of sports. If we can identify whether managers discriminate against employees based on race within a sporting context, this may teach us something about why managers discriminate against employees in the hospitality industry or education industry or any other context that we are curious about.

The main objective of this chapter is to link the economic concepts of taste-based discrimination (read: Becker) and statistical discrimination (read: Arrow) with four different lessons using sports contexts and data. Referee bias, owner bias, and fan discrimination introduce the reader to some of the economics of sports literature in this area. A summary of the nature and types of data available to scholars and teachers is nestled between the literature review and four lesson outlines incorporating different types of bias or discrimination. The chapter is clearly not exhaustive; but the lessons are meant to be exemplars of a type. Good teachers will be inspired to take an idea and explore new directions with it. The goal is to refresh the teaching-economist's tool kit with questions, pedagogy and straightforward exercises to create active and meaningful learning experiences for any student of economics.

EXAMPLES OF BIAS IN SPORT

Referee

One clear example of bias and discrimination in sports is studied by Price and Wolfers (2010). They find that the race of a referee and the race of a player impacted the number of personal fouls called in the NBA. Specifically, the results of their study suggest own-race preferences in these referees and the results were strong enough that they influenced the outcomes of games. As you can imagine, neither the NBA nor the referees were excited about these results. However, a remarkable thing happened. After considerable media attention about this academic study, referee behavior changed. Pope, Price, and Wolfers (2013) examined the performance of referees before and after the media attention and found zero evidence of racial bias for the three-year period after the results were made public. They argue that "awareness" caused a change in behavior. The lesson from this foundational study in discrimination is clear:

once humans are made aware of their own biased or discriminatory actions, they are incentivized to change their behavior.

Owner

Papers by Camerer and Weber (1999) and Coates and Oguntimein (2010) indicate that owners suffer from various types of bias and make decisions based on incomplete information. In basketball, owners tend to draft players who take a lot of shots (which does not necessarily correlate with increased wins). Harris and Berri (2016) show this is true within the WNBA. This is a form of statistical discrimination or stereotyping. Coaches or owners judge the future productivity of a player based on the number of shots they take; their presumption is that players who take lots of shots are the best players for the team. That is, these owners assume that a drafted player's performance metrics (such as wins produced or wins scored) will be high just because this player comes from a group that takes a lot of shots. This type of discrimination may lead to perverse outcomes—in this case, losses instead of wins.

Fans

Brown, Spiro, and Keenan (1991) were among the first to examine whether fan-based discrimination ended up influencing wages paid to professional basketball players. Bodvarsson and Partridge (2001) and Burdekin, Hossfeld, and Smith (2005) all consider the weight of fan-based discrimination on the composition of NBA teams (i.e., cities with larger white populations hosted teams with more white players on them). Kanazawa and Funk (2001) use Nielsen ratings to show that viewership increases for teams with more white players. Harris and Berri (2016) also examine the nature of fan preferences while studying whether the WNBA exhibits own-race bias between coaches and players. Attendance data, revenue and salary figures, minutes played, performance statistics and player characteristics, including race, are pivotal in these studies.

TYPES OF DATA

Scholars interested in baseball have an entire sabermetric society devoted to meticulous record-keeping of every action taken by every player in a game. Balls, strikes, fouls, hits, runs, errors, slugging percentages, Wins Above Replacement (WAR)... the list goes on and on. Likewise, sites such as www.baseball-reference.com, www.basketball-refernce.com, www.pro -football-reference.com, www.sabr.org, www.perfectgame.org, www.hockey -reference.com, record individual and team performance statistics the same way. Performance data on Olympic sports is available from the Olympic Library and from parent governing organizations such as www.fina.org. League websites also share performance statistics. Professional sites such as www.nfl.com, www.mlb.com, www.nba.com, www.wnba.com, and www .ncaa.org all contain downloadable publicly available data. There are also rich proprietary data sets available, too. Very few, if any industries track and record the detailed actions of their labor force this way. As indicated before, these recorded observations are not limited to just the players. It includes the actions or decisions of referees, coaches, managers and in some cases fans. All that remains for the motivated instructor is the effort required to ask questions of the data as they pertain to bias and discrimination, and then reflect on the answers provided.

TEACHING THE ECONOMICS OF BIAS AND DISCRIMINATION WITH SPORTS

How can we put these pieces together to create meaningful learning experiences? This section will introduce four exemplar lessons utilized in economics of sport courses taught on college campuses from California to Colorado.[2]

Becker's Discrimination Coefficient

Becker (1957) introduces a discrimination coefficient, d, into a firm's utility equation, such as the following:

$$U = pF(N_b + N_a) - w_a N_a - w_b N_b - dN_b,$$

where p is the price level,
F is a production function,
N_x is the number of workers in two different groups,
w_x is a wage paid to members of these groups.

If d is positive, then the employer is prejudiced against group b and the taste for discrimination will make the employer hire fewer workers from this group. One of the testable implications from Becker's model is wage differentials. Do members of a particular group earn less than others when both groups are equally productive? Any current sport with reasonably accessible salary data can serve as a laboratory for this economic concept. However, travelling back a hundred years into the history of segregated baseball in America makes this lesson unique.

Lesson: what would Satchel make today?
An entertaining and eye-opening exercise can be created with Becker's discrimination coefficient and Ken Burns' film *Baseball*. Using the 5th inning titled "Shadow Ball," students discover facts about the relative pay between key players in the Negro Leagues and their white contemporaries. The Lesson Plan in Appendix 4A uses the cases of Satchel Paige and Lefty Grove, the best white pitcher during Satchel's era. With the information provided in the documentary, students can reverse engineer the Becker discrimination coefficient by comparing the value of pitching wins between the two players and then comparing their earnings per game. The note taker can be modified to provide a step-by-step process for these calculations.

A second learning experience from the same period directs students to www .baseball-reference.com to look up Satchel's career stats. (Figure 4.1 shows the entry for Paige). Next, students must search for one or more modern day pitchers with comparable stats to forecast what Satchel might have earned if he were alive and playing baseball today. This can all easily translate into yet another lesson on how we might estimate Becker's discrimination coefficient with player data when we have reliable information on race. If the students are taking econometrics, ask them to write out a wage model and query them about the controls they would include on the right-hand side to test for employer discrimination. This leads to a terrific conversation about the nature of the data they would need to test the hypothesis of discrimination; you can also lead them through critiques of the internal and external validity of their models.

Statistical Discrimination

Lesson: do tall, top draft picks lead the pack in performance?
Lessons from men's and women's basketball are as plentiful as Temeka Johnson's and Lebron James' triple-doubles. One way to leverage the data in basketball is to explore instances of statistical discrimination. Using group averages to judge individual productivity is an example of this type of stereotyping. Students can easily download player characteristics and performance statistics from www.basketball-reference.com. For example, Figure 4.2 shows player heights, weights, and birthdates for a few professional basketball players with the last name James.

Students can access and download data for hundreds of players. They can sort the data by height and position. If they merge these data with estimates of Wins Produced from www.boxscoregeeks.com they can create a data set that allows them to investigate statistical discrimination (and many other questions). Research by Berri et al. (2005) and Harris and Berri (2016) indicate that, other things being equal, owners tend to prefer players that are tall. In fact, if you did not control for player position, you might mistakenly presume that

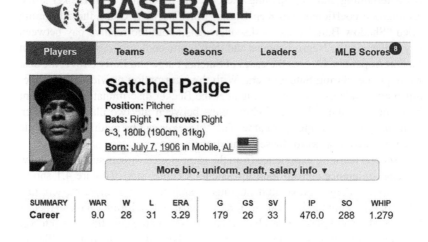

Source: www.baseball-reference.com

Figure 4.1   Satchel Paige career stats

Player	From	To	Pos	Ht	Wt	Birth Date	Colleges
Jerome James	1999	2009	C	7-0	300	November 17, 1975	Florida A&M
Justin James	2020	2020	G	6-7	190	January 24, 1997	Wyoming
LeBron James	2004	2020	F-G	6-9	250	December 30, 1984	
Mike James	2002	2014	G	6-2	188	June 23, 1975	Duquesne
Mike James	2018	2018	G	6-1	189	August 18, 1990	Lamar University
Tim James	2000	2002	F	6-7	212	December 26, 1976	Miami (FL)

Source: www.baseball-reference.com

Figure 4.2   Player characteristics

height is the single most important factor in player productivity. There is some justification for this. The tallest players in the NBA are typically Centers. They spend more time in the paint closest to the basket. This research also indicates that owners prefer players who draft early. However, if owners simply select players based on these two criteria, they may be guilty of stereotyping. Tall players, on average, take more shots than shorter players. And, first or second round draft picks also tend to take more shots on average than others. But evaluating the individual performance of a player based solely on the fact that they take more shots on average is not the best way to win games.

To drive this lesson home, students can first sort the player data by height then add position and wins produced. They can choose to estimate simple correlations within Excel, or they may opt to do so in Stata or R or any other program of their choice. They should find some correlation between height and wins produced but it will probably disappoint them if they believe—as many owners do—that tall players are the most productive players. Next, they run a regression with wins produced as the dependent variable and height, weight, position, draft position, and even age on the right-hand side. Results from such a model should lead to animated discussions about player productivity (as captured by wins produced) and height or draft position. Follow on assignments could include the development of a dream team based on whatever criteria the students think matter most. Depending on the semester in which the lesson is taught, you can post the "Faux Fantasy" team results juxtaposed alongside the real NBA or WNBA season results for even more excitement (or disillusionment as the case may be). For instructors or students interested in this analysis for women's basketball, a data set of WNBA performance statistics for the 2010–2013 draft classes, including wins produced and other player characteristics, is linked in Appendix 4B.[3]

Gender and Human Capital Wage Models

The essence of human capital wage models is that humans acquire skills and training that result in higher lifetime earnings. Sometimes the firm pays for this skill development and sometimes the workers pay for this training by accepting lower (or even negative wages) at the beginning of their careers. Labor economists have long studied a persistent gender wage gap. Even though women's labor force participation has grown more rapidly than men's in the last three decades, the gap persists. One of the reasons could be taste-based discrimination against women.

Lesson: let's dive into the elite swimming pay gap
One considerable advantage of working with sports data is the availability of performance metrics across so many different types of jobs. One sport that is only recently showing up under the microscope of the sport economist is elite swimming. Harris (2020) uses a human capital wage model to examine the determinants of wages in professional swimming. Harris models earnings as a function of age, endorsement contracts, medals earned in world competitions, Olympic appearances, college attended, and gender. Swimmer earnings are positively impacted by increased endorsement contracts, medals earned, and by the college attended. However, other things being equal, males earn two and a half times the amount females do. This result occurs even though women have a higher number of endorsement contracts on average than their male colleagues.

Students with a semester of econometrics can work with a panel data set of elite swimmer performance to investigate whether the pay gap between male and female swimmers is evidence of discrimination.[4] It is empirically difficult to identify the causality of the gender gap; but this does not mean the search for causal factors is unworthy! To simplify the learning experience, assume away endorsement income and focus exclusively on income earned from podium performances in the world championships and Olympics. Encourage the students to think about additional interacted variables that may help explain the variation in earnings they observe. Another possibility is splitting the sample into smaller sizes based on event type to see whether part of the pay gap is due to sprint versus long course performances. This exploratory lesson accomplishes two objectives. First, it introduces or re-introduces them to the gender pay gap and plants a seed about taste-based discrimination being one possible explanation. Second, it provides an additional pool of data (pun intended) to hone two-stage least squares (2SLS) and instrumental variable (IV) techniques for the empirically focused class.

Race Discrimination

Economic models of discrimination are not limited to the examination of wage differentials as in Brown et al. (1991). Several sports record minutes played per game and game starts in addition to the performance statistics of players. Berri, Deutscher and Galletti (2015) use time allocation to study whether there is a national origin bias in professional basketball in the United States and Spain. Harris and Berri (2016) use minutes played to test whether coaches exhibit own-race bias when allocating time to players in the WNBA.

Lesson: time out—why aren't the best players on the court?
Applied economists may mistakenly assume their students are comfortable and confident when presented with tables of regression results. Just as there is value in generating those tables through a hands-on research project, there is value in the practice of interpreting results. This lesson provides straightforward practice of making sense of estimated coefficients from Harris and Berri (2016). Table 4.1 defines the variables used and summarizes expected signs on the coefficients. The results are reproduced in Table 4.2. Sample questions for this lesson are included in Table 4.3. To add extra rigor, you might make the data set available and challenge the students to reproduce the results in addition to interpreting them.

Table 4.1   *Variable names for Harris and Berri (2016) own-race bias study*

Variable label	Variable name	Expected sign on estimated coefficients
PTS	POINTS	Positive
REB	REBOUNDS	Positive
AST	ASSISTS	Positive
STL	STEALS	Positive
BLK	BLOCKS	Positive
PF	PERSONAL FOULS	Negative
TOPER	TURNOVER PERCENTAGE	Negative
FTPER	FREE THROW PERCENTAGE	Positive
ADJFG	ADJUSTED FIELD GOALS	Positive
HT	HEIGHT	Positive
AGE	AGE IN YEARS	Positive
AGESQ	THE SQUARE OF AGE IN YEAR	Negative
G	GAMES PLAYED	Positive
GS	GAMES STARTED	Positive
NONWPLAYER	NONWHITE PLAYER where 1 = NONWHITE and 0 = WHITE	Positive
NONWCOACH	NONWHITE COACH where 1 = NONWHITE and 0 = WHITE	Positive
NONWPL*NONWCO	INTERACTION TERM FOR NONWHITE PLAYERS WITH NONWHITE COACHES	Negative
FBIASW	INTERACTION TERM FOR FAN BIAS FOR WHITE PLAYERS	Negative
NONWCHANGE	NONWHITE PLAYERS WITH COACHING CHANGES	Negative

CONCLUSION

Economists generally think of discrimination as flowing from tastes and preferences as in Becker (1957) or emanating from statistical discrimination or stereotyping as in Arrow (1973) and Phelps (1972). Studying discrimination makes economic sense in a world that seems more polarized now than it did 20 to 30 years ago. Discrimination manifests between males and females, heteronormative and non-heteronormative practices, old and young, and between white and non-white persons. But it is not limited to these broad categories. We might rightfully include discrimination between pregnant and non-pregnant employees,[5] married and single, native speaking and non-native

Table 4.2   Results from own-race bias study in WNBA

Variable	Model 1	Model 2	Model 3
PTS	0.412**	0.403***	0.402***
REB	0.060	0.037	0.220*
AST	0.040	0.067	0.317*
STL	−0.269	−0.277	0.287
BLK	−1.063**	−0.718*	−0.741*
PF	−1.137***	−1.120***	−0.867***
TOPER	0.077	0.86	−0.018
FTPER	0.895	1.076	3.497*
ADJFG	7.735	2.207***	3.088
HT	5.084	4.888	1.827
AGE	0.244	0.211	−0.219
AGESQ	−0.007	−0.006	0.004
G	−0.046	−0.042	0.003
GS	0.339***	0.338***	0.374***
NONW PLAYER	4.336*	4.076*	0.126
NONW COACH	5.159***	4.534**	1.915*
NONWPL*NONWCO	−4.814**	−4.842**	−0.626
FBIASW	−6.600*	−6.587*	−0.063
NONWCHANGE	−5.644***	−5.340**	−6.377**
PLAYER FE	YES	YES	NO
TEAM FE	NO	YES	YES
	R–sq 0.721	R–sq 0.720	R–sq 0.765

Notes: Models use data from 2010–2014; N=503 on 154 players. Model 1 uses player fixed effects only, Model 2 uses both player and team fixed effects, and Model 3 is an OLS model. In the sample, 56 players experienced coaching changes involving a change in the race of the coach between years, while 40 players experienced a coaching change midyear where the race of the coach changed from non-white to white or white to non-white. The midyear changes are captured by the NONWCHANGE
Dependent Variable = MGM (minutes played per game)

Table 4.3   Suggested questions for class discussion of results

1. Comment on the sign and interpret the estimated coefficient on NONWPL*NONWCO.
2. How does this result address the central question of own-race bias?
3. The authors conclude that "no evidence of own-race bias is found." Using the reported results, provide an explanation for the authors' claim.
4. Can you think of any other plausible explanations for the reported results?

speaking employees, tall and short persons, Ivy League and non-Ivy League graduates, etc. The list is, sadly, limitless. Therefore, the study of bias and discrimination is essential.

Curating lessons about discrimination within the context of sports reduces some of the stress burden on students and teachers alike. It provides some—but not complete—insulation from a subject that can be emotionally taxing. Yet, the lessons learned about the choice to discriminate within sports are directly applicable to interactions outside of sports. If a study about referee bias helped to change the discrimination of the referees, then maybe more studies about bias will amplify this effect. In a world where the COVID-19 pandemic is peeling back the veneer of "equality under the law," there is no better time to harness the power of these economic ideas. If we do, the children who learned their ABCs on Zoom may use their 123s in a world where humans view each other with less bias and treat each other with less negative discrimination.

NOTES

1. If we christen Rottenberg's "The Baseball Player's Market" from 1956 as our birth year.
2. Harris first taught economics of sport on the campus of California State University in 2003. She brought the course to Pitzer and Pomona College before ultimately reintroducing it at the United States Air Force Academy in 2016.
3. Detailed notes on the data set are available from the author upon request.
4. Students who have taken labor economics will have an advantage in this lesson.
5. See Pedriana (2009) for a summary.

REFERENCES

Arrow, K. J. (1973). The theory of discrimination. In O. Ashenfelter & A. Rees (Eds.), *Discrimination in Labor Markets* (pp. 3–33). Princeton, NJ: Princeton University Press.

Becker, G. S. (1957). *The Economics of Discrimination*. Chicago, IL: University of Chicago Press.

Berri, D. J., Brook, S., Fenn, A., Frick, B., & Vicente-Mayoral, R. (2005). The short supply of tall people: Explaining competitive imbalance in the National Basketball Association. *Journal of Economic Issues, 39*, 1029–1041.

Berri, D. J., Deutscher, C., & Galletti, A. (2015). Born in the USA: National origin effects on time allocation in US and Spanish professional basketball. *National Institute Economic Review, 232*, R41–50.

Bodvarsson, O. B., & Partridge, M. D. (2001). A supply and demand model of co-worker, employer, and customer discrimination. *Labour Economics, 8*, 389–416.

Brown, E., Spiro, R., & Keenan, D. (1991). Wage and nonwage discrimination in professional basketball: Do fans affect it? *American Journal of Economics and Sociology, 50*, 333–345.

Burdekin, R. C. K., Hossfeld, R., & Smith, J. K. (2005). Are NBA fans becoming indifferent to race? *Journal of Sports Economics, 6*, 144–159.

Camerer, D. F., & Weber, R. A. (1999). The econometrics and behavioral economics of escalation of commitment: A re-examination of Staw and Hoang's NBA data. *Journal of Economic Behavior and Organization, 39*, 59–82.

Coates, D., & Oguntimein, B. (2010). The length and success of NBA careers: Does college production predict professional outcomes? *International Journal of Sport Finance, 5*, 4–26.

Harris, J. S. (2020). It is not easy being green: Gender and earnings in professional swim. In *The Economics of Aquatic Sports* (pp. 93–98). Cham, Switzerland: Springer.

Harris, J., & Berri, D. J. (2016). If you can't pay them, play them: Fan preferences and own-race bias in the WNBA. *International Journal of Sport Finance, 11*(3), 163–180.

Humphreys, B. R. (2002). Alternative measures of competitive balance in sports leagues. *Journal of Sports Economics, 3*(2), 133–148.

Kanazawa, M. T., & Funk, J. P. (2001). Racial discrimination in professional basketball: Evidence from Nielsen ratings. *Economic Inquiry, 39*(4), 599–608.

Mills, B. M. (2017). Technological innovations in monitoring and evaluation: Evidence of performance impacts among Major League Baseball umpires. *Labour Economics, 46*, 189–199.

Pedriana, N. (2009). Discrimination by definition: The historical and legal paths to the Pregnancy Discrimination Act of 1978. *Yale Journal of Law & Feminism*, 21, 1.

Phelps, E. S. (1972). The statistical theory of racism and sexism. *The American Economic Review, 64*, 659–661.

Pope, D. G., Price, J., & Wolfers, J. (2013). Awareness reduces racial bias. No. w19765. National Bureau of Economic Research.

Price, J., & Wolfers, J. (2010). Racial discrimination among NBA referees. *The Quarterly Journal of Economics, 125*, 1859–1887.

Rottenberg, S. (1956). The baseball players' labor market. *Journal of Political Economy, 64*(3), 242–258.

APPENDIX 4A: LESSON PLANS

Lesson Plan: What Would Satchel Make Today?

ECON 476 Econ of Sport—Lesson 11, Notetaker, Dr. Jill Harris

Learning Objective:

1) Summarize different types of discrimination studied in applied work.
2) Estimate one impact of discrimination by reconciling the career of Satchel Paige with a white contemporary: if he had not played in the Negro League, what would he have earned?

List all the *player evaluations* where discrimination could be found:

1.
2.
3.

List all the *dimensions* of discrimination we might see:

1.
2.
3.

Ken Burns "Baseball" 5th Inning: *Shadow Ball* Trivia Treasure Hunt

1. Mario Cuomo loves these two plays in baseball: _____ and _____.
2. Residents of Hoovervilles could watch a baseball game for _____ a ticket.
3. Baseball crowds averaged around _____ people.
4. During the offseason, 438 exhibition games were played between the two leagues. Black players won _____ games against white players.
5. When Satchel first started pitching for the Mobile Tigers, he earned _____ per game if the turnout was good. He earned _____ if the turnout was light.
6. How many games did Satchel pitch (according to Satchel)? _____ How many of these games did he win? _____.
7. Satchel's fast ball was called the _____ _____.
8. Satchel earned roughly _____ more than his teammates.

9. Right before baseball began integrating, _____ of the players surveyed did not object to playing with black players.
10. Buck O'Neal's nickname is _____. (The player and manager of the Kansas City Monarchs)

Estimating the Impact of Discrimination: Satchel Paige, Josh Gibson, Buck Leonard

How much would Satchel have earned with no discrimination?

*   Satchel earned approximately $600 per month in the Negro Leagues, played 140 games a season and reportedly won 80% of the games he pitched.
*   Lefty Grove was the best white pitcher during Satchel's era. Lefty's team paid $100,600 to acquire him, he played 152 games a season, and won 68% of the games he pitched. He earned approximately $6,900 per month.

Use the information above to compute a rough estimate of discrimination coefficient.

Let's repeat with Josh Gibson or Buck Leonard:

Write out a formal model of discrimination in baseball during this time period. What controls would you include?

APPENDIX 4B: DATA

The link for WNBA and Elite Swim data set is available at https://jillsharrisphd .com/about.

5. Supervising sports economics research

Brad R. Humphreys and Jane E. Ruseski

INTRODUCTION

Sports economics represents a popular area for empirical research among undergraduates and graduate students. The salience of the topic for students, ample quantitative data generated by sporting events, and the relative ease of obtaining these data enhance the attractiveness of sports economics as a research area for students. In addition, sports economics is primarily an empirical field so students will have many examples of published research upon which to build their research projects.

In our experience, faculty frequently supervise sports economics research projects in undergraduate independent study courses, capstone projects, senior theses, and sports economics courses, as well as graduate research projects at various levels. This popularity of sports economics as a research topic constitutes a double-edged sword because the students being supervised are often embarking on their first substantial research project and possess little or no prior research experience. While many excellent student research projects in sports economics exist, we are also aware of, and have supervised, many less-than-successful projects.

This chapter summarizes some lessons learned based on our experience supervising sports economics research projects, provides specific examples of a structure for research projects aimed at increasing the likelihood a student successfully completes a project, and grounds this structure in the emerging literature on replicable research in the social sciences. While these lessons can be applied to ongoing empirical research projects, we recommend that students being supervised be provided with these guidelines at the outset of the project.

Project TIER, developed by Ball and Mediros (2012), is an excellent pre-existing resource for setting up an empirical research project beginning on Day One. Their website is the ideal place to direct students to on day one of an empirical research project. Project TIER, an organization devoted to promoting transparency and reproducibility in social science research, contains useful protocols for folder and file organization described in terms of a generic research project. This is an important starting point in any empirical research

project. The TIER Protocol is described at this website: https://www.projecttier
.org/tier-protocol/specifications-3-0/#overview-of-the-documentation

The protocol also contains a step-by-step list of actions that need to be
taken at the start of a replicable research project. We recommend that students
be directed to read and absorb the Project TIER protocols on the first day of
a class containing an empirical sports economics research project.

Project TIER, and much of the material discussed below, relates closely to
the replicable research initiative currently gaining traction in empirical economic research (Orozco et al., 2020). This initiative emerged following several
papers that reported very limited success in replicating the results found in
published articles. McCullough, McGeary and Harrison (2006) reported replicating the empirical results in fewer than 15 papers out of 150 papers published
in the *Journal of Money, Credit and Banking* over the period 1996–2002 with
archived code and data. Glandon (2011) reported successfully replicating the
results in only 20 of 39 empirical papers published in the *American Economic
Review* with archived code and data. Christensen and Miguel (2018) provide
a recent survey of replication issues in economics. This lack of replicability in
top peer-reviewed journals has clear implications for student research projects,
including the folly of assessing the quality of students' projects based only on
the final draft of a paper.

We describe a structured approach to supervising student research in sports
economics that emphasizes moving beyond office meetings for progress
updates coupled with a deliverable of a final draft of a paper (perhaps along
with a "rough" draft at some earlier point). We focus on the process of producing a research paper rather than the structure or anatomy of the final product
(for example, introduction, relevant literature, data and methods, results, etc.).
We assume that the student has already identified a research question and data,
although identifying an interesting question and appropriate data is also an
important part of the supervisory process.

We also identify existing resources to help in the development of such
a structured approach. Under this approach, students will face concrete
intermediate milestones throughout the project that involve thorough data
documentation, writing understandable code to clean, analyze, and report data
and results, as well as completing short, standalone components of the final
paper, with the ultimate goal of submission of the entire project at the end of
the project. In our (limited) experience, adopting this process improves the
learning experience of novice researchers and aids in the assessment of student
research projects.

A STRUCTURED APPROACH TO EMPIRICAL RESEARCH

Process-Oriented Approach to Research

Most students you will supervise on sports economics research projects will be unfamiliar with the process of doing research. They will likely proceed in an ad hoc, unorganized fashion with a laser focus on producing output such as regression results and paper drafts. Many will face the standard time constraints imposed by the academic semester – or worse, quarter – generating a sense of urgency surrounding the whole endeavor.

This lack of experience doing research, coupled with the fact that many faculty supervising sports economics research projects possess substantial research experience and instinctively perform many of the steps required to successfully complete a research project with little conscious thought, often leads to frustration for all involved. Marshall and Underwood (2019) observed that interactions between experts (research supervisors), unaware of much of their knowledge about the research process, and students, unaware of what they do not know about the research process, leads to an outcome known in the education literature as an *expert blind spot*. Based on our experience, this represents a common outcome when supervising sports economic research projects.

Marshall and Underwood (2019) developed a structured, process-oriented approach to address this problem. Providing a concrete, structured plan for a research project from the very beginning, before collecting a single data point, will help avoid common pitfalls that plague many novice researchers and result in an efficient, streamlined process. A structured approach to empirical research relates closely to the reproducible empirical research movement (Koenker and Zeileis, 2009; Ball and Medeiros, 2012). Reproducible research emphasizes that an outside researcher should be able to fully replicate all results in a paper starting from the raw data files collected at the start of the project. Ball and Medeiros (2012) called this a "soup to nuts" process. Replicable empirical research projects mean that the research supervisor can replicate all results in a research paper, simplifying evaluation. Replicable research projects also benefit our future selves at a point when whatever data were collected and regression models estimated in the past have completely slipped your mind.

Coding occupies a prominent role in the structured and replicable research approach, because coding lies at the heart of empirical economic research. Like the empirical research process, most novice researchers will also be learning to code at the same time they are learning to work with data and perform empirical research. These novice researchers will focus primarily on getting the code to be understood by the computer. While vitally important, a structured and replicable research approach goes beyond this stage and emphasizes the importance of coding in a clear way that makes the code readable by humans and allows readers to easily grasp the data analysis. Here, we also recommend concrete, specific advice on coding style for novice researchers because they will naturally focus primarily on outputs such as tables of results, and not making the process understandable and replicable by others, or their future selves.

We recognize the existence of a tradeoff between time spent working on a finished research project and time spent making the process structured, understandable, and reproducible. For novice researchers, the structured approach can substantially reduce time spent pursuing unproductive activities and performing basic activities multiple times. For experienced researchers, it can save substantial time across the publication process, given the long lags between paper submission and editorial decision, as well as the many empirical revisions requested by "Referee 2."

Systematically Organize Project Folders

We have looked on in horror many times when a student in our office or on Zoom seeking help on a research project fires up a laptop and displays a single folder crammed with scores of files containing raw and processed data, log files, scripts, pdf articles, assorted word processing documents, and other electronic detritus produced during the research process. The student scrolls endlessly through a shockingly long file list looking for something to show us, perhaps a graph or table of summary statistics, while we stare at the clock at the bottom of the screen. This should and can be avoided.

In general, folder organization and naming should reflect the research process and facilitate location of important items created during the process. Project TIER (https://www.projecttier.org/) developed a protocol for organizing folders in an empirical research projects and documenting data collection, manipulation, and analysis. This project represents an outgrowth of organizational methods described in Ball and Medeiros (2012). The TIER protocol recommends four top-level folders for all empirical research projects: a folder for the original raw data collected for the project (\original_data), a folder for scripts that manipulate and analyze the data (\analysis_files), a folder for the final analysis data set(s) (\analysis_data), and a folder for various documents generated in the research process (\documents).

Other useful folder structures exist. Knittel and Metaxoglou (2018) proposed a somewhat broader folder structure that includes storage areas for communication and background information. The key general concepts in these papers involve keeping data, analysis scripts, and writing in different folders, keeping raw data separately from data used to estimate regression models, and generous use of subfolders to make important files easy to find. Orozco et al. (2020) identified two guiding concepts for folder organization: (1) a folder should contain homogeneous items like data files, scripts/code files, documents, or documentation; and (2) folder names should make a clear distinction between project inputs and project outputs.

Purposefully Name Folders, Files, and Variables

Names matter. Advisors, collaborators, and your future self will, at some point, need to make sense of the folder structure, files, and variables that comprise any empirical research project. Your current self may know exactly what the contents of the file "blarghoct.doc" are, but your advisor, or your future self a month from now on a deadline, may not. Neither needs to waste time opening the file to see what might be in there when that deadline looms and your maximum likelihood estimation routine won't converge. Developing a purposeful system of file and variable naming can save hours of time wasted reinventing the wheel. A useful resource for naming files is a presentation prepared for the Reproducible Science Workshop by Jenny Bryan:

> One very important piece of file and folder naming advice that we strongly recommend is to never use blank spaces, special characters (&,@,%, # and the like), or punctuation (.,;) in folder or file names. This is a recipe for disaster when scripting empirical research, as statistical programs like Stata and R do not easily accommodate these characters in folder paths and file names. This will break your code. Again, friends don't let friends put spaces or garbage characters in folder and file names. Just say no.

The reproducible research literature identifies four general principles for naming folders and files. First, names should be machine readable, meaning that they should facilitate file searching and extracting information from file names only. In other words, file and folder names should contain metadata (data that provides information about other data). Second, folder and file names should be human readable, meaning that the name should contain information on the file's content. Your future self, or a collaborator, should be able to easily determine the contents of a file by the file name alone.

Third, file and folder names should work well with the default ordering in folder/file displays. The default ordering of items in all operating systems is numbers in ascending order followed by letters in alphabetical order. In practice, this means putting numeric characters first in file and folder names and left padding these numbers with zeros.

Good practice uses underscores ("_") to delimit metadata and hyphens ("-") to delimit words in folder and file titles to improve readability. The use of these delimiters, along with judicious naming of files, provides a clear and quick method of conveying all the information needed to understand the analysis process at a glance. As an example, which of the following two folder contents would you want to scan at midnight when the results in a proposal need updating before a deadline?

```
01_read-raw-price-data.do          deflateit.do
02_merge-in-state-data.do          first&secondstaiv.do
03_deflate-to-2020-dollars.do      makegraphsts.do
04_make-time-series-graph.do       othresult21.do
05_summary-stat-table.do           read 11.do
06_results-table-ols.do            runolsmodel.do
07_results-table-iv.do             scttrpl1.do
08_make-scatter-plot.do            st dt mg.do
09_robustness-check-cluster.do     sumst1125.do
10_run-all-files.do
```

Fourth, file and folder names should reflect the workflow process. Workflow describes the sequence of events that make up an empirical research project, from data collection to published paper. Note how the file naming protocol used on the left panel above reflects a workflow process. The successive scripts perform important, recognizable steps from raw data manipulation to the tabulation of regression results.

Document Everything

The replicable research literature identifies the paramount importance of documentation throughout the research process. Without thorough documentation, other researchers (including supervisors and your future self) will find it difficult to follow your workflow and replicate or understand the results. Documentation in a structured research process takes many forms, including metadata and data dictionaries for data files, comments and smart variable and function names in scripts, and comments in paper drafts.

Documentation of an empirical research project begins during the data collection stage. A number of papers (Orozco et al., 2020; Marshall and Underwood, 2019; Dekker and Lackie, 2017; Ball and Mediros, 2012) recommend the creation of metadata, data dictionaries, and other detailed documentation upon acquisition of raw data files. Metadata refers to data about data. Metadata goes beyond information contained in data dictionaries attached to Stata or SAS data files to include information that a user would need to completely understand the contents of a data file. Again, the idea behind the documentation process is that an outside researcher should be able to fully recreate the raw data acquisition process and subsequent data manipulation using only the files from the project. Many papers also recommend the use of README files – small text files containing a list and brief description of all files in a folder.

Creating a codebook for each raw data set collected represents an important, and overlooked part of the documentation process. While time consuming, creating the main codebook elements generates a deep understanding of the structure and content of a data set. Dekker and Lackie (2017) pointed out that codebooks should contain technical details such as the file layout, structure and content, along with information such as whether the data represent a sample or the population and the identification scheme for missing values.

A good codebook contains an entry for each variable in the raw data file along with the variable name and location in the raw data file. It should contain each variable's type (categorical, numeric, text, etc.), the values, corresponding labels, and label definitions for each categorical variable along with tabulations of the number and frequency of each category and the number of observations. Understanding values and labels used for categorical variables is critical. Many relatively processed data sets use a gender identification scheme of 1=male and 2=female. This can lead to big problems if one later uses that exact variable as a gender indicator variable in a regression model. Not that either of us has any personal experience with this.

Numeric variables in codebooks should have mean, standard deviation, range, and number of observations, including missing observations. For survey data, the codebook should contain the text of each question. Ideally, codebooks should be created by scripts. Learning how to write loops over variable names in your scripting language of choice is the key to scripting codebook creation.

Scripts that manipulate data, perform econometric analysis, and produce tables and figures also require documentation. In our experience, thorough documentation in script files is very important for your future self; we have both spent too much time puzzling over undocumented code we wrote months before, and sometimes had to re-do the whole thing because we could not replicate the results.

We strongly advocate against the use of spreadsheet programs such as Excel for data cleaning and manipulation and instead advocate for the use of scripts to process original format raw data files into importable data files suitable for analysis, for two reasons. First, reading raw text data into Excel involves known problems, especially with dates. The infamous Reinhart and Rogoff (2010) incident, where Excel pre-processing incorrectly parsed dates, and correcting this problem reversed the results in their *American Economic Review* paper, should be enough incentive to avoid Excel, even though students may have used it before. Second, manually changing data in cells in a spreadsheet represents an undocumented change to the data. Your future self may or may not recall the exact manipulation, breaking the chain of replicability.

Another important activity involves use of comments, in plain language, in any code file or script written as part of the research project. Orozco et al. (2020) recommend starting each script with a comment section describing, in plain language, the goal of the script, date written, author, version of the program it runs under, the computer platform, and all input and output files. Most papers on coding style note the potential to over comment scripts. For example, appending a comment to the end of each line of code is a bad idea. Commenting blocks of code is a better approach. Also, judicious use of human-readable variable names helps. Naming a variable *real_gdp_2020_dols* makes a comment such as "the variable ydefl is real GDP deflated to 2020 dollars" unnecessary. Caveat: good coding practice should also avoid long variable names. Strike a balance.

Code for Your Future Self (and Others)

We have lost count of the number of times we have written scripts to perform some empirical analysis on a data set and then returned to those files months (or years) later only to find that we have no idea what we had in mind when writing those scripts. We then spent hours or days deciphering the code, or worse, completely redoing the analysis and hoping to get the same results. We strongly suspect this occurs frequently, especially for novice researchers, over time spans as short as a few weeks.

These situations can be avoided by learning and following good coding practices. This is especially important for novice researchers, who are often learning to code and to work with data at the same time. Novice researchers will often be impatient to just get to the point where regression results get generated. Since there is a clear tradeoff between writing easy to understand and fully documented code and finishing an analysis script that generates results, novice researchers typically write undocumented code with haphazard naming conventions. Spending some more time coding correctly up front will frequently save enormous amounts of time later in the process, when the code writing was done day, weeks, or months earlier.

Space constraints prevent an extended digression on good coding practice. Many excellent papers exist containing useful coding advice. We have found the coding advice in Gentzkow and Shapiro (2014), Dekker and Lackie (2017), Knittel and Metaxoglou (2018), and Orozco et al. (2020) to be very helpful. Spending time reading the coding advice in these papers is time well spent.

In general, good coding practice means paying attention to a number of aspects including the layout of the code (no more than 80 characters per line), use of indentation (limited), sequencing of actions, variable naming (consistent, meaningful, and not too long), and documentation. Documentation plays a critical role, but good practice means making it easy to understand, not overdoing it (use comments for blocks of code, not every line, and make them easy to spot), and recognizing that variable or function naming represents a substitute for documentation in some cases.

In our experience, novice researchers struggle with many of the basic aspects of coding associated with data manipulation and cleaning. Merging data sets represents one important area where supervisors should provide thorough guidance, for example reminding students that data must be sorted before merging and mandatory tabulation of the merge indicator variables. Raw data rarely arrive in an easy to analyze format, making reshaping data sets another important, and difficult to master manipulation.

Script Everything

We repeat: script everything. Scripting lies at the heart of reproducible research. This means, ideally, you should be able to reproduce every data set underlying every figure and table in the final version of a research project by running a single batch file. This includes reading the raw data files collected for the project, all data manipulation and cleaning, deflating, and all the rest.

This means no command line data description or regression exploration. The research replication literature recommends avoiding command line or drop-down menu analysis like the plague. Write a batch file or script (.do or .R files) that reads the relevant data file and does the needed manipulation or estimation and then execute this script repeatedly instead of typing in multiple command prompt code. If you want to see what sort of results come from an alternative version of the model, just temporarily comment out the other model.

Scripting everything means no data manipulation by hand in a spreadsheet or text editor. Instead, use scripts to read the raw data files, undertake whatever manipulations are needed to transform the raw data file to a machine readable file, merging in other data files, and everything else. Taken to the extreme, scripting includes writing scripts that would download or scrape the raw data.

WORKING WITH DATA

Ball and Medeiros (2012) identified a useful distinction in types of data files: raw data files versus importable data files. Raw data files refer to electronic files in exactly the form in which they were first obtained, for example through downloading or scraping. Raw data files can take many forms, including flat text files, delimited text files, spreadsheets, or even data files already in Stata,

SAS, SPSS, or R format, depending on what the data source makes available. Best practice in reproducible research dictates keeping a read-only version of all raw data files.

For example, suppose a student you are supervising is working on a project about intercollegiate athletics. The Equity in Athletics Data Analysis (EADA) Cutting Tool (https://ope.ed.gov/athletics/#/) represents a common source of financial data for athletic programs at co-educational postsecondary institutions that receive Title IV funding. EADA data can be downloaded in Excel, SAS, or SPSS format. In this case, the raw data files would be those files downloaded from the EADA.

Importable files are transformed versions of the raw data files that can be read into econometric software such as Stata or R. If this student will perform her econometric analysis in SAS, then the raw and importable data files are the same format. If the student will perform her econometric analysis in EViews, then the raw data files differ from the importable data files, since EViews has a proprietary data file format.

Best practices in replicable research require that scripts be written to transform raw data files into importable data files. Opening up a raw data file in a spreadsheet and directly modifying data in that file violates best practice. Those changes to the raw data file are not documented and cannot be reproduced by another researcher. In other words, a researcher provided with the raw data files and documentation will have no record of changes made to cells in the spreadsheet and will not be able to replicate the results.

Data Cleaning and Visualization

Given time constraints and a focus on generating results, many novice researchers race past important steps in the empirical research process after raw data have been collected and jump directly to the regress y x-stage. This frequently leads to bad outcomes. Structured research projects force novice researchers to fully understand the structure and content of their importable data set before undertaking any econometric analysis. The process of developing codebooks described above can be beneficial in this process.

We always assume that all raw data sets contain mistakes and problems, even relatively processed raw data sets. For example, the EADA data mentioned above do not use consistent institution names over time. Many data sets use different variable names for the same values across different years or waves. Data cleaning (sometimes called validation) and visualization ensure that these issues do not lead to problems in empirical work. Missing values, and the symbols used to identify missing values, represents one common problem that thorough data cleaning can solve. Problems with missing values typically stem from a lack of standard values to identify missing values, especially in string data.

Extensive tabulation, summarization, and graphing represent the primary tools for cleaning and visualizing data. Tabulation of counts applies primarily to categorical variables, although this is also applicable to some text/string data. Tabulation is a good way to identify problems generated by missing observations. Summarization primarily applies to numeric data. Missing values in numeric data requires close attention to the number of observations over which standard summary statistics are calculated.

Data visualization means creating and viewing graphs. Scatter plots can help identify outliers and other problems such as censoring. Scatter plots of numeric variables by categorical variables can uncover miscoding and issues with missing observations. Time series plots provide a good sensibility check on variables beyond summarization.

WRITING RESEARCH PAPERS AS A PROCESS

Many student sports economics research projects take place in the context of a single semester or in some cases a quarter. Class papers, independent study projects, and capstone research projects, all involve end-of-term deadlines for submission of final versions of papers. This often leads novice researchers to focus on the final product and ignore the process of writing, including sequencing of assignments, drafting, and revisions. Novice researchers' general lack of writing experience compounds the focus on the writing product. A focus on the final product can lead to procrastination because a final draft appears to be an unattainable goal when confronted with a blank word processing document, as well as subpar final products (Marshall and Underwood, 2019).

The process writing literature in economics (Schmeiser, 2017; Marshall and Underwood, 2019) emphasizes building specific, tangible deadlines for relatively short components of the final paper into the course or project structure. In other words, break the complex task (final paper completion) into smaller, manageable sub-tasks linked to specific steps in the empirical analysis.

For example, the detailed 16-week structured empirical research project developed by Marshall and Underwood (2019) includes submission of an annotated bibliography and formal research question at the end of week three, a research proposal at the end of week six, a metadata guide or codebook at the end of week nine, a literature review at the end of week 11, and drafts of other paper sections in weeks 13 and 15. These milestones focus on submission of individual components of the final paper, not "rough" drafts, and correspond to specific components of the empirical analysis. For example, the deadline for submitting a metadata file and data dictionary corresponds to the completion of raw data collection. This process reduces the importance of the final paper, deters procrastination, and provides novice researchers with regular feedback.

Marshall and Underwood (2019) also pointed out that too many, or too frequent submission deadlines can do more harm in good. Frequent submission deadlines, for example weekly assignments, risk exceeding novice researchers' cognitive load, which can also lead to bad outcomes. The key idea involves developing a sequence of writing assignments detailed enough to clearly articulate expectations but not so exhaustive as to overwhelm novice researchers.

Schmeiser (2017) advocated a similar approach based on forcing students to become familiar with both data and literature early in the semester, culminating with a one-page research proposal in week four. The deliverables include a three to five-page progress update including an initial literature review and list of data sources in week seven, and an initial paper draft in week 10. Schmeiser (2017) also points out that students often ignore feedback and seldom read marked-up drafts with suggestions for improving the project. One possible solution involves required written responses to feedback that clearly state agreement or disagreement with the main comments.

Integrating the writing process with a structured research project requires significant investment by supervisors in creating a unified, detailed framework. One way to mitigate these costs is a gradual adoption of this approach. Requiring a completed rough draft after 10 weeks is one starting point. Another is requiring students to submit analysis scripts and metadata early on in the project.

FINAL THOUGHTS

We recognize that the process-oriented research project described in this chapter represents a substantial departure from the approach used by many research supervisors. Simply adjusting the first draft and final paper submission deadlines from last year's syllabus, urging students to come to office hours with questions or roadblocks, and hoping for the best, represents a time-tested approach that minimizes costs. Few among us received concrete advice on the research *process* in graduate school, and we all turned out okay, didn't we? Providing supervisees with detailed guidance on data collection, naming objects, coding, and process writing, along with multiple, clearly thought out milestones linked to replicability requires a substantial investment in time and effort.

We argue that this represents a high return investment for four reasons. First, we identified a number of high quality, pre-existing sources of guidance that emerged in the last few years in economics. Project TIER and many of the papers discussed in this chapter are accessible to students. Unlike five years ago, concrete and useful guidance are readily available. Second, the general unevenness of student research projects in sports economics, coupled with strong evidence of a reproducibility problem in published economic research suggests that the current standard process contains flaws. While we often recall outstanding student research projects we supervised (including those leading to publications), a large number of poor quality projects occur, even in PhD level courses. Chalking this up to lack of student effort or imagination, or simply the difficult nature of economic research, represents an unsatisfactory explanation. What if lack of adequate, clear, structured guidance constitutes the main reason for these common outcomes?

Third, adopting this approach saves substantial time for students and supervisors in the long run, despite the large set-up costs. Students will almost never, absent a complete failure to back up raw data and scripts, be forced to go back and start from square one a month into the project because some data cleaning, manipulation, inadvertent file overwriting, or file corruption issue makes their once promising preliminary results disappear. Scripting everything provides the ability to re-create an analysis data file from scratch by running a single batch file. Supervisors will be able to easily scan the project file structure, files, and analysis output files to get a complete picture on the workflow and quality of the results in the paper ("look here, you didn't sort this file before merging and used the dreaded Stata –merge m:m- (merge many to many) command!") This will save considerable time evaluating projects, and provide assurance that the results in the final paper are correct.

Fourth, frankly, adopting this process in our own work can make us all better, more productive empirical researchers. How many times have you started work on a revise and resubmit after not looking at a project for months (or years) and not been able to make heads nor tails of the data files, data manipulation, and analysis? We have, more times than we care to admit. Adopting this approach solves that problem and many others (Christensen and Miguel, 2018). In addition, journals increasingly adopt the reproducible research approach and require submission and archiving of a full set of data files and code that completely replicate all results in the published version of the paper. Adopting this approach now eliminates any costs of doing this ex post, including the risk of not being able to replicate the results after paper acceptance, and contributes to a more transparent and credible research process in the discipline

REFERENCES

Ball, R. and Medeiros, N. (2012) Teaching integrity in empirical research: A protocol for documenting data management and analysis. *The Journal of Economic Education*, 43(2), 182–189.

Christensen, G. and Miguel, E. (2018) Transparency, reproducibility, and the credibility of economics research. *Journal of Economic Literature*, 56(3), 920–980.

Dekker, H. and Lackie, P. (2017) Technical data skills for reproducible research. In L. Kellam and K. Thompson (eds), *Databrarianship*. Association of College and Research Libraries, 93, 112.

Gentzkow, M. and Shapiro, J. M. (2014) *Code and Data for the Social Sciences: A Practitioner's Guide*. Chicago, IL: University of Chicago.

Glandon, P. J. (2011) Appendix to the report of the editor: Report on the *American Economic Review* data availability compliance project. *American Economic Review*, 101(3), 695–699.

Knittel, C. R. and Metaxoglou, K. (2018) Working with data: Two empiricists' experience. *Journal of Econometric Methods*, 7(1).

Koenker, R. and Zeileis, A. (2009). On reproducible econometric research. *Journal of Applied Econometrics*, 24(5), 833–847.

Marshall, E. C. and Underwood, A. (2019) Writing in the discipline and reproducible methods: A process-oriented approach to teaching empirical undergraduate economics research. *The Journal of Economic Education*, 50(1), 17–32.

McCullough, B. D., McGeary, K. A. and Harrison, T. D. (2006) Lessons from the *JMCB* Archive. *Journal of Money, Credit and Banking*, 4, 1093–1107.

Orozco, V., Bontemps, C. Maigné, E., Piguet, V., Hofstetter, A., Lacroix, A., Levert, F., and Rousselle, J.-M. (2020) How to make a pie: Reproducible research for empirical economics and econometrics. *Journal of Economic Surveys*, 34(5), 1134–1169.

Reinhart, C. M. and Rogoff, K. S. (2010) Growth in a time of debt. *American Economic Review*, 100(2), 573–578.

Schmeiser, K. (2017) Teaching writing in economics. *The Journal of Economic Education*, 48(4), 254–264.

PART II

Teaching sports economics

6. Using guest speakers and day trips to teach sports economics

Aju J. Fenn

When I arrived at Colorado College in 2001, it was impressed upon me that I was expected to develop at least one course that incorporated guest speakers and/or field trips. At the time, I taught Principles of Economics, Research Methods, Mathematical Economics, Econometrics and Sports Economics. The easiest course to incorporate field trips and guest speakers appeared to be Sports Economics. So with some doubts about the academic value of such an approach, I turned to the business of finding speakers and trip venues. Nineteen years later and due to the pandemic, I am about to teach Sports Economics for the first time without field trips. This is the perfect time to reflect upon the positives and negatives of using field trips and/or guest speakers to teach Sports Economics. Along the way I will also reflect on strategies to recruit and develop good speakers and to be part of something positive that your students remember long after they have graduated.

ARE FIELD TRIPS RIGHT FOR YOUR CLASS?

Day trips to venues with guest speakers require careful planning, extra effort, and some resources. The first question you must ask yourself is whether this is the best approach to achieve your objectives for your sports economics class and department. A carefully planned and executed class with day trips and guest speakers can create a worthy and memorable academic experience that exceeds the best in-class lecture or discussion. If you deliver a good experience you can leverage that experience to increase enrollments in your departmental courses or to challenge your students academically. You can use day trips to venues as a reward to push them to undertake more difficult academic projects. I was first asked to teach Sports Economics while I was a visiting Assistant Professor at the University of St. Thomas. In order to take my elective Sports Economics course, students would have to take both Microeconomics and Macroeconomics classes as prerequisites. This would no doubt increase departmental enrollments. After arriving at Colorado College I discovered that a Sports Economics class with some guest speakers and a couple of day trips earned the good will and appreciation of the students. It motivated them to willingly engage in projects that ranged from literature reviews, basic data collection with analysis to learning how to make their own websites to display such information for use by subsequent cohorts of Sports Economics students. The key was to give them broad themes from the literature and allow them to develop and answer questions that were linked to our guest speakers. Students were so interested in what our guest speakers had to say that they willingly worked long hours to complete projects to get answers to questions that they had developed based on guest presentations. To them, it did not seem like work at all. I turn next to some of the challenges of organizing a day trip/guest speaker-based Sports Economics course.

WHERE DO YOU BEGIN?

When I arrived at Colorado College in 2001, I was given invaluable field trip/ guest speaker advice and information by Professor Mark Smith. He had been doing field trips for many years and shared his insights with me. He would go on to elevate field trips to an art form. He has done everything from camping out with natural resource economics students to taking students in his climate change course to the United Nations Climate change conferences. Luckily for all of us he documents all of these invaluable insights in his journal article (Smith, 2007). I will focus on Sports Economics, but if you are interested in doing day trips or field-trips in Sports Economics or any class I suggest that you read Smith (2007).

WHAT CONSTRAINTS DO YOU FACE?

The main constraints facing a day trip or field trip planner are time, talent, and other resources. How do you and your students carve out the time to take day trips? How does one find suitable guest speakers and set them up for success? Who is going to pay for the associated transportation and potential venue costs? Let us consider each of these questions.

Time

Colorado Colleges operates on a modular block plan where students take one course at a time and faculty teach one course at a time over a three-and-a-half-week period consisting of 18 days. Classes meet for approximately three hours per day. Given such a time intensive framework, engaging teaching requires creative alternatives to chalk and talk. One of the advantages of the block plan is that students have fewer scheduling conflicts with a day trip or a field trip. On a semester or quarter system, advertising the timing of day trips in advance of course registration will enable interested students to minimize scheduling conflicts. J-term (January term) or an early summer class may also be windows where students have fewer conflicts with other courses. It is not always possible to eliminate all conflicts for all students, but advertising in advance and providing quality field trips does incentivize students to free up their schedules. One also has to consider the availability of speakers during your class window. More on that later.

Talent

Which speakers should you invite? How do you reach them and convince them to speak to your class? What will they speak about and how will it enhance the academic content of your Sports Economics course? These are all valid questions. I will deal with the first question here and the other three in subsequent sections of this chapter.

You may begin by inviting the athletics director for your school and any neighboring schools that play in a different division. If the local division one athletics director is not available, perhaps an associate or assistant athletics director may have the time. Coaches or assistant coaches from division 3, 2 or 1 programs may also be an accessible resource. All of the above speakers can speak to the economics of amateur sports and Title IX issues. Another accessible resource for speakers is the local youth soccer, baseball, lacrosse, or hockey league directors.

Next you may consider front office general managers for the local AAA baseball team or minor league soccer, football, or semi-pro sports teams. These executives are quite happy to speak to your students both because they have an opportunity to represent their organizations, attract fans and because it may enhance the service part of their résumés. I will go into detail on how to recruit speakers later on.

Other Resources

In addition to time and guest speakers, you may require transportation and other resources to travel to venues such as the local NBA arena or NFL stadium. If the college or university does not have a bus or van with a driver, you may consider asking students to ride share with others that have cars. Finally, if cost is still an issue, a visit to the dean may be in order. Alternatively, you may work with the alumni office to solicit funds for the class.

If you feel like you can clear the above hurdles you will be interested in the rest of this chapter which will outline the details of setting up a guest speaker and field trip-based class.

FINDING, RECRUITING, AND PREPARING GUEST SPEAKERS

The obvious choices for guest speakers are front office personnel from major league teams in your area. The challenge is they are often quite busy and have to be persuaded to speak to your class. Front office executives from minor league teams are usually easier to recruit. Other potential speakers include college athletics directors and marketing executives, relevant speakers from sports consulting firms, sports agents, executives from sports broadcasting networks and the directors of youth sports leagues. The preferred approach to recruiting speakers is via an introduction. However, using the correct pitch when directly contacting speakers can also yield positive results.

I received an offer for an introduction to a Major League Baseball (MLB) executive during the 2001 Colorado College fall conference, which is a kickoff event to the annual school year. During my introduction to the college members, my chair mentioned that I had an interest in sports economics. During a mixer right after that event I was approached by a trustee of the college who offered to put me in touch with a close friend of his who was an executive for the Colorado Rockies. I gladly accepted. Through the years I have had former students, staff, and faculty offer me potential speakers because they knew I taught Sports Economics and welcomed guest speakers. The moral of the story is to put the word out that you teach Sports Economics and are interested in potential guest speakers.

The best way to do this is to let faculty colleagues, staff and administrators know of your desire to find and recruit guest speakers. You may do this in person as an aside after a department or all-college faculty meeting. Contact the college development or advancement office and request a meeting to discuss the opportunity to bring alumni back to campus to speak about sports, sports marketing, or related topics. In most cases the development office will be eager to help as they are often looking for meaningful ways to engage alumni. Perhaps a speaker can also do a campus-wide talk in the evening after speaking to your class in the morning or afternoon. As previously stated, do not overlook your institution's own athletic department. Begin by inviting your Athletics Director (AD) and asking them if they have any suggestions for other ADs or college conference officials from the area. If your institution is in a small town, contact some of the major businesses who sponsor college athletics through your college's athletics department to recruit executives who will usually be happy to speak about why they sponsor college athletics. This approach is usually successful because you have an introduction to the potential speaker through somebody known to them.

The next approach is to contact potential speakers directly. A respectful email containing an official invitation to discuss potential speaking opportunities is a great way to start this conversation. You may begin by introducing yourself professionally and describe your course briefly. Then the letter should politely request an opportunity to meet with the speaker to see if you can tailor the speaking opportunity to their interests and strengths. Explain that while you can give the students textbook knowledge, only speakers from the real world can provide valuable insights into the workings of the sports industry. Most executives view a speaking opportunity at an academic college or university as a positive. After the email letter you may follow up with the person in a week or so to see if they are available. If they are not available, you may ask them if there is someone else in their organization or another organization that would make a good guest speaker.

The last source of guest speakers is to invite academic scholars from neighboring institutions to visit and discuss their sports economics research. I recall a year when I was responsible for a guest speaker series. I invited speakers for general campus talks but also had them speak to my sports economics class. In 2021, due to the COVID-19 pandemic, all my guest speakers spoke to my students via Zoom. This lowered the travel costs associated with bringing speakers to campus. The lesson being, instructors facing significant budget or time constraints, may use Zoom to bring guest speakers to their students. Doing so lowers the time and monetary costs associated with bringing speakers to class. The only drawback to using Zoom in 2021 was that students did not get to visit the Broncos training facility and Coors Field. The onsite visits give students a feel for the behind-the-scenes aspects of running a professional sports team. It also seems to motivate them to work harder in class because they know that the field trips are a special experience that most of them enjoy. Once you have a slate of speakers, the next step is to prepare them for a successful experience.

I always ask speakers to speak on aspects of their professional roles that they are most comfortable speaking about. Once I have some idea of their topic, I work with the class to provide the economic models and concepts ahead of time. The very first time Joe Ellis of the Broncos visited my class he chose to speak about revenue streams and expenditure outlays for the Denver Broncos. I was able to prepare the class for his talk by reviewing the revenues and expenditures model from the sports economics text by Leeds et al. (2018). Each year Hal Roth and Brian Gaffney of the Colorado Rockies deliver an excellent presentation of the economic structure of each of the major and some of the minor league sports teams in the USA. They cover up-to-date details of revenue sharing agreements, salary caps, luxury taxes, etc. Sometimes a presentation like this one needs little additional set up other than prompting students to think of research topics for their course presentations. When I have

National Football league (NFL) agents visit my class, I go over transactions costs and the principle-agent problem to prepare the class for their talks.

Travis Tygart, the CEO of the Unites States Anti-doping agency is a regular visitor to my class. He has even hired a student or two from the college. He provided me with an article by Michael Shermer (2008) that takes a game theoretic approach to the problem of doping. The article shows that for a two-athlete sport, in the absence of credible doping detection and penalties, the Nash equilibrium is for both athletes to dope. On the other hand, after the introduction of a credible threat of doping detection and punishment, the Nash equilibrium for both athletes is not to dope. Sometimes your speakers will have excellent resources for your class. I have had athletic directors speak about the importance of Title IX. Sometimes I have students debate whether college athletes should be paid after the guest speaker has departed. Last but not least, every speaker leaves with a small gift bag of some college swag and a thank you card signed by the entire class. It is important to convey our gratitude for their time and effort.

PREPARING SPEAKERS FOR THEIR VISIT

I usually meet with some first-time speakers or communicate over email to discuss the topic and scope of their talk. Other details may include their instructional needs, such as photocopies, or audio-visual needs. I get logistics worked out ahead of time. Then I lesson plan to introduce the relevant concepts ahead of time. Once I have the details and dates set with my speakers, I send them an official letter, via email, confirming both the time and topic. The letter also includes detailed instructions to get to campus and from the parking lot to my office. I also give them my cell phone number for last minute communications.

PREPARING THE STUDENTS AND HOLDING THEM ACCOUNTABLE

If your guest speakers have a good experience, they are likely to return. You may even be able to persuade them to speak on different topics as they become comfortable with the way that your classes conduct themselves. Defining student expectations clearly is helpful because it also signals to students that the guest speakers and their material are to be taken seriously. The speakers are not there to entertain the students. It is important to set a tone that the class is about academics and not sports.

I usually convey my general expectations to students on the first day of class and then remind them about specific details before each speaker or field trip. I explain to my students that they are the beneficiaries of the engagement and professionalism of former cohorts of sports economics students. I remind them to dress professionally for guest speakers, arrive early to class and have meaningful questions prepared for each speaker. Their grades in part are based on in class participation and discussion. I also hold them accountable for guest speaker material by placing questions on exams. I remind students that they are representatives of the college and want to represent themselves and their institution well.

INTRODUCING THE SPEAKERS AND THANKING THEM

I will usually keep an eye out for my speakers so that I can meet and greet them in my office prior to class. I get them a bottle of water, ask them if they need to use the restroom, and make sure that they have their laptop or photocopies handy. The key is to make them feel comfortable and appreciated.

As class time approaches, I escort them to class. Most students tend to be early or on time, thanks to my gentle reminders. I kick things off with a brief introduction of the guest speaker's educational and professional background and ask the class to join me in welcoming them. Then I turn things over to the speaker and retreat to a corner of the class so that I can serve as a moderator or assist with classroom technology. Once their talk is concluded, I thank them briefly and present them with the small gift bag and pre-signed thank you card. Gifts include coffee mugs with the college and department logo and perhaps a title such as distinguished guest lecturer. While all of these executives are highly respected in their fields, most of them appreciate being welcomed into academe to share their wisdom. A coffee mug or water bottle with the appropriate credentials gives them subtle bragging rights of sorts.

ORGANIZING DAY TRIPS

A day trip is an off-campus trip where the class visits a sports facility and benefits from experiential learning. The two trips that my sports economics class takes are to the Denver Broncos stadium or training facility, and to the Colorado Rockies stadium. The academic focus of each trip is a talk by front office executives. At the Broncos, the topics have ranged from revenue and expenditure streams of an NFL team to building a winning franchise. The talk at the Rockies Stadium usually covers the details of US major and minor leagues financial structure and compensation. These talks are followed by a tour of the facility and usually conclude with lunch before we depart. While we are touring the stadium, students get to see how different seats are priced at different levels. They get to see the players' locker rooms and training facilities. Sometimes we have even seen a player or two. I remind the reader to consult Smith (2007) for a much more detailed look at organizing field trips.

The day trips are set up well before the class begins and students know these dates on the first day of class. You must check with your institution to comply with all day trip and off-campus policies. We have an office of field study that must be notified ahead of time. If possible, arrange a single bus or van with a professional driver so that you can keep all your students together. In some instances I have had students who need to drive separately or leave early. I provide them with detailed locations and our arrival time. I also communicate with the sports teams about these students. If you cannot afford a bus or a van, examine the possibility of organizing your class into a caravan of cars.

Our trips are in the mornings, so I provide bagels and juice for my class. Well-fed students are less cranky and more attentive. I tend to schedule my day trips on Fridays so that I have the weekend to recover and reset for class. I have strict picture and social media policies that comply with the team's wishes. Students do take pictures of themselves in the dugout, the clubhouse, and on the edges of the field. It is great to see them having fun while representing themselves and the college in a respectful manner. I remind them about the appropriate attire, timeliness, and class participation the day before the trip. I have a few examples of less than acceptable behavior that I cite to clarify my expectations.

If you have organized a successful day trip, you will know it from the smiles on your students' faces and their sincere gratitude. Day trips are a lot of work but conversations with alumni reaffirm that they are most appreciated and remembered. My students may not always remember the concepts of operating at the margin, but they do remember how to be professional and how to present themselves.

After each iteration of my class I survey my students for feedback on the guest speakers and the day trips. I also get in touch with speakers after a week or two to get their thoughts on how I could make the experience better for them.

CONCLUDING REMARKS

A class like this takes a lot of time to set up. Successive iterations of the class have substantially lower time costs as you develop a good roster of speakers. Unlike classes where you do all of the teaching, a class like this seems to fly by because students are so engaged, and you are not on your feet all of the time. Not all courses lend themselves to the field trip and guest speaker approach, but those that do shine brightly. Be careful to start small and simple with a few guest speakers and perhaps a single day trip. Then learn from your errors and successes. I am happy to discuss what I know with any professor that is inter-ested in trying out this method.

REFERENCES

Leeds, M.A., von Allmen, P., & Matheson, V.A. (2018). *The Economics of Sports* (6th edn). Routledge. https://doi.org/10.4324/9781315167947

Shermer, M. (2008). The doping dilemma. *Scientific American*, 298(4), 82–89. http://www.jstor.org/stable/26000562

Smith, M. G. (2007). Case studies on location: Taking to the field in economics. *Journal of Economic Education*, 38(3), 308–317.

7. Sports and the law: using court cases to teach sports economics

Victor A. Matheson

INTRODUCTION

As a part of an undergraduate economics curriculum, sports economics is a relatively young field. As such, the discipline has fewer "tried and true" teaching methodologies as compared with other economics courses, such as principles and intermediate macro and micro. The purpose of this chapter is twofold. First, it lays forth a rationale for the use of court cases in teaching a sports economics class. Second, it provides an overview of the most important cases related to sports economics. Even those teachers who choose not to directly include the study of court decisions in their class need a working knowledge of sports law because of the critical impact that many court decisions have had on the development of the US professional and collegiate sports industries.

So, why study court cases in an economics class? The most obvious answer is that the courts have played a crucial role in the economic development of American sports. To the average American sports fan, it may not seem that the Supreme Court has anything to do with their enjoyment of the game they watch on television on Sunday afternoons, but nothing could be further from the truth. High school basketball stars who jumped straight to the NBA, such as Kevin Garnett and LeBron James, can thank Spencer Haywood and the Court for their decision in his favor, which opened the door for non-college graduates to enter the league. The stunning success of the US Women's National Soccer team over the past three decades is a direct result of court enforcement of the provisions of Title IX of the Education Amendments of 1972, which barred gender discrimination in athletic programs at college institutions. When the local baseball team signs new stars or loses talent to big-spending clubs, this can be traced directly back to the decision in *Flood v. Kuhn* that, at least in part, ushered in the era of free agency in Major League Baseball. Tiger Woods' spectacular golf career hinged on his ability to play on public golf courses as a child, a privilege denied to African Americans only a few years before his birth. Indeed, the courts have examined everything from ticket scalping to television contracts to the use of golf carts in professional tournaments, touching nearly every aspect of modern spectator sports.

Many topics typically covered in a sports economics class cannot help but cover legal issues. For example, baseball's antitrust exemption is discussed in nearly every textbook covering sports economic issues. What better way to discover the origin of this admittedly strange exemption than to read the court's original reasoning? The same idea applies to franchise movement, labor relations, free agency, and a host of other subjects.

Beyond this, however, the use of court cases in an undergraduate economics class is valuable in numerous other ways. First, court classes allow students to develop critical reading and reasoning skills. Most written court decisions present a clear view of the competing differences of the two parties as well as an explanation as to how the court arrived at its final decision. In many cases, a dissenting opinion is also recorded, providing yet another viewpoint from the court. Students who read these opinions learn to read and analyze the decisions carefully in order to follow the logic of the court. In addition, in many of the cases related to sports law, the written opinions also present interesting historical background of the sport, leagues, and teams involved in the case.

Court cases also allow the instructor to present readings outside the standard textbooks that are accessible to most undergraduates. Many sports economics classes are taught as a lower-level elective or as part of a sports management curriculum, and therefore the students are unlikely to have taken a course in econometrics, or even statistics, as a prerequisite. Therefore, many students may lack the mathematical or statistical background to fully understand many of the classic journal articles in the field, but a professor may wish to present material that rises above the level of *Sports Illustrated* or ESPN.com. Court cases neatly fit into a niche between the popular press and the rigorous analytical complexity of most scholarly articles. Of course, court opinions are typically filled with technical issues regarding the appeals process, court jurisdiction, and descriptions of the lawyers involved in trying the case. Much of this minutia of the legal process is of interest only to the legal scholar. Therefore, a teacher using court cases should select them carefully and attempt to strip down the opinions in order to make the decisions more easily accessible to the non-legal expert and in a way that the reasoning of the court can be more plainly seen.

Finally, students seem to respond positively to the experience. Many economics majors strongly consider law school after graduation, so an opportunity to read legal opinions is of great interest to them. Even those students not pursuing a career in law find the cases interesting. Most have heard of the great legal cases, such as *Brown v. Board of Education*, but have no idea what the whole legal system is about. Furthermore, the increasingly contentious Supreme Court confirmation process has introduced the general public to legal terms such as *stare decisis*, but without much idea about what they mean or why they are important. A sports economics course with a focus on legal issues not only provides this type of information but also broadens the course to fit better within a liberal arts education rather than being a narrow specialty field of interest to sports junkies but few others.

A SPORTS LAW PRIMER FOR SPORTS ECONOMISTS

So, what cases should be covered in an economics class or what cases should a sports economist at least have some basic knowledge of? In a true sports law class, a great deal of time would be spent on things such as contract law and liability. While player contracts and personal injury lawsuits might be the bread and butter of many lawyers, they are of less interest to sports economists. For an economist, the field of sports law is probably best broken into four subject areas: baseball's antitrust exemption; antitrust and labor relations; leagues, members and rivals, and antitrust; and sports and discrimination regarding race, gender, and disability. The following sections of this chapter will discuss these topics in turn and will discuss how these cases can be used in a sports economics classroom. Finally, this chapter concludes with an appendix with a reasonably long list of potential legal cases that may be used in a sports economics class.

BASEBALL'S ANTITRUST EXEMPTION

The "Holy Trinity" of baseball cases, *Federal Base Ball*, *Toolson*, and *Flood*, are probably the best-known sports economics cases as well as an ideal starting point to introduce students to the legal cases. They are short and the court's reasoning is clear but very "controversial" (which is just a polite way to say "obviously and completely wrong in every aspect"). Therefore, it is easy to generate discussion on the topic.

So, what is the story behind the *Federal Base Ball* case? The idea that com-petition among competing firms promotes general welfare is one of the central tenets of economics. A cartel is a group of firms which, though officially independent, make decisions as a group. The Sherman Act of 1890 and subse-quent federal antitrust laws prohibit firms from conspiring with one another to prevent competition, and the very first decisions made by the Court regarding the antitrust statutes took steps to eliminate the formation of cartels.

However, sporting events and leagues present an unusual problem to the Court and to economists. Sports teams are competitors on the field but part-ners in business. For a game to take place, the two competitors must agree to compete with each other, and in order for a sports league to run smoothly, a great deal of cooperation between teams, who are competitors in the game, must occur. While economists would undoubtedly condemn a situation where the primary providers of a commodity, such as steel or oil, in separate cities around the country, got together to decide how their product was to be distributed among the consumers in each of the cities, in the case of a national sports league, without such agreements the league would cease to function. The questions that face the Court in this section are to what extent are leagues' agreements with one another "ancillary" in nature; that is, a necessary part of producing the final product in an efficient manner, and what agreements are "naked" restraints designed only to reduce competition at the expense of consumers and labor (players).

The Supreme Court first addressed the issue of antitrust in relation to sports leagues in *Federal Base Ball Club of Baltimore, Inc. v. National League of Professional Base Ball Clubs et al.*, (1922). The Federal League was formed in 1914 as an attempt to compete with the established National and American Leagues. In a novel attempt to break into the market, the Federal League sued the two established leagues for antitrust violations. The Federal League's first lawsuit was filed in the District Court of Northern Illinois under Judge Kenesaw Mountain Landis who stated that attacks on baseball "would be regarded by this court as a blow to a national institution." By the time Landis issued a ruling, the Major Leagues had reached agreements with all but one of the Federal League teams, driving the league out of business following the 1915 season. Five years later, Landis went on to become the first commissioner of Major League Baseball.

Following Landis' ruling, the remaining team, the Baltimore Terrapins, filed suit separately. While the Supreme Court acknowledged baseball engages in commerce and that the commerce consists of teams traveling across state lines to play opposing teams, nevertheless the court decided that baseball did not qualify as interstate commerce as the interstate travel was a "mere incident, not the essential thing." Since the federal antitrust statutes only apply to interstate commerce, as opposed to "purely state affairs," this ruling established the infamous "antitrust exemption" enjoyed by Major League Baseball since that time.

This decision has been widely criticized by legal and economic scholars as well as by future members of the court. Subsequent court decisions made baseball's exemption increasingly difficult to justify. The Supreme Court consistently denied other industries, particularly other sports, the right to use the Federal Baseball ruling as a precedent. Somehow the Court was able to see that other sports were inter-state commerce while it maintained the fiction that baseball was not.

The court had its next chance to address the antitrust issue in *Toolson v. New York Yankees* (1953). Toolson was a relatively unknown minor league player for the New York Yankees who objected to baseball's reserve clause that indefinitely bound players to specific teams. The majority argued that, as set forth by the *Federal Baseball* decision, in enacting the antitrust laws Congress intended professional baseball to be exempt. In addition, Congress had plenty of time since *Federal Baseball* to change the law and by not doing so gave tacit approval to the previous decision. Justices Burton and Reed broke from the majority arguing that even if baseball in the 1910s did not constitute interstate trade, the tremendous growth in the popularity of the sport over the intervening 40 years, and in particular the growth of radio and television revenues given the fact that people in New Jersey clearly listen to New York Yankees games, certainly made baseball interstate commerce and placed the leagues within the purview of federal antitrust statutes by the 1950s. While not commenting on the legality of Major League Baseball's reserve system, they called upon the court to reverse the *Federal Baseball* decision and lift the league's antitrust exemption.

Over the next several years, the court's logic became increasingly strained. In *United States v. International Boxing Club* (1955), the US antitrust division brought suit against the great heavyweight boxer Joe Louis and a group of boxing promoters, charging an attempt to monopolize the boxing business. The defendants argued that as a sports organization it should be exempt from the antitrust laws due to the court's previous rulings in *Federal Baseball* and *Toolson*. The Court divided into three factions. Chief Justice Warren, writing for the majority, stated that the court should not extend this exemption to boxing. While the Court passed on another opportunity to overturn its previous decision, Warren went so far as to suggest that if the current court had the duty to hear *Federal Baseball* for the first time, it likely would not have granted the original exemption. Still, the majority concluded that legal concept of *stare decisis*, that is "let the old decision stand," took precedence over correcting a mistake of a previous Court.[1]

The Court's second faction, Justices Burton and Reed, while concurring with the majority that boxing should not be granted an exemption to the nation's antitrust laws, expressed that they would also have overturned the *Federal Baseball* decision and eliminated baseball's exemption at the same time.

The third prevailing opinion, summed up best by Justice Frankfurter (and joined by Justice Minton) in the first sentence of his dissent said that,

> It would baffle the subtlest ingenuity to find a single differentiating factor between other sporting exhibitions, whether boxing or football or tennis, and baseball insofar as the conduct of the sport is relevant to the criteria or considerations by which the Sherman Law becomes applicable to a "trade or commerce."

In their opinion, baseball and other sports should be treated identically, and given the fact that the Court had already granted immunity to baseball would extend that immunity to boxing as well.

In *Radovich v. National Football League* (1957), the court concluded that baseball was not only different from individual sports such as boxing but also other team sports such as football. Bill Radovich, an all-Pro offensive lineman for the Detroit Lions, left the NFL in 1946 for an unaffiliated team in California due to a family illness. The NFL, like the other major professional sports of the day, had not yet expanded to the West Coast. When Radovich was blacklisted at the urging of the NFL by west coast teams, Radovich filed his ultimately successful antitrust suit against the league.[2] Even though both baseball and football were team sports playing across state lines, baseball remained exempt from antitrust laws for allegedly not being interstate commerce while football was not exempt. Stripped of their antitrust protection, the NFL, fearing another antitrust lawsuit, began to deal in earnest with their players for the first time. The NFL Players Association, which had been formed just a year before the ruling, immediately won concessions from owners including a league-wide minimum wage, payment to injured players, medical insurance, and a retirement plan.

The case of *Flood v. Kuhn* (1972), brought to an end any hopes that the Supreme Court would overturn its decisions in either *Federal Baseball Club v. National League* or *Toolson v. New York Yankees,* which established major league baseball's antitrust exemption. Along with *Federal Baseball* and *Toolson, Flood* is the third case of what is known as "baseball's antitrust trilogy." While three of the justices would have overturned the previous cases, five others voted to continue the exemption and leave the next move in the hands of Congress. In this decision, Justice Blackmun gives a thorough summary of the cases that sprang from *Federal Baseball* and *Toolson,* explaining how the Court arrived at an antitrust exemption for baseball alone and why the Court felt it appropriate that Congress and not the Judiciary should remove the exemption. The Court also made it clear that baseball should be considered a unique exception to the antitrust laws and that *Federal Baseball* should once and for all be laid to rest as a precedent for exempting other sports.

In his plea to the court to lift the reserve clause, Flood states, "I am not a piece of property to be bought and sold, irrespective of my wishes." His words recall the Dred Scott[3] case over a century earlier where black slaves were determined to be property and nothing more. It therefore comes as no surprise that Justice Thurgood Marshall comes to Flood's defense considering Marshall's history as a civil rights lawyer in the 1950s and 1960s and his position as the first African American member of the Supreme Court. In his stinging dissent, Marshall asks the Court to right its past wrongs and let Flood to make his case without allowing Major League Baseball to hide behind its long-standing antitrust exemption. What is most striking about Marshall's dissent, however, is his prescient statement to Flood near the end of his comments where he warns that Flood may not have prevailed even if *Federal Baseball* had been overturned. Marshall points out the federal labor laws and federal antitrust laws run counter to one another, and since the Major League Baseball Players Association had begun collective bargaining with the league shortly before Flood was traded, Flood would have to balance his contention that the league was violating antitrust laws with the fact that the players were forming an effective union. Indeed, in this respect, *Flood v. Kuhn* also ushered in the modern era of league/player relations as many of the subsequent cases involving leagues and their players have centered on the issue of collective bargaining.

While Flood was unsuccessful in his bid to force free agency on the league through the antitrust laws, Major League Baseball players had to wait only a short time to gain that right. Despite winning the Flood case, MLB came under severe pressure, due to the case, to enter into a collective bargaining agreement with the players. The agreement signed between the players and the owners in February 1973, less than one year after the Flood decision, both altered the reserve clause and established an arbitration panel to hear players' grievances.

In October 1975, the Players Association filed grievances on behalf of Andy Messersmith and Dave McNally, alleging that by playing out the final year of a renewal contract, they had satisfied the conditions necessary for free agency. In *Kansas City Royals v. MLB Players Association* (1976), the US Court of Appeals for the Eighth Circuit upheld the arbitration panel's decision granting these players free agency.

While *Flood v. Kuhn* established that the "business of baseball" was exempt from the antitrust laws, it left open the question of what exactly constituted the scope of the exemption. Appeals Court rulings in several cases appeared to grant an expansive view of the exemption. In cases such as *Finley v. Kuhn* (1978) and *Professional Baseball Schools and Clubs v. Kuhn* (1982), various appeals courts concluded that the "business of baseball" includes such things as franchise location, player allocation, and game scheduling. In a pre-trial motion hearing in *Piazza v. MLB* (1993), however, a case that involved whether or not MLB could legally block the move of the Giants franchise from San Francisco to Florida, District Court Judge John Padova muddied the water by holding that, in his opinion, the Supreme Court meant only to exclude the reserve clause from antitrust prosecution. Before the contradiction between Padova and other Appeals Court rulings could be worked out in the courtroom, however, Piazza and MLB settled out of court, leaving open the scope of MLB's antitrust exemption.

Since this case was decided, Congress has acted to limit the antitrust exemption enjoyed by Major League Baseball. Twenty-six years after *Flood v. Kuhn* – a year after Mr. Flood's death from cancer – Congress passed the "Curt Flood Act of 1998" guaranteeing major league players protection under the federal antitrust statutes in their labor dealings with baseball owners. Since the Curt Flood Act specifically exempted only MLB's antitrust exemption with respect to labor and since subsequent court decisions such as that in *MLB v. Crist* (2003)[4] have granted the more expansive view of the exemption, the clear implication is that baseball still enjoys a unique exemption from the antitrust laws that govern the other American sports as well as the rest of American industry.

In terms of introducing this material in the classroom, assigning the "Holy Trinity" along with at least one other case like *Radovich*, where the Court chose not to extend the antitrust exemption to other sports, seems to be an effective set of readings that balances class time along with learning goals. It is also possible to assign the later cases that establish post-*Flood* that the antitrust exemption still holds. However, to me at least, these cases seem to be somewhat of a letdown both in terms of the impact on the growth of the sports industry in the US and in student interest when compared with the original cases.

ANTITRUST AND LABOR RELATIONS

After starting with baseball's antitrust exemption, there are basically two directions to go depending on the other topics your course covers. You can discuss antitrust behavior with respect to sports labor markets with specific attention paid to how the presence of unions affects the Court's thinking, or you can explore more general topics related to overall antitrust issues. Here, cases related to antitrust and labor unions will be examined first.

As noted previously, the notion that competition among different firms promotes general welfare is one of the central tenets of economics. A cartel is a group of firms which, though officially independent, makes decisions as one body. The "Sherman Act of 1890" and subsequent federal antitrust laws prohibit firms from conspiring with one another to raise prices, and the very first decisions made by the Court regarding the antitrust statutes took steps to eliminate the formation of cartels.

From an economic point of view, however, labor unions are essentially identical to a cartel in that they are formed by workers joining together to create bargaining power in an effort to raise their wages. From the very beginning, it was clear that Congress had no intention of including labor unions under the antitrust umbrella, and workers were specifically excluded from prosecution under antitrust laws under Section 6 of the "Clayton Act of 1914".

The protection of labor unions from antitrust law, however, also spills over and provides industry with a similar protection as long as the firm(s) is engaged in collective bargaining with a union. This two-way protection is known as the "non-statutory labor exemption" to the antitrust laws and was inferred by the courts in order to facilitate collective bargaining.

The reasoning for providing companies with this sort of reciprocal protection is clear. Suppose a sports labor union negotiated a contract with a league that provided for some version of the reserve clause in exchange for higher salaries. It would be unfair for the union to then turn around and sue the league by claiming the reserve clause is a violation of the antitrust laws. In the words of the Supreme Court in *Brown v. Pro Football* (1996),

> As a matter of logic, it would be difficult, if not impossible, to require groups of employers and employees to bargain together, but at the same time to forbid them to make among themselves or with each other *any* of the competition-restricting agreements potentially necessary to make the process work or its results mutually acceptable. (Emphasis in original)

As predicted by Justice Marshall in his dissent to *Flood v. Kuhn*, following the Flood decision, the one primary role of the courts in organized professional sports moved from deciding whether certain league policies violated antitrust rules to whether the restrictive rules were part of fairly negotiated labor agreements.

In *Haywood v. NBA* (1971), the Supreme Court determined that the NBA, unlike baseball, could not claim an exemption from antitrust laws in order to protect its rules requiring that player be at least four years removed from high school before entering the league. Spencer Haywood, a member of the 1968 US Olympic team, had joined the rival American Basketball Association (ABA) after only two seasons in college. After one season in the ABA, Spencer joined the Seattle Supersonics of the NBA in violation of the NBA's age policies. The court ruled that the NBA's age limit was an unreasonable restraint of trade and constituted a group boycott by the teams in the league of Haywood's services.[5]

The Haywood ruling ushered in the current era of underclassmen, and for many years high school students, entering into the NBA draft. However, to many current students, this ruling may seem odd because they are likely to know that NBA rules (in place since 2005) currently prohibit high school students from entering into the NBA without being at least one year removed from high school – such players are known as "one and done" players. The NFL requires players to be at least three years removed to enter the NFL draft. How can these age restrictions be legal when the Court specifically ruled them illegal in *Haywood v. NBA*?

The answer lies in the non-statutory labor exemption to antitrust. At the time of Haywood's case, the NBA did not have a collective bargaining, which had been fairly bargained with the players union, that specifically addressed the age of the players. That rule had been unilaterally imposed on the players by management, and therefore it was not exempt from antitrust rules. And a group of teams with significant market power in the basketball players market banding together to restrict Haywood's access to this market is a clear violation of antitrust.

Other age limit cases have come before the Court since Haywood's day. Maurice Clarett was a star running back as a freshman for the Ohio State University football team, helping the team win the 2002 NCAA national title. Prior to his sophomore year, he was found to have accepted payment as a player in violation of NCAA rules and was suspended from the team by the NCAA. He attempted to enter into the professional draft but was prohibited from doing so by NFL rules that limited the draft to players who had completed at least three seasons of college football. Unable to play in the NCAA due to rules on amateur eligibility and unable to play in the NFL owing to age rules, he sued, protesting the NFL's age limits. In *Clarett v. NFL* (2004), he lost his case as the Court ruled that the age restrictions were part of a fairly negotiated collective bargaining agreement between the players union and the league. More recently, Olivia Moultrie sued the National Women's Soccer League for the right to join the league as a 15-year old player.[6] In this case, given the lack of a collective bargaining agreement restricting the age of players, Moultrie won a preliminary injunction in the case and the league quickly settled.

Numerous other restrictions on players have been tested in the courts. In the NFL, Radovich's legal victory in 1957 eliminated the reserve clause from the NFL but, in 1963, the Rozelle Rule was instituted, which required teams acquiring a free agent to compensate the team losing the free agent by an amount determined by the league commissioner. Of course, if the level of compensation is set high enough, the Rozelle Rule serves as a *de facto* reserve clause. In *Mackey v. NFL* (1976), the NFL Players Association (NFLPA) sued the league, charging that the Rozelle Rule was an unfair restraint of trade, just as the reserve clause was. The Eighth Circuit Court of Appeals did indeed find that the Rozelle Rule was anti-competitive and, most importantly, had never been agreed upon in fair bargaining between the league and the union so was not covered by the non-statutory labor exemption. Similarly, the NFL player draft was deemed anti-competitive in *Smith v. Pro Football* (1978) since it reduced the salaries for rookie players and since the plaintiff had been drafted prior to the first collective bargaining agreement between the league and its players in 1968. In both of these cases, care must be taken, however, to differentiate between the notion of economic competition and competition on the field. While a league rule such as a reverse order draft is designed to promote competitive balance on the field, it is anticompetitive from an economic stand-point as it reduces the number of buyers for a particular player to a single team.

Obviously the non-statutory labor exemption is a knife that cuts both ways, and players have fared more poorly in subsequent court decisions, however. Rookie point guard Leon Wood lost his complaint against the NBA's draft and salary cap in *Wood v. NBA* (1987) since both items were part of the current NBA collective bargaining agreement. Similarly, the NFL players were unable to force the NFL through antitrust action to accept their demands for expanded free agency in *Powell v. NFL* (1989) since the players and owners had at one time engaged in collective bargaining. Despite a breakdown in negotiations, the court decided that the non-statutory labor exemption was still in place until the union actually disbanded in late 1989 (as affirmed by *McNeil v. NFL* (1991)). The NFL players again lost an antitrust case in *Brown v. Pro Football* (1996) regarding compensation of reserve players due to the presence of collective bargaining.

From a teaching perspective, *Wood v. NBA* (1987) is a particularly nice case to examine. Leon Wood was an Olympian and a first round draft pick who was chosen by the Philadelphia 76ers, who were already at the salary cap for the team. Thus, they were only able to offer Wood an NBA minimum contract, well below what Wood would have been able to negotiate in a free market. But because the draft and salary cap were part of the collective bargaining agreement, Wood lost his case.[7] The Court's opinion is short, clearly shows the consequences of the non-statutory labor exemption to antitrust, and deals with things such as salary caps and the draft, which students still know about today.

LEAGUES, MEMBERS AND RIVALS, AND ANTITRUST

The next broad area of law that is of interest to a sports economist is not whether certain leagues or labor unions are subject to antitrust law but rather, if an organization is subject to such laws, what types of activities run afoul of the law and what is legal? One major area of court interest has been whether to consider leagues as single entities which can make economic decisions as a group or whether each team should be considered an individual unit that is not allowed to collude with the other teams in its league to make decisions on pricing, output, and other economic variables.

For example, much of the financial success of the NFL is due to the large national television contract that the league negotiates with broadcasters on behalf of its individual teams. Of course, having the league negotiate television contracts rather than individual teams effectively reduces the number of sellers from 30 to 1, a clear act of collusion that reduces competition. Indeed, in *U.S. v. NFL* (1953) the court found selling media rights as a league was anticompetitive and violated antitrust laws. Congress then intervened and granted the league (and subsequently other sports leagues) an exemption to the antitrust laws that allowed the NFL to negotiate television rights as a league. As part of this exemption, however, Congress ordered the NFL to not place their games in direct competition to college and high school football. The current NFL schedule, which does not have either Friday night or Saturday games (until late in the season when the college season is over), is a direct result of this restriction.

The role of league versus teams played a prominent role in *Fraser v. Major League Soccer* (2000). Major League Soccer (MLS) was formed in 1996 as the top American soccer league following the demise of the previous top league, the North American Soccer League (NASL), in 1984. MLS was very specifically formed as a single entity league where all teams would be owned by the league rather than by individual franchise owners. The league set very strict salary caps and players were under contract to the league rather than to an individual team, eliminating any competition between teams for a player's services. The players argued that this lack of competition was illegal on the face of it and sued for judicial relief. (Note that the players did not form a players union until 2006, so the league was not protected by the non-statutory labor exemption.)

While syndicate ownership (that is, the ownership of more than one team in a league by a single investor) has potential problems related to on-field competition (witness the infamous 1899 Cleveland Spiders), the court noted that such an organizational structure is not illegal, and individual "branches" or subsidiaries of the same company are under no obligation to compete with one another.

The court also noted that since no other "major" league existed at the time of the formation of MLS, is was difficult to argue that MLS reduced salaries for top American soccer players when no American market existed for them previously.

Finally, the court stated, that MLS (unlike the NFL, for example) could not be guilty of antitrust behavior since MLS did not have significant market power in the market for soccer talent. While it was the only "major league" buyer of players in the United States, numerous minor leagues also existed in this country, and dozens of other leagues that competed for American players existed in the rest of the world. Therefore, if one considers the relevant market to be the international market for soccer talent, as the court did, MLS was by no means a monopoly. While this case is long and complicated, in makes for a good case for students since the Court does give three separate reasons why they find in favor of MLS over the players. Even students somewhat confused by the complexity of the case are likely to be able to come up with at least one of these reasons with a careful reading of the Court's decision.

The definition of the relevant market also played an important role in several other prominent court cases. As noted previously, in 1955, the Supreme Court ruled in *U.S. v. International Boxing Club* (1955), that boxing was not baseball and therefore was not exempt from antitrust. The Court remanded the case back to the District Court for trial. The case found itself before the Supreme Court again in *International Boxing Club v. U.S.* (1959). The antitrust division of the federal government accused International Boxing Club, including its premier fighter, Joe Louis, of monopolizing the market for championship boxing. The group indeed promoted 25 of the 27 championship fights that occurred over the period of the government's complaint. International Boxing argued, however, that championship bouts are but a small part of the boxing industry and that they therefore controlled only a small portion of the sport. The Court sided with the government's claim that championship matches are a distinct subset of the boxing industry as a whole, and therefore International Boxing's monopolization of this sub-market was illegal under antitrust laws.

Similarly, in *NFL v. NASL* (1982), the North American Soccer League successfully challenged the NFL's restriction that its owners could not own another sports franchise. While the group of NFL owners had nothing like a monopoly on capital overall, the court identified a specific sub-market of "sports capital." By not allowing its owners to purchase other franchises, the NFL was shutting off a significant portion of the nation's "sports capital" from the rival NASL. The NFL subsequently changed its ownership rules such that a NFL owner could purchase another sports franchise in his or her own market or another sports franchise in a market where no other NFL team resides. Thus, NFL former owners Paul Allen (Seattle Seahawks) and Malcolm Glazer (Tampa Bay Buccaneers) were allowed to become owners of the Portland Trailblazers and Manchester United, respectively, since the NFL does not have franchises in these cities. Similarly, Robert Kraft is allowed to own both the NFL's New England Patriots and MLS's New England Revolution since it is not plausible to presume that Kraft would be using his MLS franchise to try to steal business from the local NFL franchise (since he owns both.)

In *American Needle v. National Football League* (2010), the Court again affirmed that belonging to a league does not shield teams from antitrust scrutiny. When the 32 teams in the NFL colluded to deny American Needle, a sportswear company, the ability to compete for a contract to produce NFL-branded merchandise, the cartel was found in violation of antitrust laws.

Another set of issues commonly addressed by the courts related to antitrust involve existing leagues' responses to new leagues. Established leagues have generally dealt with rivals in three ways: merger, cut-throat competition, and expansion. For example, the established National League merged with the newly formed American League to form MLB in 1901, and the NBA and

National Hockey League (NHL) each absorbed four teams from the rival ABA and World Hockey League (WHL) following their rivals' demise. Competition, whether fair or unfair, drove the Federal League out of business in 1915, killed the United States Football League (USFL) in 1985 as well as the Xtreme Football League (XFL) in 2004, and led to the Negro Leagues gradually disappearing following the integration of MLB in the late 1940s and early 1950s. Expansion played a role in the NFL's response to the rival American Football League in the early 1960s and MLB's response to the proposed Continental League in the late 1950s and early 1960s. The courts were involved in many of these rivalries.

Of course, *Federal Baseball* dealt directly with the competition aspect. Unfortunately, thanks to the court's decision to exempt baseball from antitrust law, one will never know how the court would have regarded MLB's attempts to drive the Federal League out of business. Courts in general have not been kind to rival leagues that attempted win in court what they could not achieve in the marketplace since the intent of antitrust law has always been to protect competition, not to protect competitors.

This sort of court reasoning is apparent in *AFL v. NFL* (1960). In this case, the upstart AFL contended that the NFL was complicating its entry into the national professional football market by expanding its own league into potential AFL cities. For example, both Minnesota and Dallas were granted expansion franchises soon after the AFL announced plans to locate teams in these cities. (Note that Minnesota and Dallas both still play in the NFC today.) The court responded that the NFL was not duty-bound to make entry into the market easy for the AFL and that the country still had enough existing viable cities to allow the AFL to begin play. Expanding into markets that might be attractive to potential competitors was not considered predatory behavior on the part of the NFL.

In 1967, the ABA was formed to compete with the NBA. Competition for players (like the previously discussed Spencer Haywood) between the leagues led to sharply higher player salaries so that, starting from roughly equal levels in 1967, by 1972, the average professional basketball player earned nearly three time that of his NFL or MLB counterpart. In 1976, the NBA merged with the rival ABA absorbing four of that league's teams. The NBA Players Association, fearing the loss of the competing league would bring an end to escalating pay scales, brought an antitrust suit against the NBA in *Robertson v. NBA* (1975) to block the merger.[8] The merger of the only two significant providers of professional basketball certainly seemed anti-competitive on the face of it and, in the wake of the *Haywood* ruling, the writing was on the wall. The NBA settled with the players and granted them free agency in exchange for the players dropping the suit.

Professional hockey players in the US also earned free agency (at least in part) in the US through a court decision involving a rival league. The World Hockey Association formed in 1972 to compete against the long-established NHL. The new league immediately began to stock its rosters with existing NHL player, the highest profile of which was all-time great, Bobby Hull. When the NHL took actions to prohibit the movement of players to the WHA, the local Philadelphia WHA team challenged the NHL in court. In *Philadelphia World Hockey Club v. Philadelphia Hockey Club* (1972), the Court determined that hockey was subject to antitrust laws and couldn't prevent player movement to another league. The WHA itself had no reserve clause and the NHL countered with limited player free agency within the NHL, but NHL players didn't gain true free agency as part of their collective bargaining agreement until 1995.

The court has been similarly unkind to leagues that attempt to enforce rules on their own members. In *Los Angeles Coliseum v. NFL / Oakland Coliseum v. Oakland Raiders* (1984), the Court stated that on antitrust grounds, the NFL could not block the move of the Oakland Raiders to Los Angeles. This ruling effectively prohibited sports leagues (except MLB which is, of course, exempt from antitrust action) from blocking the movement of franchises to new venues or metropolitan areas. The stark difference between MLB and other leagues is reflected in the fact that 21 teams (spread across three leagues) have moved to new cities in the NHL, NBA, and NFL since 1982, while only a single MLB has changed location since then.

Even winning an antitrust case is no guarantee that a new league will be successful. In 1983, investors began the USFL which was designed as a spring-time rival to the NFL. The USFL was quite successful in attracting talent (including players such as Herschel Walker, Jim Kelly, and Doug Flutie) but was less successful in generating sufficient revenues to keep the league profitable. In *United States Football League v. National Football League* (1985), the Court determined that the NFL did indeed play a role in the USFL's demise by engaging in predatory behavior, including attempts to have exclusive dealing contracts with broadcasters. The trial jury found accusations by the USFL to be believable that any network giving a contract to the USFL would be punished by the NFL through various means. However, the same jury that found the NFL guilty of predatory behavior also determined that the USFL's financial difficulties were also largely of its own making and awarded the league only $1 in damages (which was trebled to a similarly unhelpful $3 under antitrust law). The USFL ceased operation immediately after the damage award was announced.

Students (as well as professors) may find *USFL v. NFL* (1986) of particular interest due to the involvement of one particular individual. The owner of the New Jersey Generals, one of the most prominent franchises in the league, had been particularly adamant in moving the league from the spring to the fall into direct competition with the NFL and college football, stating that, "If God wanted football in the spring, he wouldn't have created baseball." One possible rationale for the switch may have been a ploy to force a merger between the NFL and the strongest USFL franchises, as had recently occurred in mergers between the ABA and NBA and the NHL and WHA. Of course, the architect of this disastrous move that ultimately bankrupted the league was none other than future US President, Donald Trump.

Finally, at least three major court decisions have addressed the NCAA cartel. Interestingly, while the teams in many sports leagues have spent decades lobbying Congress to allow them to collude, certain teams in the National Collegiate Athletic Association (NCAA) were actively attempting to break up the NCAA's cartel, at least with respect to television rights, if not with respect to enforcing amateurism on players. Prior to the mid-1980s, the NCAA limited the number of television appearances that any individual school's football team could broadcast. The University of Oklahoma, among the most successful teams at the time, sued the NCAA in order to negotiate with broadcasters for more television appearances. In *NCAA v. Board of Regents of the University of Oklahoma* (1984), the Supreme Court affirmed that sports leagues were a unique exception to other industries in that a certain degree of cooperation is required between nominal competitors in order to produce the product. Therefore, the Court held that the NCAA's control of things, such as playing rules, player eligibility, etc., were appropriate behavior for the NCAA in order to make college football run smoothly. The Court ruled, however, that the NCAA's monopoly power should not extend into the economic realm of whether a school can appear on television or how much a school could charge for tickets or broadcast rights. For an economist, the Court's ruling had obvious results. The elimination of the NCAA cartel led to a massive expansion of the number of televised games,[9] and the increase in supply initially led to a significant decrease in the price of broadcasting rights for college football. Of course, over the long run, the value of college football's (and other sports') media rights skyrocketed, leading to top programs generating in excess of $200 million in total revenue by the early 2020s.

Later cases have taken aim at the NCAA's labor cartel that enforced amateurism on college players despite the massive growth in revenues being generated by these players. UCLA basketball star Ed O'Bannon successfully sued the NCAA for using his likeness in an Electronic Arts video game after he had graduated. While *O'Bannon v. NCAA* (2015) left the NCAA's amateurism rules in place, the Court did force schools to at least allow its members to offer stipends to players (that may exceed $5,000 per year) to players to cover the full cost of attendance (to include things such as extra food or laundry or transportation). In addition, O'Bannon and the other members of the class action lawsuit settled with Electronic Arts for $40 million. Of course, rather than share revenue with the players for use of their likenesses going forward, the NCAA instead simply decided to cancel licensing agreements with video game makers.[10]

Following the O'Bannon decision, West Virginia University running back Shane Alston led a group of athletes to sue the NCAA for the right to receive additional money to cover other education-related costs (such as books, lab fees, or scholarship money for postgraduate work). The decision in *Alston v. NCAA* (2021) was a resounding defeat for the NCAA. The Court's majority decision was adopted unanimously by the US Supreme Court, but students are more likely to instead enjoy reading Justice Kavanaugh's concurrence to the case, which eviscerates the NCAA's amateurism model and argues what economists have said for decades, that the NCAA is a cartel engaged in price fixing to drive down the cost of it primary input – athletic talent.[11] Given the recent timing of this decision, along with the natural and obvious interest college students have in intercollegiate athletics, it hard to recommend a Court decision more highly than the Kavanaugh's concurrence in the case, although care must to taken to explain the fact that this opinion goes well beyond the decision signed by the rest of the Court and does not necessarily mean that a majority of the Court would be willing to sign a decision that would effectively end enforced amateurism in the NCAA. Finally, while the *Alston* case had nothing to do directly with athletes' rights to profit off their name, image, and likeness (NIL), which was the issue at the heart of the *O'Bannon* case and was in the background of Maurice Clarett's NCAA violations that led him to seek early entry into the NFL, the writing was on the wall. Within weeks of the *Alston* decision, the NCAA dropped its long-standing ban on players receiving NIL payments.

SPORTS AND DISCRIMINATION

Sports have played an important role in the area of civil rights. Athletes such as Jesse Owens, Joe Louis, Jackie Robinson, Arthur Ashe, Mohammad Ali, Babe Zaharias Didrickson, Billy Jean King, Megan Rapino, and Colin Kaepernick have all become important figures in the fight for racial and gender equality both in sports as well as in society as a whole. Once again, the courts have played an important role in providing for a "level playing field" for women, minorities, and even the disabled.

Brown v. Board of Education (1954) established that racial segregation was illegal in public schools. *Dawson v. Baltimore* (1955) and *Holmes v. City of Atlanta* (1955) extended the prohibition of segregation to publicly owned and operated swimming pools, beaches, parks, and golf courses opening up opportunities for minorities to participate in sports such as tennis, swimming and golf. *Daniel v. Paul* (1969) extended the prohibition of segregation to privately owned "public accommodations." In other words, if customers are routinely granted admission to a recreational facility but without being granted ownership or control of the facility as in a true "private club," then private owners could also not discriminate. This ruling opened up semi-private or public/private golf courses, tennis clubs, and swimming facilities to minorities while only allowing discrimination at truly private members-only country clubs. Beyond these few cases, however, the courts have played only a minor role in eliminating racial discrimination in professional sports as most sports and leagues had begun to voluntarily desegregate well before legal action was undertaken.

The courts have played a much more important role in the enforcement of Title IX of the Education Amendments of 1972, which was intended to prevent gender discrimination in federally funded educational programs. The provision of athletic opportunities for women has been among the most visible results of Title IX and among the most contentious. By far the most important case involving Title IX is *Grove City College v. Bell* (1984). Grove City College was a private, conservative, religious college that did not wish to provide athletic teams for female students. Grove City claimed that they were not subject to Title IX since they received no direct funding from the federal government. The Supreme Court disagreed, citing the fact the many Grove City students received federally subsidized financial aid. In effect, Grove City was indirectly receiving federal money through their students, and the college would have to abide by Title IX regulations if it were to continue to accept students receiving federal financial aid. While this at first appeared to be a victory for the proponents of financial aid, the Court very specifically limited the portions of the college were subject to Title IX restrictions to the financial aid department itself. Although the financial aid would be used to fund general operations of the college including the athletic department, the Court either did not understand or did not concern itself with the economic concept of fungibility and limited the enforcement of Title IX to only the financial aid department. Congress later passed amendments to Title IX reversing this portion of the Court's ruling. This is an interesting case for both economists in general and for students. As noted by above, the key question, "Was this a win or a loss for proponent of Title IX?" is a mixed one, and the concept of fungibility is an important one in economics.

Beyond the *Grove City* case, other Title IX cases, such as *Kelley v. Board of Trustees, University of Illinois*

There are also several cases involving the rights of transgender or intersex athletes to compete as women. Cases of Olympic hopefuls such as Caster Semenya have been handled by the Court of Arbitration in Sport (CAS) and, to my knowledge, do not have written decisions that would work in the format suggested in this chapter, but I would welcome a revision if possible. The most prominent recent case, *Soule v. Connecticut Association of Schools* (2021), seeks to ban transgender athletes from competing as females as a Title IX violation. This litigation was ongoing at the time this chapter was written.

Finally, the case of *PGA Tour v. Martin* (2001) delves into the realm of discrimination by disability status and is of interest to many sports economists owing to the large amount of media attention it received at the time. Casey Martin was a talented professional golfer with a recognized disability that made it difficult to walk long distances. Martin sued the Professional Golfers' Association (PGA) for the right to use a cart on the pro tour. The PGA argued that the use of a cart would fundamentally alter the nature of the sport, while Martin contended, and the court agreed, that a cart would be a reasonable accommodation for his recognized disability. This is a good case for students where the arguments are easy to follow and the dissent by Antonin Scalia may also be of interest.

CONCLUSIONS

Reading decisions written by the Courts can be a valuable addition to the classroom in sports economics or sports management classes. It can promote critical reading skills, and can expose students to how the legal system works. In addition, legal opinions have often been crucial in the development of professional and collegiate sports in the US, and in many cases the most important current issues facing sports are under litigation, which means that court decisions will usually address "hot button" topics.

If you would like to use cases in your class, they are easy to find online for free at places such as caselaw.findlaw.com, openjurist.org, or law.justia.com or through paid subscription services such as Lexis-Nexis or WestLaw, which may also be available at your institution. Cases can be found through a simple Google search or by using search functions within legal websites. Searching for a case such as *Flood v. Kuhn* will bring up numerous court references so you will typically want to use the decision from the highest level court and you will want to use the final court decision rather than written decisions of individual motions or other preliminary published rulings that may be available. In the appendix to this chapter, I have provided a list of cases of potential interest to instructors of sports economics along with brief descriptions and case designation numbers for the best version of the case to read. Written court decisions are not copyrighted, so you are free to deliver these cases to your students with few limitations. Enjoy!

NOTES

1. Of course, the concept of *stare decisis* played a crucial role in what is perhaps the Supreme Court's most famous decision, *Brown v. Board of Education* (1954). In this case, the Court chose not to "let the old decision stand" and overturned *Plessy v. Ferguson* (1896) which had established the legality of segregation. The Court recognized that, in practice, the notion of "separate but equal" established in *Plessy v. Ferguson* led to distinctly unequal treatment for minorities. *Stare decisis* continues to play a crucial role in important modern cases. While a majority of current Supreme Court justices likely believe that *Roe v. Wade* (1973), which established a constitutional right to abortion, was wrongly decided, the decision facing the Court today is whether righting a (perceived) previous wrong is more important than respecting standing precedent.
2. Although the NFL had no teams on the West Coast, the league could still exert its influence by threatening to block the ability of players on unaffiliated teams to get promoted into the NFL if their team allowed Radovich to play.
3. In *Dred Scott v. Sanford* (1857), the Supreme Court ruled that Dred Scott, a black slave, remained the property of his master despite having lived for an extended time in Illinois and Wisconsin, areas in which slavery was outlawed. The Court ruled that as a Negro and as a slave, Scott was not a citizen and therefore did not have the right to sue for his freedom. The Court went even further by declaring the Missouri Compromise of 1820, which restricted slavery in frontier territories, unconstitutional. The Court's decision outraged Northern abolitionists and led directly to the nomination of Abraham Lincoln as the Republican candidate for President in 1860. In the end the Courts decided both Dred Scott and Curt Flood were indeed pieces of property to be bought and sold.
4. In this case, the local government in Tampa successfully sued MLB on antitrust grounds to prevent the contraction of the Tampa Bay Devil Rays by the league.
5. The *Haywood* case is also interesting in that the Court issued a "stay" preventing Haywood from being removed from the team while the Court was making its decision. A stay is an order by a court to prohibit a decision from being immediately enforced and is typically issued when there is uncertainty about the outcome of a case and if a particular decision would have irreversible consequences for one of the parties. The most familiar type of stay is a stay of execution. Obviously, the Court can't later exonerate a death row inmate if the inmate has already been put to death. In the *Haywood* case, if Haywood is not allowed to play and the Court later finds he should have been able to play, Haywood's skills may have deteriorated due to lack of action and there is no way to compensate the Seattle Supersonics for Haywood's absence. If Haywood is allowed to play and the Court later finds he should not have been able to play, the NBA can simply retroactively have the Supersonics forfeit those games, and Seattle can decide whether or not to play Haywood knowing the potential consequences.
6. Once again, the NCAA's amateurism rules played an important role in this case. Moultrie had appeared several years earlier in a Nike ad during the Super Bowl. She could not accept money for her appearance without forfeiting her ability to play in college based on the Name/Image/Likeness rules in place by the NCAA at the time. So, she took the money and declared herself a professional.
7. While Wood's playing career didn't turn out the way he had planned, he had a long career in the league as a referee.

8. The namesake "Robertson" in this case is NBA Hall-of-Famer Oscar Robertson, the first player to average a triple-double in league history, and a player widely considered to be the best guard of the early decades of the NBA.
9. For example, NBC's contract with Notre Dame to broadcast all of that school's games on nationwide television led some to derisively call the network the "Notre Dame Broadcasting Network."
10. Imagine that – cancelling a profitable contract solely because you don't want to share any of the profits with the people who make those profits possible…
11. A 9–0 Supreme Court decision is quite remarkable in an era of partisanship where you probably couldn't get a unanimous court to agree on the definition of a ham sandwich. It was also a huge win for the "so-called sports economists" who lent their expertise to the case over the hired guns, including Nobel Prize winners, bought and paid for by the NCAA.

APPENDIX 7A

Case	Year	Court	Topic	Specifics
Federal Base Ball Club of Baltimore v. National League (259 U.S. 200)	1922	SCOTUS	Baseball's antitrust exemption	Baseball determined to not be interstate commerce so was not subject to antitrust rules.
Toolson v. New York Yankees (346 U.S. 356)	1953	SCOTUS	Baseball's antitrust exemption	Court reaffirmed baseball's antitrust exemption.
US v. International Boxing Club (348 U.S. 236)	1955	SCOTUS	Baseball's antitrust exemption	Baseball's antitrust exemption not extended to boxing.
Radovich v. NFL (352 U.S. 445)	1957	SCOTUS	Baseball's antitrust exemption	Baseball's antitrust exemption not extended to football.
Flood v. Kuhn (407 U.S. 258)	1972	SCOTUS	Baseball's antitrust exemption	Court reaffirmed baseball's antitrust exemption while admitting Federal Baseball was a mistake.
Kansas City Royals v. Major League Baseball Players (532 F.2d 615)	1976	8th Cir.	Free agency	Court affirmed arbitrator Peter Seitz's decision granting Andy Messersmith and Dave McNally free agency.
Finley v. Kuhn (569 F.2d 527)	1978	7th Cir.	Baseball's antitrust exemption	Baseball's commissioner has powers granted by MLB that do not violate antitrust laws.
Professional Baseball Schools and Clubs v. Kuhn (693 F.2d 1085)	1982	11th Cir.	Baseball's antitrust exemption	Baseball's antitrust exemption extends to minor league baseball.
Piazza v. MLB (831 F. Supp. 420)	1993	E.D. Pa.	Baseball's antitrust exemption	Judge ruled that baseball's antitrust exemption does not extend to relocation, but this claim was never tested by a higher court.
MLB v. Crist (331 F.3d 1177)	2003	11th Cir.	Baseball's antitrust exemption	Baseball's antitrust exemption extends to relocation and contraction decisions.
Haywood v. NBA (401 U.S. 1204)	1971	SCOTUS	Age limits	NBA's age limit deemed a violation of antitrust laws and Haywood allowed to play until case is concluded.

Case	Year	Court	Topic	Specifics
Clarett v. NFL (369 F.3d 124)	2004	2nd Cir.	Age limits	NFL's age limits allowed because they were part of CBA.
Philadelphia World Hockey Club v. Philadelphia Hockey Club (351 F. Supp. 457)	1972	E.D. Pa.	Free agency	Court rules that NHL can't prevent current player under contract from signing with rival league.
Mackey v. NFL (543 F2d 606)	1976	8th Cir.	Rozelle Rule and free agency	The Rozelle Rule found to be a violation of antitrust laws as it was imposed before negotiated CBA.
Smith v. Pro Football, Inc. (593 F.2d 1173)	1978	D.C. Cir.	Draft	Draft (at the time) was a violation of antitrust laws as it was imposed before a fairly negotiated CBA.
Wood v. NBA (809 F.2d 954)	1987	2nd Cir.	Draft and salary cap	Wood can't sue for personal damages caused by draft and salary cap because they are part of CBA.
Powell v. NFL (888 F.2d 559)	1989	8th Cir.	Free agency	Players unable to force NFL into free agency in court due to existence of a CBA.
McNeil v. NFL (790 F.Supp. 871)	1991	D. Minn.	Union decertification	Players are eventually allowed to decertify their union in order to take NFL to court for antitrust violations.
Brown et al. v. Pro Football, Inc. (518 U.S. 231)	1996	SCOTUS	Non-statutory exemption to antitrust	Practice squad players are determined to be covered by CBA even though they weren't part of CBA.
United States v. NFL (116 F. Supp. 319)	1953	E.D. Pa.	Team collusion	Court rules NFL teams can't negotiate TV contracts as a league. Congress later grants them a limited exemption to antitrust.
Fraser et al. v. Major League Soccer (284 F.3d 47)	2002	1st Cir.	Single entity, market definition	MLS found not guilty of monopolizing market for players for three reasons – single entity, relevant market, and no reduction in competition.

Case	Year	Court	Topic	Specifics
International Boxing Club v. United States 358 U.S. 242	1959	SCOTUS	Market definition	Championship boxing determined to be a distinct market that International Boxing monopolized.
NFL v. North American Soccer League (459 U.S 1074)	1982	SCOTUS	Market definition	NFL's cross ownership rules deemed illegal and that there exists a special market for "sports capital."
American Needle v. NFL (560 U.S. 183)	2010	SCOTUS	Team collusion	Court ruled that NFL teams could not collude in awarding merchandise contracts.
AFL v. NFL (323 F.2d 124)	1963	4th Cir.	Rival leagues	NFL is allowed to make life difficult for rival league by expanding into attractive markets for AFL.
Robertson v. NBA (389 F. Supp. 867)	1975	S.D. N.Y.	Rival leagues, free agency	The NBA players blocked the merger of the NBA and ABA until the NBA granted the players free agency.
Philadelphia World Hockey Club v. Philadelphia Hockey Club (351 F. Supp. 457)	1972	E.D. Pa.	Rival leagues, reserve clause	The NHL unsuccessfully attempted to block its players from moving to the rival WHA.
Los Angeles Memorial Coliseum v. NFL (726 F.2d 1381)	1984	9th Cir.	Franchise movement	The NFL unsuccessfully attempted to block the movement of the Oakland Raiders to Los Angeles.
United States Football League v. NFL (644 F. Supp. 1040)	1986	S.D. N.Y.	Rival leagues	The NFL was found to have engaged in predatory behavior, but the USFL was awarded only $1 in damages leading to the bankruptcy of the league.
NCAA v. Board of Regents of the University of OK (468 U.S. 85)	1984	SCOTUS	Leagues vs. teams	Sports require some level of collusion to exist, but this does not extend to setting the number of television appearances a team can have.
O'Bannon v. NCAA (802 F.3d 1049)	2015	9th Cir.	Amateurism in college	NCAA cannot use name, image, or likeness of athletes after graduation without compensation.

Case	Year	Court	Topic	Specifics
Alston v. NCAA (594 U.S. __)	2021	SCOTUS	Amateurism in college	NCAA cannot prevent schools from offering enhanced educational benefits to athletes.
Dawson v. Baltimore (350 U.S. 877)	1955	SCOTUS	Segregation	Segregation at public beaches illegal.
Holmes v. Atlanta (350 U.S. 879)	1955	SCOTUS	Segregation	Segregation at public golf courses illegal.
Daniel v. Paul (395 U.S. 298)	1969	SCOTUS	Segregation	Segregation at privately owned public accommodations illegal.
Grove City College v. Bell (465 U.S. 555)	1984	SCOTUS	Title IX	Schools with students receiving federally funded grants must abide by Title IX requirements but only in the specific program or activity that was benefited by the grant.
Kelley v. Board of Trustees, University of IL (35 F.3d 265)	1994	7th Cir.	Title IX	Title IX does not protect male teams from being eliminated if men are overrepresented in athletics.
Cohen v. Brown (101 F.3d 155)	1996	1st Cir.	Title IX	Cutting men's and women's programs at the same time does not satisfy Title IX if women are already underrepresented.
O'Connor v. Board of Education of School District 23 (545 F. Supp. 376)	1982	N.D. Ill.	Title IX	Title IX does not require boys' teams to allow girls to play if a girls' team is available.
Clark v. AZ Interscholastic Association (695 F.2d 1126)	1982	9th Cir	Title IX	Title IX does not require boys to be able to play on girls' teams as long as boys have other playing opportunities.
Soule v. CT Association of Schools (No case # - ongoing)	2021	2nd Cir.	Title IX	Title IX does not prevent schools from allowing transgendered athletes to participate as females.
PGA Tour v. Martin	2001	SCOTUS	Americans with Disabilities Act	Casey Martin's use of a cart was ruled a reasonable accommodation for recognized disability that didn't fundamental alter the nature of golf.

8. Making sports economics inclusive: why you aren't teaching sports economics well if women are not part of your story

David Berri

The premise of this chapter is quite simple. Millions of women are fans of sport. Millions of women play sports. But historically, the stories told about sports – which are predominantly told by men – frequently ignore women. As a consequence, women often do not feel the conversations about sports include them.

This history has impacted the way in which we both study and teach sports economics. If you look out upon your students in these classes and primarily just see men looking back at you, this isn't because women aren't interested in sports. It is because our discussions about sports often exclude women. It is hoped this brief chapter can be a step forward in making the sports economics environment a more inclusive space.

A HISTORY OF IGNORING WOMEN IN ECONOMICS

As anyone who teaches sports economics knows, the stories told in this class are not just about sports (much to the dismay of some students!). Our subject matter is also about economics. Unfortunately, the story of women and sports often mirrors the history of women and economics. To see this, let's take a brief journey through time.

The year is 1776. In this year, Adam Smith publishes *An Inquiry into the Nature and Causes of the Wealth of Nations* in 1776.[1] According to Milton Friedman (1977), Smith's work is "the beginning of scientific economics". Fifteen years later, Robert Heilbroner (1992) described *The Wealth of Nations* as "the outpouring not only of a great mind, but of a whole epoch." And it is not just these two men. Today we have both an *Adam Smith Society*[2] and an *Adam Smith Institute*.[3] Yes, when it comes to economics the story begins with Smith and, for many, what they think about Smith captures much of what they think about economics.

Much has been said about what Smith said in 1776. Less has been noted about what he failed to say. A quick search of the pdf of this seminal work reveals that the word "man" appears 272 times in Smith's work. He also used the word "men" 195 times. When it comes to the other half of the population, though, Smith is mostly silent. The word "women" appears only 18 times. And "woman"? In the entire book Smith only uses this word twice.[4] These simple statistics make it clear that Smith's book about the functioning of a nation's economy didn't have much to say about women. And yes, that means Smith mostly ignored half the population.

One can see this quite clearly when we consider one of the more famous quotes from the book (volume I, p. 48):

> It is not from the benevolence of the butcher, the brewer, or the baker that we expect our dinner, but from their regard to their own self-interest.

This simple statement captures the idea that markets create positive outcomes for society despite the fact market participants are not trying to do this. Unfortunately – when we consider Smith's life – it is immensely inaccurate. As Marcal (2016) notes, Smith spent much of his life living with his mother. So, Smith didn't get his dinner from the butcher, the brewer, or the baker. He got his dinner from his mother. And it isn't a stretch to say his mother wasn't making Smith's dinner purely out of her own self-interest.

It is not surprising that Smith failed to note the true source of his dinner. Again, his book almost completely ignores women. Unfortunately, Smith's example has been followed in the economics profession for the last 245 years.

Betsey Stevenson and Hannah Zlotnik (2018) did a study of eight prominent textbooks in economics. They found that, on average, 77% of the people mentioned in these books are men. When these books mention business leaders, the percentage who are men jumps to 94%. A similar percentage is seen when it is policymakers (92%) or economists (93%). This choice does not reflect the world we observe. As Lennon (2013) notes, about 20% of leadership positions across many business sectors and government positions are held by women. Yes, that isn't very good. But economic textbooks still exaggerate how often men are leaders.

The failure of economics to adequately represent women in the stories it tells likely contributes the fact women are not well represented in economics. In the 2020 Report of the Committee on the Status of Women in the Economics Profession (CSWEP) (Chevalier, 2020) it was noted that women are 34.1% of undergraduates in economics despite the fact women are 57% of all undergraduates. Furthermore, women have been roughly a third of all undergraduate majors in economics since 1995 (the first year CSWEP began tracking data).

When we turn to professors, we see the same lack of representation. CSWEP reports (Chevalier, 2020) that only 14.7% of full professors in economics are women. That number increases to 30.6% for assistant professors. However, over all, fewer than 25% of all faculty in economics are women.

The lack of representation in the textbooks and in the classroom likely contributes to the lack of women choosing the major. As Stevenson and Zlotnick observe,

> ... there is a large literature on stereotype threat that suggests that an inability for women to see themselves in economics may make them less interested in the field. Most promisingly, a recent study showed that brief exposure to female economics alumnae led more women to continue on to a further economics class (Porter and Serra, 2017). (Stevenson and Zlotnick, 2018)

Of course, stereotype threat is not the only issue in economics. Surveys show that women also face an alarming amount of sexual discrimination in the field. A survey (Chicago Booth Review, 2019) by the American Economic Association of 9,000 economists in 2019 revealed that 48% of women say they have faced discrimination. A similar percentage of women have said they have refused to speak up at their place of employment or a conference because they feared they would face harassment or discrimination.

In sum, it appears economics often ignores women. And when it is not ignoring women, it is often subjecting women to discrimination. All of that likely leads women to avoid the field of economics.

Like the entire discipline of economics, sports economics also tends to ignore women. Most of the articles written in *The Journal of Sports Economics* and the *International Journal of Sports Finance* (the two top journals in this field) are written by men and these tend to focus on men's sports. Out of the 65 scholars who are members of at least one of the journals' editorial boards, only three are women. And the textbooks also have a similar focus on men's sports.[5] Even this chapter about women in sports is written by a man and edited by two other men.

A HISTORY OF BANNING WOMEN FROM SPORTS

Just as economics has had trouble moving on from the focus of Adam Smith, it appears many sports economists today follow the approach taken by the first economist to write about sports.

Thorstein Veblen published "The Theory of the Leisure Class" in 1899. In this seminal work, Veblen discusses at length the behavior of the wealthy respect to sports. Consider the following quote (p. 118):

> It is perhaps truer, or at least more evident, as regards sports than as regards the other expressions of predatory emulation already spoken of, that the temperament which inclines men to them is essentially a boyish temperament. The addiction to sports, therefore, in a peculiar degree marks an arrested development of the man's moral nature. This peculiar boyishness of temperament in sporting men immediately becomes apparent when attention is directed to the large element of make-believe that is present in all sporting activity. Sports share this character of make-believe with the games and exploits to which children, especially boys, are habitually inclined. ... It is noticeable, for instance, that even very mild-mannered and matter-of-fact men who go out shooting are apt to carry an excess of arms and accoutrements in order to impress upon their own imagination the seriousness of their undertaking. These huntsmen are also prone to a histrionic, prancing gait and to an elaborate exaggeration of the motions, whether of stealth or of onslaught, involved in their deeds of exploit.

Veblen's last observation about the "histrionic, prancing gait" of men hunting definitely brings to mind any number of Bugs Bunny cartoons starring Elmer Fudd! Beyond that humorous visual, though, Veblen's general observation about the behavior of people in sports is just as true today as it was in 1899. Sports very much are make-believe and the people engaged in sports are often acting out childhood fantasies.

There is, though, something missing from Veblen's quote. Veblen tale about the behavior of people in sports focuses solely on men. Perhaps this made sense in 1899. The popular sports in 1899 – boxing, horse racing, college football, professional baseball – were generally played by men. In fact, women were actively discouraged from playing any sports at all when Veblen was writing at the end of the nineteenth century.

As Mansky and Wei-Haas (2016) report, Baron Pierre de Coubertin – the founder of the Olympic movement – argued the Olympic Games were brought back for "the solemn and periodic exaltation of male athleticism". He went on to add that he did this for "female applause as reward." Coubertin defended his decision to relegate women to spectators by arguing that "as no women participated in the Ancient Games, there obviously was to be no place for them in the modern ones."

Coubertin went on to note that the bodies of women simply could not handle the stress of athletic contests (Mansky and Wei-Haas, 2016):

> It is indecent that spectators should be exposed to the risk of seeing the body of a woman being smashed before their eyes. Besides, no matter how toughened a sportswoman may be, her organism is not cut out to sustain certain shocks. Her nerves rule her muscles, nature wanted it that way.

In general, discriminatory attitudes often come from a place of ignorance and half-truths and Coubertin's proclamations about women and sports are no exception. As Schultz (2018, pp. 10–11) reports, there were Olympic games in ancient Greece that only had men competing. But we also know from history and mythology that women have participated in sports for thousands of years. For example, there is evidence that women played sports both in ancient China and in Mesoamerica. Women also competed in sports in Ancient Greece. In fact, Greek and Roman myths often told stories of women competing in athletic contests. Artemis was the goddess of the hunt and archery. There is the story of the Amazons, the athletic women who today are part of the DC Comics story of *Wonder Woman*. And then there is the story of Atalanta.

As Schultz (2018, p. 11) notes, Atalanta[6] was a mythological athlete who said she would marry a man who could defeat her in a footrace. As the story tells, this eventually happened but only when Aphrodite – the goddess of love – intervened.

The story of Atalanta is quite similar to the real story of Khutulun. As Mackenzi Lee (2018, pp. 29–30) recounts the tale, Khutulun was the great-great-granddaughter of Ghengis Kahn. In the thirteenth century this Mongolian princess asked to have some input into who she would marry. Specifically, a contest was arranged where a prospective husband would wager 100 horses on a wrestling contest with Khutulun. If the man won, he would marry Khutulun. If she won, she kept the horses. As the story goes, Khutulun amassed 10,000 horses in these wrestling matches. One suspects that if Khutulun met Coubertin she probably could have explained to him in terms he would understand why sports were for women!

Of course, women in Ancient Greece could have done the same. Although there were male-only Greek Olympic contests, the ancient Greeks also had athletic events for women. Schultz (2018, p. 11) reports that there were the Herean Games (for the goddess Hera), as well as athletic contests for women in both Sparta and Cyrene.

Although women have a long history of competing in sports, in the nineteenth century many men agreed with Coubertin about what playing sports would do to women. Mansky and Wei-Haas (2016) offer this quote from historian Kathleen E. McCrone:

> A woman's ovaries and uterus were believed to control her mental and physical health, according to historian Kathleen E. McCrone. "On the basis of no scientific evidence whatsoever, they related biology to behavior," she writes in her book *Playing the Game: Sport and the Physical Emancipation of English Women, 1870-1914*. Women who behaved outside of society's norm were kept in line and told, as McCrone writes, "physical effort, like running, jumping and climbing, might damage their reproductive organs and make them unattractive to men."

In 1898, the *Journal of Physical Education* (published in Germany) offered a similar sentiment (Schulz, 2018, p. 17):

> ... violent movement in the body can cause a shift in the position and loosening of the uterus as well as prolapse and bleeding, with resulting sterility, thus defeating a woman's true purpose in life, i.e., the bringing forth of strong children.

There were definitely women who defied the silly notion that playing sports would harm women. One year after James Naismith invented the game of basketball in 1891 at Springfield College in Massachusetts, Senda Berenson introduced basketball (Hult and Trekell, 1991) to the women of Smith College (just 25 miles away). This means women were playing basketball almost from the beginning. But not many women.

By 1899, universities such as Stanford banned women's basketball from intercollegiate competition.[7] Although women's basketball carried on at the local level throughout the nation (Hult and Krekell, 1991), banning women from playing organized, competitive basketball continued to be a popular pastime in the first years of the twentieth century. As Agha and Berri (2021) report, in 1908 the American Athletic Union (AAU) said women shouldn't play basketball in public. Such a public display in front of men was considered at the time as damaging to "the standard of womanhood." Six years later, the American Olympic Committee also argued that women shouldn't be allowed to play basketball at the 1916 Olympic Games.

One man – James Sullivan – was involved in both the AAU and the American Olympic movement decisions. As Shelton (2017) notes, Sullivan didn't just keep women from playing basketball. He also wanted to keep women out of the Olympics entirely.

> Even though women had hoped to be allowed to compete in championships, one man – James E. Sullivan – had control of both the American Olympic Committee and the Amateur Athletic Union, and he staunchly believed women had no place in formal competitions and refused to allow it again and again. ... American women had wanted to join the Olympics in 1912 but were refused. The decision rested on Sullivan, who was said to be obsessed with rules and regulations, and even in 1914, under his control, the AAU voted that women could not take part "in any event in which they would not wear long skirts."

Sullivan was hardly the only man doing his best to keep women from playing sports. Jennifer Ring (2009) argues that A.G. Spaulding – who did much to popularize the sport of baseball in the nineteenth century – also did much to keep women off the baseball diamond. As Ring notes, Spaulding in 1911 very much defined baseball as an exercise in "manhood" (Ring, 2009, p. 54):

> Base ball is the American game par excellence, because its playing demands Brain and Brawn, and American manhood supplies these ingredients in quantity sufficient to spread over the entire continent. No man or boy can win distinction on the ball field who is not, as man or boy, an athlete, possessing all the qualifications which an intelligent, effective, playing of the game demands.

Ring (2009, p. 33), though, notes that baseball was not historically defined in terms of men. Women were playing baseball at colleges in New England states in the middle of the nineteenth century. By the 1890s, though, softball and baseball were designated as "female" and "male" sports and women were discouraged from playing the latter (Ring, 2009, p. 33).

In the United Kingdom we see a very similar story. Just as women were playing baseball in the nineteenth century, women in England were definitely playing soccer.[8] Back in 1881 the Glasgow Herald printed a story about a match between women from England and Scotland. The First World War dramatically increased the popularity of women's matches and by 1920 there was a soccer game that had 53,000 fans in attendance. Soon after, though, the men of the English Football Association decided they couldn't tolerate women playing football. In 1921, this organization decided that this game was "quite unsuitable for women and not to be encouraged" (Coletta, 2015).

The English Football Association wasn't just offering an opinion on women playing soccer. As Coletta (2015) reports, this organization told both referees and coaches that if they allowed women to play on the men's fields that they would lose their licenses. Effectively, the men banned women's soccer. And this ban stayed in place until 1972.

All of these stories illustrate how women were systematically prevented from playing sports in the past. And that history has led to a belief that sports are primarily a male domain. Consequently, the sports stories told today still focus almost entirely on men's sports.

THE MYTH AND REALITY OF WOMEN IN SPORTS TODAY

How much do men focus on men when they talk about sports? In the late 1990s, ESPN SportsCenter devoted about 2% of its coverage to women's sports (Cooky, Messner, and Musto, 2015). Maybe one could argue this made sense. The WNBA only started playing in 1997. Women also were participating in professional tennis and golf. But other professional leagues – such as National Pro Fastpitch and the National Women's Soccer League – didn't exist yet. There were – thanks to Title IX – many opportunities for women to play college sports. But since Title IX had only been passed in 1972, women's college sports did not seem to have a huge following roughly 25 years later.

By 2014, women's sports appeared to be bigger. There were more professional leagues. Women's college sports – especially in basketball and softball – appeared to have a bigger audience. Therefore, one would expect the coverage of women's sports to increase. But as Cooky, Messner, and Musto (2015) note, in 2014 ESPN SportsCenter still only devoted 2% of its coverage to women's sports.

A simple classroom exercise can confirm this basic finding. Open up the main website of ESPN on any given day and start looking at the stories on the front page. Simply scrolling down the page will reveal that the vast majority of stories are about men's sports. And it isn't just ESPN's website that fails to cover women's sports. As Berri (2017d) observed, you are more likely to find pages dedicated to sports involving animals on popular sports websites than you will find pages dedicated to women's sports.

An obvious explanation for this is that the sports media tends to be dominated by men. According the Women's Media Center (2019), 90% of print sports coverage is produced by men. On the wire services, men produced 86% of the content in sports while on the internet that percentage fell to 79%.

These percentages also reflect who is employed. As the Women's Media Center (2019) reports:

> Women comprised 10 percent of sports editors in 2017 and 9.5 percent in 2014. During the same period, women made up 16.6 percent and 12.4 percent, respectively, of columnists; 11.5 percent and 12.6 percent, respectively, of reporters; and 20.4 percent and 19.2 percent, respectively, of copy editors/designers.

All of this tells a clear story. Men dominate the sports media. Therefore, that coverage skews towards men's sports.

Of course, maybe this is just economics. Aren't men the vast majority of sports fans? If the market is dominated by men, shouldn't the coverage of sports primarily focus on men's sports?

Unfortunately, surveys undermine that story. According to a Gallup survey (Jones, 2015), 59% of adults in the United States identify as sports fans. With respect to gender, 66% of men and 51% of women say they are fans of sports. If these ratios hold true for 2019, then there are currently 66 million women in the United States who identify as sports fans. And women are 44% of all sports fans.

This percentage is similar to the number of high school and college athletes who are women. In 2018–19, about 7.9 million high school students participated in high school athletes.[9] Of these, 3.4 million were girls; or about 43% of all high school athletes. At the NCAA level there were nearly 500,000 athletes in 2018–19 with women comprising 44% (219,447) of this total.[10]

In sum, whether we look at fans or athletes, women are a significant part of sports. So why doesn't the coverage reflect this? There is anecdotal evidence that there is significant demand for women's sports. For example:

- US women's soccer tends to get higher television ratings than US men's soccer. As Hess (2019) noted, the highest rated soccer match in US history was the 2015 FIFA Women's World Cup between the USA and Japan. The 2019 FIFA Women's World Cup final attracted 15.6 million English-language viewers, higher than the 12.5 million US English language viewers for the FIFA Men's World Cup final in 2018.
- This same disparity is seen in the professional ranks. In 2019, an average Major League Soccer broadcast had 266,000 viewers (Nwulu, 2019). In 2020, though, the average National Women's Soccer League game had 383,000 viewers (Cash, 2020).
- We see a similar story in tennis. Raviprakash, Wray, Lee, and Westcott (2020) report:
  In sports where men's and women's games have relatively equal marketing support, their commercial impact has been roughly equivalent. Tennis, for which the prize money at Grand Slam events is the same for women as men, is arguably the best example. In the United States, TV ratings for tennis grand slams—a major driver of pay TV subscriptions and advertising revenues—have been slightly higher for women than men.
- Berri (2019) notes a similar story in softball. The 2015 College World Series for softball (played by women) had much higher ratings than the 2015 College World Series for baseball (played by men).

Each of these anecdotes suggest there is interest in women's sports. Despite these ratings, though, the sports media's coverage of women's sports remains quite scarce. And many men continue to think that sports are primarily for men.

THE QUIZ!

One suspects that many men are not aware that so many women are athletes and sports fans. There is reason why this might be the case. And it is called "The Quiz!"

Molly Cosby (2016) described "The Quiz" as follows:

Once a woman's team preference (in football) is known, she better prepare for questions aimed at her like rotten tomatoes. Football is used as an example here, but in reality, women get interrogated about basically every sport. Some men have some sort of indigenous behavior to examine a woman's knowledge of her sports team to decide whether or not she deserves the right to root for her team. This implies they are the experts and have the right to administer the test.

Chelsey Ranard (2018) also noted how often women's fandom is tested by male sports fans:

> Sometimes it's hard to be a female sports fan just being surrounded by other fans. Someone will inevitably ask you how long you've been a fan, why you're a fan, and some even test you with questions to prove your fandom. Women are accused of being bandwagoners, of liking a sport because their significant other watches, or are constantly having things explained to them without prompting.

Gina Lehe – who is one of five women who are part of the leadership position for the College Football Playoff[11] – indicated she is very reluctant to tell men what she does for a living "because inevitably they will want to quiz her to see if she passes some kind of test" (Killion, 2018).

It is certainly not uncommon for professors to give tests and quizzes. Although professors do this often, we are all aware this activity isn't a reason why people like being around us.

"The Quiz" is essentially a barrier to entry for women in the sports world. It makes them reluctant to confess their interests. And obviously, if women think this will happen in your classes, they are not going to be anxious to sign up for the course.

BRINGING WOMEN INTO SPORTS ECONOMICS

Obviously a first step in making your sports economics class a more inclusive environment is to make sure you are not interrogating people for being in the classroom. But one can do much more.

Let's start with something very basic. As noted, men started playing organized sports before women. Consequently, it is not uncommon for men's sports to be the default. If a television station announces it is broadcasting "college basketball" you can be sure that refers to a men's game. If it was a women's game, the listing for the television station would say "women's college basketball". This even occurs in sports such as gymnastics where the competitions involving women are much more popular. Television stations refer to a broadcast of a men's gymnastics meet as "gymnastics". If women are competing, the television listing will say "women's gymnastics".

Obviously college professors can't fix what happens in television broadcasting. Nevertheless, in the classroom the obvious solution to this discrepancy is to get in the habit of saying "men's basketball" and "women's basketball". And it is important to emphasize that if you are talking about college sports, the participants are "men" and "women". Colleges and universities do not have "boys" and "girls" teams. The participants are adults. So if you say "men's basketball" you should not also say "girls' basketball". This approach trivializes what the women on your sports teams are doing.

Understanding the language one should use in talking about women's sports is only the first step. Sports economics often appears to mirror the coverage of sports we see at ESPN. In other words, most of the stories told center on men's sports. But let's imagine you wanted to change this in the classroom and start talking about women in sports.

Obviously, understanding the history of women in sports and the gender-biases we see in the sports media is a good place to start. But there are many other stories one can tell. What follows is a sample a few of the stories you could start telling to make your course more inclusive.

Title IX and the Myth of Reverse Discrimination

In 1972, President Richard Nixon signed into law the following addition to the Civil Rights Act of 1964: "No person in the United States shall, on the basis of sex, be excluded from participation in, be denied the benefits of, or be subjected to discrimination under any educational program or activity receiving federal financial assistance."[12]

This statement does not mention sports. But its impact on the sports programs of high schools and colleges was immediately clear. If your institution received federal funding, you could no longer just offer athletic opportunities to boys and men and exclude girls and women.

Given how little girls and women participated in sports before 1972, one might think the views of those who lived in the time of Veblen were correct. Sports were for men. In fact, many might have thought that girls and women simply weren't interested in sports. The data, though, tell a very different story. According to Andrew Zimbalist (2001) in 1971, 294,015 girls played high school sports. By 1973 – one year after Title IX – the number was 817,073. And by 1978 – just six years after Title IX – that number was 2.08 million.

There are two explanations for these numbers. It could be that suddenly girls just became interested in playing high school sports. Or – and this is far more likely – it took government action to end a history of discrimination. In other words, prior to the 1970s there were millions of girls who wanted to play sports but were simply never given the same opportunities as boys.

We see the same pattern at the college level. In 1971, Zimbalist (2001) reports that 31,852 women played college sports. By 1977 there were 64,375 women playing college sports. In just six years, the population of women playing college sports more than doubled.

As already noted, today girls and women are more than 40% of the athletes playing in high school and college. So, it appears Title IX has made sports a much more inclusive space. But has this come at the expense of declining opportunities for boys and men? Are men victims of reverse discrimination?

To answer these questions, we need to first address how Title IX is enforced. Averett and Estelle (2013) pointed out that after Title IX was passed it wasn't clear to anyone exactly how to make schools comply. In 1979, though, the Department of Health, Education and Welfare established what came to be known as the "three-prong test".[13] This test is described by Averett and Estelle (2013) as follows:

- Proportionality Test: "provides a composition of athletic opportunities to men and women that is proportional to the gender composition of the student body."
- Program Expansion Test: "demonstrate consistent program expansion for women."
- Accommodation of Interest Tests: "show accommodation of student interests or abilities."

Anderson and Cheslock (2004) noted that although there are three prongs, it is the first prong that gets the most attention. Perhaps one reason for this is that the last two prongs are not easy to establish objectively. The words "consistent program expansion" and "accommodation of student interests" seem rather hard to measure. In contrast, whether or not opportunities are proportional to the gender composition of the student body is an objective standard. As Zimbalist (2001, p. 63) notes: "… the proportionality criterion is quantifiable by nature and has therefore been relied on more heavily than the other two standards in judging compliance."

Once again, women are currently 44% of all student athletes. When Title IX was passed, women were 43.1% of students.[14] The next year, that percentage rose to 44.1%. So, if this was 1973, then the percentage of athletes that are women in college sports would almost exactly match the gender composition of the students on college campuses.

Unfortunately, it is not 1973. By 1979, women were already more than 50% of all students. And today women are 57% of the students on college campuses. That suggests, in general, schools are not in compliance with this first prong of the test.[15]

Both Anderson and Cheslock (2004) and Averett and Estelle (2013) investigated how many schools were in compliance with Title IX. Both studies found that more than 80% of schools were not in compliance. Furthermore, Anderson and Cheslock (2004) presented evidence that to the extent that schools were trying to comply they were not doing so by cutting men's teams.

So, why are the majority of schools not making sure the athletic opportunities for women in college are matching the gender composition of the student body? According to Averett and Estelle (2013) there is a simple explanation. The law indicates a school will lose federal funding if they don't comply. But as these authors reported in 2013, that has never happened. And Nancy Hogshead-Makar – lawyer and head of Champion Women (https://championwomen.org/) – said in an interview with the author in 2020 that this remains true to this day.

Because Title IX doesn't appear to be strictly enforced, it seems unlikely that many men's sports are really being cut to comply with this law. In other words, it is not plausible that increased opportunities for women have come at the cost of fewer opportunities for men. For example, between 2002–03 and 2018–19, 37,328 girls' athletic teams were added at high schools around the country and the total number of female participants grew by 546,000. At the same 35,554 boys' teams were added and the number of male participants grew by 545,000, almost exactly the same level of growth as in girls' sports (NFHS, 2021). The story is similar for the NCAA where the increase in the number of women's teams from 4,279 in 1982 to 10,660 in 2019 has been accompanied by an increase in men's teams from 6,746 to 9,226 and an increase in over 115,000 male college athletes over the same time period (NCAA, 2021).

So why have some men's programs been cut? Donna Lopiana – founder of Sport Management Resources – offered this explanation when schools were cutting men and women's sports in 2020. Although schools cited the COVID pandemic, Lopiana had a different explanation (Baker, 2021):

> There are a bunch of schools who say they have to cut in the name of financial exigencies, but the problem is that at the same time they're pleading poor, they're spending up the wazoo to protect their one or two revenue-producing sports. ... COVID is an excuse to redistribute resources to continue to participate in the insatiable arms race. In football and basketball, there are no limits to expenditures. We have seven and eight figure salaried coaches. We build lavish football-only, athlete-only facilities. No one is saying no. There's no national governance organization that says, I'm going to cap coaching expenditures, or I'm not going to allow you to build a building that all students can't use. Without any restraints, everyone just continues to spend whatever is possible to spend.

Just as we see with the response to COVID, there is reason to suspect for decades smaller men's programs have not been cut in response to Title IX. Again, schools generally don't comply with Title IX. Furthermore, schools engaged in an arms race in men's basketball and football have a reason to shift spending from smaller men's sport into the two sports that dominate the attention of athletic directors.

Table 8.1   Attendance in the early years of the WNBA and NBA

Season	WNBA year	Average attendance, WNBA	NBA year	Average attendance, NBA
1	1997	9,661	1946–47	3,142
5	2001	9,110	1950–51	3,576
10	2006	7,480	1955–56	4,498
20	2016	7,655	1965–66	6,019
21	2017	7,716	1966–67	6,631
22	2018	6,746	1967–68	6,749
23	2019	6,528	1968–69	6,484

Note: Data compiled by authors from Across the Timeline (for WNBA data) and basketball-reference.com and http://www.apbr.org/attendance.html (for the NBA data)

The Demand for Women's Sports

Perhaps athletic directors are wise to cut programs to invest in football and men's basketball. The market has clearly said these sports are what fans demand. And when it comes to evaluating the popularity of sports, we should always just look at the demand data. Right?

Well, maybe we need to do more. Consider the WNBA and the NBA. The WNBA reached its 23rd season in 2019. That year, average game-day attendance was 6,528. This was more than 11,000 less than what an average NBA team attracted in 2018–19 (Statista[16] says average NBA attendance was 17,857 that year). Just from these two numbers it is clear, professional men's basketball is immensely more popular than professional women's basketball. And when we consider that the WNBA is the most popular women's professional league in North America, it seems fairly clear that men's sports are much more popular than women's sports. The market has spoken, and that market says men's sports is better than women's sports!

At least, that is the story you would tell if you didn't know any history. Of course, at this point we should know that we can't ignore history if we want to tell the entire story.

The NBA started in 1946–47.[17] As Table 8.1 notes, the early years of the NBA were grim. The NBA didn't average 5,000 fans per game until its 13th season. It wasn't until its 20th season that average attendance reached 6,000 fans. And when we compare the WNBA's 23rd year to the NBA's 23rd year we see the women are doing slightly better.

Of course, in recent years WNBA attendance has declined.[18] That might suggest that demand for women's basketball is falling. But it turns out this is mostly a supply issue. In 2017 the New York Liberty averaged 9,889 fans per game while playing in Madison Square Garden. The next year, James

Dolan – the owner of the Liberty (and Madison Square Garden) – moved the Liberty's home games to the Westchester County Center. This arena only held 5,000 fans (Alvarez, 2018). It was also located in White Plains, New York; or more than 30 miles away from Madison Square Garden. Not surprisingly, attendance in 2018 fell to 2,823 per game and 2,239 the following season.[19]

The Washington Mystics made a similar move. In 2018, the Mystics attracted 6,136 fans per game. The next season the Mystics won the WNBA title. Their attendance, though, fell to 4,546.[20] Did the team suddenly become less popular? No, the Mystics essentially sold out all their home games. The problem was their new arena in 2019 only held about 4,500 fans. Like the Liberty, the Mystics intentionally reduced the supply of tickets they sold.

Much of the decline we see in attendance is linked to the choices made by Washington and New York. As a consequence, 2019 attendance data in the WNBA doesn't tell us much about the league's popularity. A better picture can be found when we look at the television data.

We noted earlier the Major League Soccer's broadcasts averaged 266,000 viewers per game in 2019. The broadcasts – on FOX, ESPN, and Univision – pay MLS $90 million per season (Young, 2020). Such a deal dwarfs the $25 million the WNBA gets per season from ESPN (Ourand, 2016). Given these dollars, one would expect the WNBA's ratings to pale in comparison to MLS.

But that is not what the numbers say. Moran (2019) reported that across the first half of the 2019 season the WNBA averaged more than 300,000 viewers per game. And in 2020, Cathy Engelbert (the league's commissioner) announced a 68% increase in television ratings relative to the previous season (Negley, 2020). In other words, although attendance is falling (again, mainly due to supply issues), television ratings suggest that the WNBA is increasing in popularity.

Before we get too excited, though, perhaps there is another way to look at the story. Perhaps one might argue that we would expect more attendance and more television viewers today because population is much larger. Since 1969, population in the United States has grown from about 200 million to more than 330 million. Shouldn't the WNBA have far more fans today than the NBA in 1969?

Before we leap to that conclusion, we need to do more than just look at the size of the market. We also need to consider the entertainment options in 1969 compared with today. Fifty years ago, there were essentially three television networks. There were no video games, no internet, and no videos streaming into people's houses. When it came to sports, there were also far fewer options in-person and on television. Yes, population has grown but one could argue entertainment options have grown much faster. And that means, the WNBA has far more to compete with in finding an audience today.

In essence, the WNBA should be quite pleased with how far it has come. That is not, however, the story the WNBA often tells. At least, it is not the story told by the NBA, the WNBA's partner. Adam Silver is the current commissioner of the NBA. In 2015 – when the WNBA was less than 20 years old – Silver offered this observation about the WNBA.

> We thought we would have broken through by now. We thought ratings and attendance would be higher. (Adler, 2015)

Once again, relative to the NBA when it was less than 20 years old, the WNBA was doing quite well in 2015. Three years later, though, Silver was still not impressed with the WNBA's progress. Consider the following two quotes:

> ... this is a business issue, and we still have a number of teams losing money. ... We haven't figured out a winning formula, to be quite honest. (Bonesteel, 2018)

> On average (we've lost) over $10 million every year we operated. (Feinberg, 2018)

Some perspective is needed for those statements. First, the NBA also told ESPN (Windhorst and Lowe, 2017) that even after the league's television deal had increased substantially that a number of NBA teams couldn't earn a profit. And second, even if the $10 million losses were real (and given the statement about the NBA's profits we should have doubts), the NBA's revenues are over $8 billion. A $10 million profit or loss would be – in the grand scheme of the NBA – essentially meaningless. The league routinely spends this amount on players who don't even play.

Beyond these issues, it is useful to compare Silver's statements about the early years of the WNBA to the statements of Maurice Podoloff in the 1950s. Podoloff was the first president of the NBA and led the league when it was – as noted earlier – doing much worse than the WNBA today. Here is how Podoloff reacted to those early poor attendance numbers (Surdam, 2012, p. 29),

> We are getting some very bad publicity due to the fact that some of our team managers are just a bit too scrupulously honest in giving attendance figures to radios and newspapers. If you can avoid giving the figures out, do so. If however, you must announce figures, a little padding will be forgiven.

The difference is quite clear. Silver went out of his way to tell people he thought the WNBA was struggling even though – when compared with the early history for the NBA – this take could be disputed. Podoloff saw NBA teams honestly report their poor attendance figures and immediately told them that bad-mouthing your product in public – even if what you say is true – is really just bad marketing.

Podoloff also had a very different take on what the owners thought about losses. Here is testimony he gave to Congress in 1957 (Surdam, 2012, p. 8)

… if we produce sports, we want to have an audience, and the receipts are a measure of our success. But I will tell you one thing; I have seen more than one team owner and manager come off the floor on the verge of tears. He didn't moan and groan because he had lost money. He moaned and groaned because he lost the game.

In the early years of the NBA, it wasn't just the case that attendance was low. Of the first 23 franchises to participate in the NBA, 15 went out of business by the mid-1950s (Berri and Engst, 2021). Despite this failure rate, Podoloff didn't think owners cared as much about profits as they did about winning.

And there is good reason to think Podoloff was very much right. At least, NBA owners historically acted like they agree with Podoloff. In 1983, the NBA instituted a cap on payrolls (commonly called a salary cap). Later on, the NBA instituted caps on individual rookie pay and individual veteran pay. Economists suspect these caps are all about limiting the pay to players. The owners, though, argue these caps are necessary. The basic argument is that owners are so focused on winning that their spending on talent will cause the NBA to lose money. Certainly that was the argument the NBA made back in 1983 when the first cap was proposed (Dupree, 1983).

Unfortunately, many WNBA owners today seem to lack this same focus. Women's basketball doesn't seem to suffer so much from a gap in demand as a gap in ownership enthusiasm. Consider what James Dolan – owner of the New York Knicks and New York Liberty – said to "Real Sports" on HBO in 2015 (Mather, 2017):

It [the Liberty] hasn't made money. Its prospects of making money, at that time and even today, are still slim.

Yes, this is the same owner that appeared to sabotage his own team's attendance numbers by moving his franchise out his own arena to a much smaller venue in a different city. These are not the decisions of an owner that is placing winning above profits.

The WNBA seems to have owners that are far focused on cutting costs than they are on winning games. And we can see that with the next story we tell.

The Gender–Wage Gap

It is well known that a gender–wage gap exists in the overall economy. According to Bleiweis (2020), in 2018 women on average earned about 82 cents for every dollar that men make. Blau and Kahn (2017) note that even when we consider a wide variety of human capital and occupational differences between men and women, a significant unexplained portion of the gap remains. This suggests discrimination still remains a significant part of the labor market for women.

Although the gender–wage gap we see in the overall economy is significant, it pales in comparison to what we see in professional basketball. Consider for a moment the highest paid players in the NBA and WNBA.

In July of 2017, Stephen Curry and the Golden State Warriors agreed to a five-year super-max contract that would pay Curry $201 million.[21] A few weeks earlier, the Warriors won their second NBA title in three years. And Curry was widely considered (and this is confirmed by the data)[22] one of the team's best players. Because of this deal, Curry was scheduled to be paid $43 million in 2020–21.[23] Given a 72-game season,[24] Curry was scheduled to be paid $597,311 per game.

The highest paid player in the WNBA in 2021 is Diana Taurasi – the person who leads all WNBA players in history in scoring and is known as the "Michael Jordan of the WNBA". After signing a maximum deal in 2021, Taurasi was schedule to be paid $221,450.[25] This means that Curry, who is not the "Michael Jordan of the NBA" and does not lead all players in NBA history in scoring, is scheduled to be paid more than twice as much per game than Taurasi will receive for an entire season. And Curry gets this per game money whether he plays in the games or not.

Given these numbers, Taurasi is paid about 0.5 cents for every dollar Curry is paid. If we look at the average player in the WNBA and NBA that gender–wage gap is essentially the same. According to Basketball-Reference, the average NBA player in 2020–21 is paid $7.9 million. Meanwhile, according to the WNBA, the new collective bargaining agreement signed in 2020 will increase average wages in the WNBA to about $130,000.[26] This means the gender–wage gap in professional basketball in North America is such that women are paid 1.6 cents for every dollar a man makes.

Is this really just discrimination? We already noted that the WNBA's attendance today is quite comparable to what the NBA's attendance was at the same point in its history. But relative to today, the professional women do not draw as well as the men. We can see the same story when we look at the revenue data. According to Badenhausen (2020), the NBA generated $8.8 billion in revenue in 2019–20. Meanwhile, an estimate of WNBA revenue says that league revenue for the women is merely $70 million.[27]

Given these figures, it is not surprising that the women are paid much less than the men. If the entire league only takes in $70 million, it is simply not realistic to expect Taurasi to be paid the same wage as Curry. If the organization doesn't even have the money, there is no way it can pay the workers any more. Right?

Well, not exactly. The NBA's collective bargaining agreement says the players should receive about 50% of league revenue. WNBA players, though, are not doing quite so well. Again, the average wage is $130,000. With 12 players on the roster of 12 teams, that means the 144 players in the WNBA are paid $18.7 million; or about 27% of the conservative estimate of league revenue. And that is after the WNBA players received a significant raise!

A few months after Curry signed his super-max deal, Berri (2017b) noted that WNBA players were receiving – as a percentage of league revenue – far less than their NBA counterparts. Here is how a few players reacted to this news.

Skylar Diggins-Smith (two-time member of the All-WNBA First Team with a 2018 salary of $115,500):

> Players in the NBA get about 50% of the revenue. For women, the percentage is in the twenties. So, before we even talk about base salary or anything like that, we don't even get paid the same percentage of the revenue that we bring in, which is kind of unbelievable. People try to hijack this issue and say that women's basketball may not be as interesting a game, because they disparage women in sports, period. But we don't even make the same percentage of revenue! And jersey sales … we don't get any of it. The men do. And I have had a top-five jersey for three or four years in the WNBA. (Wealthsimple, 2018)

Natalie Achonwa (member of the 2015 WNBA All-Rookie team with a 2018 salary of $52,265):

> It's not just that we want more money, it's not that we want to compare ourselves to NBA players and what they make, we understand. We're the most educated professional sports league, most of the WNBA players are college graduates, we understand that it's not that, we just feel like they should give us more money. NBA [players] get 50 per cent of their revenue, we make less than 25 per cent of it [22 per cent]. We want a bigger piece of the pie. (Ewing, 2018)

Kelsey Plum (the number one pick in the 2017 WNBA draft with a 2018 salary of $52,263):

> I'm tired of people thinking that us players are asking for the same type of money as NBA players. We are asking for the same percentage of revenue shared within our CBA. NBA players receive around 50 percent of shared revenue within their league, whereas we receive around 20 percent. (Ellentuck, 2018)

Plum's pay as the number one pick in the draft is especially interesting. Plum was a star player at the University of Washington. Berri (2017c) noted the cost of attending the University of Washington – which is all the NCAA technically pays its athletes – was $49,986. This means that in her second WNBA season Plum was paid less than $3,000 more than she was paid as a senior in college.

What would a player like Plum be paid if the WNBA paid like the NBA? Again, we are not talking about changing the WNBA's revenue. All the players said they wanted is the same split in revenue.

Once again, it is estimated that WNBA revenue is $70 million. A 50% split would give the players $35 million. With 144 players (12 players on 12 teams), that means the average salary would be $243,056. Yes, a 50% split would mean the average player would make more than Diana Taurasi – the highest paid player in the WNBA – was scheduled to make after the new Collective Bargaining Agreement (CBA) in 2020.

Obviously, Taurasi should be paid at least as well as the average. But if she was paid like Curry, she would be paid quite a bit more. Curry's 2020–21 salary is 5.43 times higher than the average. If Taurasi was paid 5.43 times better than the average WNBA player, then she would be paid $1,320,375.

Such numbers are not about increasing the WNBA's revenue. It is simply about giving the WNBA players the same split in the revenue we see in the NBA and then also imposing the same distribution in pay. Such a change would likely benefit the WNBA. In 2015, Diana Taurasi illustrated how much higher pay for its stars would help. Because the WNBA pays so little, many of its stars also play in leagues in Europe and Asia. These leagues pay substantially more than the WNBA. How much more? UMMC Ekaterinburg – Taurasi's team in Russia – paid Taurasi $1.5 million in 2015. They also paid her an additional $107,000 – or her WNBA salary at the time – to skip the 2015 season (Fagan, 2015). So, the "Michael Jordan of the WNBA" was paid by a Russian team to *not* play in the WNBA.

Taurasi is not the only player to make such a choice. As Agha and Berri (2021) note, in 2019 there were 49 American-born WNBA players playing a second season outside of North America. And this has been the case throughout the history of the WNBA. The players definitely do not consider these jobs outside the WNBA as second-best. As Candace Parker put it (TooFab Staff, 2020):

> It's funny because everyone would ask me, "What's your off-season job, what's your summer job?" Actually, this is my summer job, the WNBA, because I feed my daughter overseas … the money over there is 10–20 times more than you would make here.

Having players think of the WNBA as just their "summer job" is not the only consequence of the WNBA's low wages. In 2019, Breanna Stewart – the 2018 league MVP (most valuable player) – tore her Achilles playing the final of the Euroleague (Metcalfe, 2019). This injury caused the 2018 league MVP to miss the entire 2019 season.

Table 8.2   Income and payroll in the NBA from 1951 to 1957

Season	Total income	Total payroll	Percentage paid to players
1951–52	$1,533,457	$530,475	34.6%
1952–53	$1,648,544	$650,614	39.5%
1953–54	$1,559,567	$682,592	43.8%
1954–55	$1,578,064	$733,332	46.5%
1955–56	$1,798,884	$745,728	41.5%
1956–57	$1,776,181	$768,972	43.3%

Source: Rod Fort's Sports Business Page. Originally taken from the Committee on the Judiciary. House of Representatives. Organized Professional Team Sports. 85th Cong. 1st sess. Part 3. 1957. P. 2928

So why doesn't the WNBA persist in paying such low wages? Mark Cuban – owner of the Dallas Mavericks of the NBA – offered an answer (Berri, 2018c):

> The difference is the total amount of revenue. It's not a gender issue. It's just like we paid a lower percentage to the men until the revenues went up. And when our revenues went up, we were able to pay a higher percentage.

That seems like a plausible story. At least, it is plausible if you had no knowledge of NBA history. Back in the 1950s the NBA testified before Congress. As part of this testimony, the NBA noted its total income and payroll from 1951–52 to 1956–57.

As Table 8.2 indicates, NBA revenue in 1951–52 was only $1.5 million while the league paid $530,475 in salaries. Two things stand out from those figures. First, the NBA was initially a very small business. In 2020 dollars, $1.6 million in revenue in 1955 is worth less than $16 million.[28] That means, in 1955 the NBA was earning less than 25% of the revenue the WNBA is likely earning today. Despite being much smaller – and contrary to Cuban's assertion – in 1954–55 the NBA reported paying 46.5% of its revenue to its players.

The current WNBA deal doesn't expire until the 2027 season, or when the WNBA will be 31 years old. In 1982–83 the NBA was in its 37th season, or just six years older than the WNBA will be when the current collective bargaining agreement ends. Back in 1983, the NBA told the *Washington Post* (Dupree, 1983) that its players were receiving 59% of league revenue. At this point, the NBA was only averaging about 10,000 fans per contest[29] and the league claimed it was losing money.

Again, we have reason to be skeptical of the NBA's claims about losses. Nevertheless, there is reason to think the NBA was not quite the business it is today. Herb Simon bought the Indiana Pacers for just $10.5 million in 1983 (Kravitz, 2019); or about $28 million in today's dollars.[30] According to Simon, he only bought the team because people in the city begged him to step in and prevent the team from moving to Sacramento. Simons also noted they asked five other people before they asked him (Kravitz, 2019). In other words, people were not anxious to invest in the NBA in 1983.

Despite the fact the NBA was still a struggling league in 1983, it still paid much better than the WNBA pays today. So, contrary to the story told by Cuban, low pay in the WNBA is really not about the level of revenue.

We should note that despite the condition of the NBA in 1983, this investment definitely worked out for Simon. According to Forbes, the Pacers are now worth $1.5 billion.[31] This is not because the Pacers became a remarkably successful franchise. This team has never won an NBA title and it is obviously in one of the smallest markets in the league. Nevertheless, Simon's reluctant investment in 1983 has led to a very impressive return.

Would an investment today in the WNBA lead to similar returns? Your answer might depend on how you perceive the athletes the WNBA employs.

Who is the Best?

Here is a fun topic to discuss in class. Who are better athletes? Men or women?

Before you have the students answer this question, ask this question: Who is the best boxer in the world?[32]

According to Campbell (2020) of CBS Sports, the following are the top five boxers in December of 2020:

1.   Canelo Alvarez: Super Middleweight (weight limit is 168 pounds)
2.   Naoya Inoue: Bantamweight (weight limit is 118 pounds)
3.   Errol Spence, Jr.: Welterweight (weight limit is 147 pounds)
4.   Terence Crawford: Welterweight (weight limit is 147 pounds)
5.   Vasiliy Lomachencko: Lightweight (weight limit is 135 pounds)

Tyson Fury is an undefeated heavyweight champion. He is also 6 feet, 9 inches in height and weighs 254 pounds. It is very unlikely any of the five men listed above could last very long in a fight with Fury. In fact, because a man the size of Fury could seriously hurt these smaller men, such a fight wouldn't even be allowed. Weight requirements in boxing are strictly enforced because it is believed a bigger man would have a distinct advantage over a smaller man.

All of that means if we were listing the "best" boxers in the world, a man like Tyson Fury has to rank ahead of the five men listed above. In fact, we can probably argue that almost any heavyweight fighter would be ranked ahead of any of these five fighters. And yet, men are willing to argue that all of these heavyweights are not "better" fighters than Alvarez, Inoue, Spence Jr., Crawford, or Lomachencko.

It is not just boxing analysts that make this argument. The market also seems comfortable with the idea the best boxers are not necessarily the greatest in an absolute sense. In 2015, Floyd Mayweather fought Manny Pacquiao. As Parkinson (2020) notes, this fight is the richest fight in history. The fight earned more than $400 million (Rafael, 2015). It was also fought for the welterweight title, or a title held by boxers who weigh less than 147 pounds. Furthermore, both fighters were relatively old. Mayweather was 38 years old when he entered the ring to face the 36-year-old Pacquiao.

So, how can a fight between two little old guys be the richest fight in history? Again, the issue isn't who is the absolute best. The issue is who is "best in class". Both Mayweather and Pacquiao had demonstrated throughout their careers that – relative to the competition they faced – they were two of the greatest fighters in history. Sure, neither would have a chance against Fury or any other heavyweight. But that is not relevant to boxing experts or the fans willing to pay to see the fight.

We see the same issue when it comes to many men's sports. College football games often draw higher television ratings than NFL games despite the fact no college team would have much of a chance against an NFL team. In addition, Little League World Series games can get higher ratings than a Major League Baseball game despite the fact little boys would have no chance against Major League talent.

When it comes to sports, men are perfectly comfortable with the idea that "best" only means "best in class". One doesn't have to be the greatest in an absolute sense.

Given this approach, let's talk about the greatest basketball player in 2018. In the NBA, the sportswriters declared James Harden was the league MVP for the 2017–18 season. Harden is 196 cm tall (6 ft. 5 in.) which is similar to the height of Sylvia Fowles (198 cm), Breanna Stewart (193 cm), and Elena Delle Donne (196 cm). As Table 8.3 reports, these three women were named the WNBA MVP in 2017, 2018, and 2019 respectively. Could any of these women be as good as Harden?

All of these women are similar in height to Harden. So, one might imagine in a game of one-on-one they might be able to hold their own. Or maybe we can't imagine that is true. Returning to our story from boxing, it ultimately doesn't make any difference. Once again, boxers are evaluated in terms of their competition. All that matters is "best in class", not best in an absolute sense. Therefore, whether Fowles, Stewart, or Delle Donne could defeat Harden in a game is irrelevant. We don't care of Floyd Mayweather can beat Tyson Fury in a fight. And we also shouldn't care if a WNBA player can defeat an NBA player.

In deciding who is "better" we should look at how each player has fared relative to their competition. As Table 8.3 indicates, after 11 NBA seasons

Table 8.3   *Comparing four MVPs in basketball (as of 2020)*

	James Harden (2018 NBA MVP)	Sylvia Fowles (2017 WNBA MVP)	Breanna Stewart (2018 WNBA MVP)	Elena Delle Donne (2019 WNBA MVP)
Height (cm)	196	198	193	196
Age	31	35	26	31
Years played	11	13	4	7
First Team All-League	6	3	2	4
MVP awards	1	1	1	2
Championships won	0	2	2	1
Finals MVP	0	2	2	0

Harden was named to the All-NBA first team six times. The 2018 MVP award was the only time Harden earned such an honor. And Harden has never won an NBA title. The closest he has come is reaching the finals in 2012 with the Oklahoma City Thunder. Harden, though, was not a starter on that team.

One could argue the three women listed in Table 8.3 are a bit more accomplished. Elena Delle Donne is virtually the same age as Harden (they were born ten days apart in 1989). Typically, women do not enter the WNBA early,[33] so it is not surprising Delle Donne has only played seven WNBA seasons. Despite playing four fewer seasons, Delle Donne has been named league MVP twice and also won a WNBA title.

Stewart is much younger than the other players listed. But in just four WNBA seasons she has already been league MVP and won two NBA titles. Stewart was also the named the Finals MVP for both of these championship teams.

Fowles is the oldest of the group and has only been named to the All-WNBA first team three times. But in addition to being a league MVP, Fowles – like Stewart – has also been part of two WNBA title teams. And like Stewart, Fowles was named the Finals MVP for both of her title teams.

Once again, Harden has never been named a Finals MVP because he has never won an NBA title. That suggests he is not quite as good as these three players who have all hoisted a trophy.

Then again, titles are team accomplishments, and we wish to compare individual players. Fortunately, basketball productivity can be quantified. Specifically – as we briefly noted earlier – we can measure how many wins each player produces in the WNBA and NBA.[34] This is because – as noted by Berri (2017a) – basketball is not really complicated:

> Basketball is a fairly simple game. Teams win because they a) acquire possession of the ball without the other team scoring (i.e., grab defensive rebounds, create turnovers); b) keep possession of the ball (i.e., avoid turnovers, grab offensive rebounds); and c) turn possessions into points (i.e., shoot efficiently from the field and the line).

As Berri (2008) detailed, the simplicity of basketball allows one to take a player's box score statistics and measure how many wins the player produces, i.e. the player's Wins Produced. When we take this step, we see the following for 2018:

- James Harden (2017–18): 16.59 wins produced
- Sylvia Fowles: 9.12 wins produced
- Breanna Stewart: 6.97 wins produced
- Elena Delle Donne: 6.77 wins produced

Okay, there we have it. The three women combined to produce 22.86 wins while Harden – by himself – produced 16.59. That has to mean that Harden is better than all three. Right?

Well, not quite. Harden had more opportunity to produce wins. An NBA season is 82 games long while the WNBA only plays a 34-game schedule. Per 34 games, Harden produced only 6.88 wins in 2017–18. And that exaggerates a bit his production relative to Stewart since an NBA game is 48 minutes while WNBA games are only 40 minutes long. Despite this advantage, both Fowles and Stewart did more per 34 games than Harden. And if Harden's advantage in minutes is taken into account, Delle Donne also did more than Harden.[35]

As Table 8.4 reveals that when we look at all WNBA and NBA players in 2018, Harden was only the seventh most productive player. Not only was Harden not more productive than either Fowles or Stewart in 2018, he also didn't match the production of Courtney Vandersloot or Diana Taurasi. Perhaps the latter result is not surprising since – once again – Taurasi is also known as the "Michael Jordan of the WNBA".

One should note that Stewart also didn't match Fowles but did surpass the productivity of Delle Donne. That was not true in 2019, when Delle Donne produced 9.55 wins (and – as noted – Stewart didn't get to play). Stewart also didn't come close to matching Fowles in her 2017 MVP season (Fowles produced 9.67 wins while Stewart only produced 4.09 wins).

Of course, if we were to compare college basketball careers, few could match what Stewart did. Stewart starred at the University of Connecticut from 2013 to 2016. In all four years, Stewart's team won the NCAA title. Stewart was a big part of these four titles, producing 33.98 wins across her college

Table 8.4   The best basketball players in 2018

Rank	Players in 2018	Wins produced per 34 games	WNBA/NBA team
1	Sylvia Fowles*	9.12	Minnesota Lynx
2	LeBron James	7.94	Cleveland Cavaliers
3	Courtney Vandersloot*	7.25	Chicago Sky
4	Ben Simmons	7.00	Philadelphia 76ers
5	Breanna Stewart*	6.97	Seattle Storm
6	Diana Taurasi*	6.88	Phoenix Mercury
7	James Harden	6.88	Houston Rockets
8	Elena Delle Donne*	6.77	Washington Mystics
9	Andre Drummond	6.65	Detroit Pistons
10	Candace Parker*	6.42	Los Angeles Sparks

Note: *WNBA Player

career.[36] Although impressive, her college teammate – Napheesa Collier – produced 36.79 wins at Connecticut from 2015–16 to 2018–19. And Sabrina Ionescu finished her four-year career at the University of Oregon with 39.71 Wins Produced. Ionescu also finished with 26 triple-doubles, a mark that more than doubled the previous record (a man set the original record). She is also the first woman or man to finish a college career with more than 2,000 points scored, 1,000 rebounds, and 1,000 assists.[37] So, maybe Ionescu was the greatest college basketball player in history.

Regardless of whether you rank Ionescu or Stewart (or Collier!) as the best, the point we are making remains. If you are going to discuss the "best" in basketball you have to consider both men and women.

The same story would be told about soccer. In September of 2020, Christiano Ronaldo scored both goals in Portugal's 2–0 win over Sweden. This gave Ronaldo 101 goals in his international playing career. As Pugh (2020) noted after this performance:

> One of the greatest players of all time and looks set to surpass (Ali) Daei's record with ease. If he does, the record is likely to stand for years given the lack of modern-day stars anywhere near him in the list.

Unfortunately for Ronaldo, this statement is only true if you ignore the fact women play soccer. In January of 2020, Christine Sinclair scored her 185th goal in international play (FIFA, 2020). This broke the record of 184 set by Abby Wambach. Ronaldo might catch Daei. But it is very unlikely he is catching Sinclair, Wambach, or many of the other women who have more than 100 goals in international play (there are more than two dozen).

Yes, that means a list of the top soccer players in the world must include women. Unfortunately, too often we see headlines like the Pugh (2020) article: "Top 10 international goal scorers of all time ..." If you don't include the word "men" in this statement ... well, your list is very wrong.

The same story can be told about tennis. Ultimate Tennis Statistics[38] offers a list of the tennis players with the most grand slam victories. Topping the list is Roger Federer and Rafael Nadal. Both of these men have won 20 grand slam titles. Of course, these totals can't be considered "the most". Margaret Court (24 titles), Serena Williams (23 titles), and Steffi Graf (22 titles) have all won more than Federer and Nadal.[39] So if you are listing the "best" tennis players you have to look at more than just the men who have played.

Remember, the best boxers are not always the biggest. And yes, they aren't always men either. To illustrate, who was the best "Ali" to ever fight? Muhammed Ali is famous for saying he was "The Greatest". But his daughter – Laila Ali – was undefeated when she retired from boxing in 2007. In contrast, her father lost five times in his career. One could argue that "The Greatest" wasn't even the greatest in his own family!

So Many More Stories!

Talking about discrimination, Title IX, the gender–wage gap, and even "The Greatest" athletes is just the start of what one can do with women's sports in a sports economic course. There is so much more one can do. Essentially, many stories sports economists tell about men's sports can also be told about women's sports. And when you are thinking of the stories you tell in class you should consider if a story from women's sports might help you both tell the story and make your class more inclusive.

For example:

- One can look at competitive balance in men's college sports by looking at Peach (2007). For women's college basketball one can look at Treber, Levy, and Matheson (2013).
- One can discuss decision-making in the NBA draft by discussing the research of Berri, Brook, and Fenn (2011). Or one can discuss decision-making in the WNBA draft by discussing Harris and Berri (2015).
- One can look at how minutes are allocated in the NBA by reviewing Berri, Deutscher, and Galletti (2015). Or one can look at Harris and Berri (2016) and examine the same issue for the WNBA.
- One can look at the extent of economic exploitation in Major League Baseball by looking at ... well, so many articles. But for now, let's say Berri (2019). Or one can look at the extent of economic exploitation in the

All-American Girls Professional Baseball League in Giddings and Haupert (2019).

- One can talk about measuring the productivity of a pitcher in baseball by looking at how Fielding Independent Pitching Earned Run Average (ERA) is discussed in Bradbury (2007). Or one can talk about Fielding Independent Pitching ERA for National Pro Fastpitch by looking at Berri (2018a).[40]

Of course, data from women's sports also allow one to discuss topics specific to gender studies. Once again, women tend to occupy only about 20% of leadership positions in politics, business, and academia.[41] Is this because men are better leaders than women? The study of coaching in women's softball by von Allmen (2013) certainly didn't find this. Another study of both college and professional basketball coaches also failed to find that men are better coaches than women (Darvin, Pegoraro, Berri, 2018).

What about the idea that men perform better than women under pressure? That is definitely not the story told by Cohen-Zada, Krumer, Shapir, and Rosenboim (2017). The authors looked at an extensive data set of men and women professional tennis players. As they noted:[42]

"Our research showed that men consistently choke under competitive pressure, but with regard to women the results are mixed," says Dr. Mosi Rosenboim of BGU's Department of Management. "However, even if women show a drop in performance in the more crucial stages of the match, it is still about 50 percent less than that of men."

"The purpose of this study is to shed additional light on how men and women respond to competitive pressure and use its conclusions to better understand the labor market," says Dr. Danny Cohen-Zada of BGU's Department of Economics. "For example, our findings do not support the existing hypothesis that men earn more than women in similar jobs because they respond better than women to pressure."

Toma (2017) examined free throw shooting by men and women in both college and professional basketball. This study also failed to find evidence that men are better under pressure than women.

All of these studies are made possible because – just like we see in men's sports – there is extensive data in women's sports. For example, Basketball Reference has a page dedicated to the WNBA[43] while Her Hoop Stats provides extensive data for the WNBA and NCAA women's basketball.[44] Of course, the NCAA also has data on NCAA women's basketball, as well as data on every other women's college sport.[45] One can also find data for the National Pro Fastpitch league, National Women Soccer League, the National Women's Hockey League, and so on. Yes, the numbers for women are not always as easy to find as they are for men's sports. But if you search, the statistics are out there. And with all those numbers come even more stories.

CONCLUDING THOUGHTS

Economics has a long history of focusing on men and excluding women. The same is true when we look at the history of sports. So perhaps it is not surprising that sports economics historically has focused on men.

Women, though, are very much a part of the story of sports. More than 40% of both athletes and fans are women. The dominance of men in the sports media and the habit of men to quiz women when they enter this space might prevent many men from seeing how much women are involved in and like sports. But that doesn't change the fact that millions of women are part of the world of sports.

All of this means if you are teaching sports economics, you are not telling the entire story if women are not part of your stories. And there are so many stories one can tell when one spends some time thinking about women in sports. Discrimination, demand for sports across time, the impact of coaching, how athletes perform under pressure, and even identifying "the greatest" athletes are all topics that are better informed by a discussion of women in sports.

Hopefully this chapter has given instructors a few ideas. One last piece of advice though, for those who will be adding women sports to their classes. Be sure to leave gender stereotypes out of your discussion. This goes beyond the issue of who is likely to choke and whether women can coach. You also shouldn't tell stories that men are more likely to be risk-takers or women would be better off if they were assertive like men. The differences in outcomes we see between men and women – both within sports and outsides of sports – are generally about culture and society and not about biology. If you don't see this … well, a book such as *Delusions of Gender* (Fine, 2011) is a good place to start thinking about these issues.

Making your class a more inclusive environment isn't just about doing the right thing. It is about making sure your class accurately represents the world of sports. If you do this, both the women and men in your class will end up with a better educational experience.

NOTES

1. For those who don't wish to buy the book, Adam Smith's *The Wealth of Nations* is available here: https://www.econlib.org/library/Smith/smWN.html
2. https://www.adamsmithsociety.com/
3. https://www.adamsmith.org/home
4. Smith only says "invisible hand" once. The book really isn't about "invisible hands". But that is a story for another day!

5. Berri (2018a) includes a chapter on women and sports. But it is fair to say that this textbook – with a woman playing softball on the cover – includes more stories on men's sports than it does on women's sports. Leeds, von Allmen, and Matheson's (2018) textbook also specifically discusses discrimination in women's sports and the impact of Title IX, but only one out of 12 biographical sketches features a female athlete.

6. This is also the name of an Italian Serie A football (or soccer) team. And yes, the team is named after the mythical woman.

7. In 2020, Coach Tara VanDerveer set the all-time record for coaching wins in women's college basketball at Stanford; the place that once banned women from playing the game.

8. The story of the early history of women's soccer in England and how men banned the sport is told in Amanda Coletta (2015).

9. https://www.nfhs.org/articles/participation-in-high-school-sports-registers-first -decline-in-30-years/

10. NCAA: https://www.ncaa.org/about/resources/research/diversity-research

11. As Killion (2018) reports:
    There are five women in senior leadership positions, running the College Football Playoff: (Allison) Doughty, Chief Operating Officer Andrea Williams, Director of Stadium and Game Operations Nikki Epley, Senior Director of Operations and Logistics Laila Brock, and Senior Director of External Relations and Branding Gina Lehe. Add in Patricia Ernstrom, executive director of the Bay Area Host Committee, and the championship game is a lesson in what a workplace can look like if the boss has an open mind when it comes to hiring and the door to advancement is unlocked.

12. The discussion of the Civil Rights Act of 1964 and the specifics of Title IX can be found in Averett and Estelle (2013).

13. Averett and Estelle (2013).

14. Source: https://nces.ed.gov/programs/digest/d19/tables/dt19_303.10.asp

15. Source: https://nces.ed.gov/programs/digest/d19/tables/dt19_303.10.asp

16. Source: https://www.statista.com/statistics/193632/average-regular-season-home -attendance-per-team-in-the-nba-since-2006

17. The NBA began as the Basketball Association of America (BAA) in 1946. The BAA and National Basketball League merged in 1949 to form the NBA. When we think of the history of the NBA, though, we tend to begin with the BAA where six different NBA franchises originated.

18. The records for attendance in WNBA happened in the first few years of the league. This is primarily because the WNBA often just gave tickets away in its first seasons. That is a far less common practice today.

19. Source: https://www.acrossthetimeline.com/wnba/attendance.html

20. Source: https://www.acrossthetimeline.com/wnba/attendance.html

21. The NBA has a veteran salary cap that limits what an individual player can receive. Wojnarowski (2017) notes that a "supermax" deal is one that crosses the $200 million threshold. Curry's deal was the first to do this.

22. When the Warriors won the title in 2015, Curry led the team with 19.0 Wins Produced. No other player on the team produced ten wins that season. In 2017, the Warriors were led in Wins Produced by Kevin Durant (14.4 Wins Produced). But Curry's 13.0 Wins Produced was second on the team. Complete Wins Produced data for the NBA from 1973–74 to 2019–20 can be found at Rod Fort's Sports Business Pages. This data also comes with an explanation of this measurement and

references to even more discussion (https://sites.google.com/site/rodswebpages/codes).

23. According to Basketball-Reference.com, Curry's 2020–21 salary is $43,006,362.
24. Due to COVID, the NBA season in 2020–21 was shortened from 82 games to 72 games.
25. Source: https://www.spotrac.com/wnba/free-agents/
26. Source: https://www.wnba.com/news/wnba-and-wnbpa-reach-tentative-agreement-on-groundbreaking-eight-year-collective-bargaining-agreement/
27. As Berri (2020) details, we know the WNBA gets $25 million from its ESPN television deal. There is also another deal with the CBS sports cable channel. In addition, the league gets money from the sale of tickets, Fan Duel, Twitter, Tidal, local broadcasting deals, merchandise sales, WNBA League Pass, and sponsorships deals. Berri (2020) says a conservative estimate of all this places league revenue at $60 million. A league source, though, says maybe that estimate should be $70 million.
28. Source: https://www.bls.gov/data/inflation_calculator.htm
29. Source: http://www.apbr.org/attendance.html
30. Source: https://www.bls.gov/data/inflation_calculator.htm
31. Source: https://www.forbes.com/profile/herb-simon/?sh=6f7b2b992c1f
32. This story follows from Berri (2018b).
33. As the WNBA notes (https://www.wnba.com/faq/), a woman has to be at least 22 years of age to be drafted by the WNBA. In contrast, NBA players can enter the league after one-year of college. Anthony Davis played just one season at the University of Kentucky before entering the NBA in 2012. Davis is about 6-months older than Jewel Lloyd, the Rookie of the Year in the WNBA in 2016. By the time Lloyd won this award, Davis was already a veteran of four NBA seasons.
34. Berri and Krautmann (2013) explains how Wins Produced can be calculated for a WNBA player. This measure builds on the methodology detailed in Berri (2008) and Berri, Schmidt, and Brook (2006). More on how Wins Produced is calculated can be found at Rod Fort's Sports Business Pages.
35. An NBA game is 8 minutes longer. Hence, NBA players can play 20% more minutes per game than WNBA players. If we adjust for that bias, then Harden produced only 5.7 wins; a mark less than Delle Donne, Liz Cambage, and Sue Bird.
36. Stewart is not the only woman to win four NCAA titles in basketball. Her teammates Morgan Tuck and Moriah Jefferson also won four titles with her. And Jefferson produced 31.9 wins at Connecticut, or a total that nearly matched Stewart's productivity. In sum, Stewart didn't win these titles by herself.
37. Source: https://goducks.com/sports/womens-basketball/roster/sabrina-ionescu/8584
38. Source: https://www.ultimatetennisstatistics.com/record?recordId=GrandSlamTitles
39. Source: https://sports.yahoo.com/most-grand-slam-tennis-singles-040047235.html
40. Bradbury (2007) refers to Defensive Independent Pitching Statistics (DIPS). This builds on the early work of McCracken (2001). Fielding Independent Pitching ERA is just another name for DIPS ERA.
41. This was noted by Benchmarking Women's Leadership in the United States. This was a report prepared by the University of Denver: Colorado Women's College in 2013. http://www.womenscollege.du.edu/media/documents/BenchmarkingWomensLeadershipintheUS.pdf

42. American Associates, Ben-Gurion University of the Negev. "Male athletes more likely to choke under pressure." *ScienceDaily*, 10 November 2016. www .sciencedaily.com/releases/2016/11/161110124555.htm
43. https://www.basketball-reference.com/wnba/
44. Source: https://herhoopstats.com/ Her Hoop Stats does require a very modest fee of $20 per year.
45. Source: https://stats.ncaa.org/ Be forewarned, the NCAA stat has historically been a bit hard to navigate.

REFERENCES

Adler, Lindsey. 2015. "NBA Commissioner: We Thought The WNBA Would Have Broken Through By Now." *BuzzFeed*, (September 17). https://www.buzzfeednews .com/article/lindseyadler/nba-commissioner-we-thought-the-wnba-would-have -broken-throu

Agha, Nola, and David Berri. 2021. "Gender Differences in the Pay of Professional Basketball Players." In Ali Bowes and Alex Culvin (eds), *The Professionalisation of Women's Sport: Issues and Debates*. Emerald, pp. 53–70.

Alvarez, Anya. 2018. "Liberty's End: How a Great New York Team Was Banished to the Suburbs." *The Guardian*, (May 25). https://www.theguardian.com/sport/2018/ may/25/libertys-end-how-a-great-new-york-team-was-banished-to-the-suburbs

Anderson, Deborah J., and John J. Cheslock. 2004. "Institutional Strategies to Achieve Gender Equity in Intercollegiate Athletics: Does Title IX Harm Male Athletes?" *American Economic Review*, 94(2): 307–311.

Averett, Susan L., and Sarah M. Estelle. 2013. "The Economics of Title IX Compliance in Intercollegiate Athletics." In Eva Marikova Leeds and Michael Leeds (eds), *Handbook on the Economics of Women in Sports*. Edward Elgar Publishing, pp. 175–212.

Badenhausen, Kurt. 2020. "NBA Team Values 2020: Lakers and Warriors Join Knicks In Rarefied $4 Billion Club." *Forbes*, (February 11). https://www.forbes.com/ sites/kurtbadenhausen/2020/02/11/nba-team-values-2020-lakers-and-warriors-join -knicks-in-rarefied-4-billion-club/?sh=21070e972032

Baker, Carrie. N. 2021. "Athletes Win First Round in Title IX Challenge to Cuts to Women's Sports." *Ms. Magazine*, (January 12). https://msmagazine.com/2021/01/ 12/athletes-title-ix-lawsuit-university-iowa-womens-sports/

Berri, David. 2008. "A Simple Measure of Worker Productivity in the National Basketball Association." *The Business of Sport*, 3: 1–40.

Berri, David. 2017a. "Boston Celtics Help Clear a Path for LeBron James Back to the NBA Finals." *Forbes*, (August 23). https://www.forbes.com/sites/davidberri/ 2017/08/23/the-boston-celtics-help-lebron-james-get-back-to-the-nba-finals/ #75117206cee2

Berri, David. 2017b. "Basketball's Growing Gender Gap: The Evidence the WNBA Is Underpaying Players." *Forbes*, (September 20). https://www.forbes.com/sites/ davidberri/2017/09/20/there-is-a-growing-gender-wage-gap-in-professional -basketball/#435aea1536e0

Berri, David. 2017c. "Women Are Also Exploited by College Basketball." *Forbes*, (November 5). https://www.forbes.com/sites/davidberri/2017/11/05/women-are-also -exploited-by-college-basketball/#4c9357097848

Berri, David. 2017d. "Some Popular Sports Sites Appear to Cover More Animals than Women." *Forbes*, (November 29). https://www.forbes.com/sites/davidberri/2017/11/29/some-popular-sports-sites-appear-to-cover-more-animals-than-women/#4ff573135466

Berri, David J. 2018a. *Sports Economics*, (May). New York: Worth Publishers/Macmillan Education.

Berri, David J. 2018b. "Who Is the Best Basketball Player Right Now? Learning a Lesson from Boxing." *Forbes*, (June 13). https://www.forbes.com/sites/davidberri/2018/06/13/who-is-the-best-basketball-player-right-now-learning-a-lesson-from-boxing/#d558b8160d52

Berri, David. 2018c. "Mark Cuban Is Wrong About Why WNBA Pay Is So Low." *Huffington Post*, (December 4). https://www.huffingtonpost.com/entry/opinion-mark-cuban-wnba-pay_us_5c05a726e4b0cd916faef969

Berri, David. 2019. "ESPN and College Softball: How Time and Consistent Coverage Can Dramatically Change a Fan Base." *Softball America*, (March 18). https://www.softballamerica.com/stories/espn-and-college-softball-have-dramatically-changed-a-fan-base/

Berri, David. 2020. "Basketball's Gender Wage Gap Narrows (but doesn't vanish!)" *Winsidr*, (February 22). https://winsidr.com/2020/02/12/basketballs-gender-wage-gap-narrows-but-doesnt-vanish/

Berri, David J. and Anthony Krautmann. 2013. "Understanding the WNBA On and Off the Court." In Eva Marikova Leeds and Michael Leeds (eds), *Handbook on the Economics of Women in Sports*. Edward Elgar Publishing, pp. 132–155.

Berri, David and Steve Engst. 2021. "The Economics and Finance of Professional Basketball." In Karen Weaver (ed.), *Sport Finance*. Kendall-Hunt Publishers.

Berri, David J., Martin B. Schmidt, and Stacey L. Brook. 2006. *The Wages of Wins: Taking Measure of the Many Myths in Modern Sport*. Stanford, CA: Stanford University Press.

Berri, David J., Stacey L. Brook, and Aju Fenn. 2011. "From College to the Pros: Predicting the NBA Amateur Player Draft." *Journal of Productivity Analysis*, 35(1): 25–35, February. On-line citation: DOI 10.1007/s11123-010-0187-x.

Berri, David J., Christian Deutscher, and Arturo Galletti. 2015. "Born in the USA: National Origin Effects on Time Allocation in US and Spanish Professional Basketball." for special issue of *National Institute Economic Review*, May. R41–R50.

Blau, Francine D., and Lawrence M. Kahn. 2017. "The Gender Wage Gap: Extent, Trends, and Explanations." *Journal of Economic Literature*, 55(3): 789–865.

Bleiweis, Robin, 2020. "Quick Facts about the Gender Wage Gap." *American Progress*, (March 24). https://www.americanprogress.org/issues/women/reports/2020/03/24/482141/quick-facts-gender-wage-gap/

Bonesteel, Matt. 2018. "Adam Silver: One of the WNBA's Problems is that Not Enough Young Women Pay Attention to It." *Washington Post*, (April 20). https://www.washingtonpost.com/news/early-lead/wp/2018/04/20/adam-silver-one-of-the-wnbas-problems-is-that-not-enough-young-women-pay-attention-to-it/?utm_term=.37dd184f2cc7

Bradbury, John C. 2007. "Does the Baseball Labor Market Properly Value Pitchers?" *Journal of Sports Economics*, 8(6): 616–632, December.

Campbell, Brian. 2020. "Boxing Pound-for-Pound Rankings: Errol Spence Jr. Passes Terence Crawford as Top Welterweight Fighter." *CBS Sports*, (December 21). https://www.cbssports.com/boxing/news/boxing-pound-for-pound-rankings-errol-spence-jr-passes-terence-crawford-as-top-welterweight-fighter/

Cash, Meredith. 2020. "TV ratings for North America's Top Women's Soccer League are up a Whopping 493%. Here's How they Succeeded as Other Sports are Losing Viewers." *Insider*, (October 29). https://www.insider.com/nwsl-viewership-up-493 -percent-despite-sports-ratings-struggles-2020-10

Chevalier, Judy. 2020. "The 2020 Report of the Committee on the Status of Women in the Economics Profession." *American Economic Association*, (December 16). https://www.aeaweb.org/about-aea/committees/cswep/survey/annual-reports

Chicago Booth Review. 2019. "A Climate of Discrimination in Economics." (May 29) https://review.chicagobooth.edu/economics/2019/article/climate-discrimination -economics

Cohen-Zada, D., A. Krumer, O. Shapir, and M. Rosenboim. 2017. "Choking under Pressure and Gender: Evidence from Professional Tennis." *Journal of Economic Psychology*, 61: 176–190.

Coletta, Amanda. 2015. "A League of their Own: The Most Dominant Soccer Team in 1920 was Full of Female Factory Workers." *New York Times*, (June 5).

Cooky, C., M. A. Messner, and M. Musto. 2015. "It's Dude Time!" A Quarter Century of Excluding Women's Sports in Televised News and Highlight Shows." *Communication & Sport*, pp. 1–27.

Cosby, Molly. 2016. "Should Women Go Through Stricter Security Screenings to Enter Sporting Events?" *The Ladies League*, (January 25). https://www.theladiesleague .org/single-post/2016-1-25-should-women-go-through-stricter-security-screenings -to-enter-sporting-events

Darvin, Lindsey, Ann Pegoraro, and David Berri. 2018. "Are Men Better Leaders? An Investigation of Head Coaches' Gender and Individual Players' Performance in Amateur and Professional Women's Basketball." *Sex Roles*, 78(April): 455–466.

DuPree, David. 1983. "NBA: Red Ink and a Bleak Future." *Washington Post*, (March 15). https://www.washingtonpost.com/archive/sports/1983/03/15/nba-red-ink-and-a -bleak-future/198bd65f-4062-4372-95e4-388b22c77666/

Ellentuck, M. 2018. "Liz Cambage Tells us 5 Ways the WNBA is Failing its Players." *SB Nation*, (August 16). https://www.sbnation.com/wnba/2018/8/16/17693052/liz -cambage-interview-wnba-players-problems-fixing

Ewing, Lori. 2018. "After Standout Rookie Season, Nurse Frustrated by Lack of Exposure for WNBA." *The Canadian Press*, (August 31). https://www.cbc.ca/ sports/olympics/kia-nurse-standout-rookie-wnba-season-lost-1.4806930

Fagan, Kate. 2015. "Taurasi to Rest, Skip the WNBA Season." *ESPN.com*, (February 3). https://www.espn.com/wnba/story/_/id/12272047/diana-taurasi-opts-sit-2015 -wnba-season

Feinberg, Doug. 2018. "WNBA Crossroads: League Looks to Cut Losses, Hire President." *USA Today*, (December 28). https://www.usatoday.com/story/sports/ wnba/2018/12/28/wnba-looks-for-new-president-profitability-in-2019/38809289/

FIFA. 2020. "The World Hails Record-Setting Sinclair." January 30. https://www.fifa .com/womens-football/news/the-world-hails-record-setting-sinclair

Fine, Cordelia. 2011. *Delusions of Gender*. WW Norton.

Friedman, Milton. 1977. "The Invisible Hand." In *The Business System: A Bicentennial View*, pp. 2–13. Hanover, New Hampshire: Amos Tuck School of Business Administration.

Giddings, Lisa A. and Michael Haupert. 2019. "Earning Like a Woman: Salaries versus Marginal Revenue Products in the AAGBPL and MLB: 1947–1952." *Journal of Sports Economics*, 20(2): 198–217.

Harris, Jill and David Berri. 2015. "Predicting the WNBA Draft: What Matters Most From College Performance." *International Journal of Sport Finance*, 10 (November): 299–309.

Harris, Jill and David Berri. 2016. "If You Can't Pay Them, Play Them: Fan Preference and Own-Race Bias in the WNBA." *International Journal of Sport Finance*, 11 (August): 163–180.

Heilbroner, Robert. 1992. *The Worldly Philosophers*, 6th edn. Touchstone.

Hess, Abigail Johnson. 2019. "US Viewership of the 2019 Women's World Cup Final was 22% Higher than the 2018 Men's Final." *CNBC.com*, (July 10). https://www .cnbc.com/2019/07/10/us-viewership-of-the-womens-world-cup-final-was-higher -than-the-mens.html

Hult, Joan S. and Marianna Trekell (eds). 1991. *A Century of Women's Basketball: From Frailty to Final Four*. Reston, VA: AAHPERD Publications.

Jones, Jeffrey. 2015. "As Industry Grows, Percentage of U.S. Sports Fans Steady." *Gallup Marketplace*, (June 17). https://news.gallup.com/poll/183689/industry -grows-percentage-sports-fans-steady.aspx

Killion, Ann. 2018. "College Football's Title Game Largely Run by Woman." *San Francisco Chronicle*, (November 23) https://www.sfchronicle.com/sports/ annkillion/article/College-football-s-title-game-largely-run-by-13417462.php

Kravitz, Bob. 2019. "In his Own Words: Pacers Owner Herb Simon Discusses his Team, Arena Upgrades, State of the NBA and More." *The Athletic*, (May 8). https:// theathletic.com/968170/2019/05/08/in-his-own-words-pacers-owner-herb-simon -discusses-his-team-arena-renovations-state-of-the-nba-and-more/

Lee, Mackenzi. 2018. *Bygone Badass Broads*. Abrams the Art of Books.

Leeds, Michael, Peter von Allmen, and Victor Matheson. 2018. *Economics of Sports*, 6th edn. Routledge.

Lennon, Tiffani. 2013. *Benchmarking Women's Leadership in the United States*. University of Denver – Colorado Women's College.

Mansky, Jackie and Maya Wei-Haas. 2016. "The Rise of the Modern Sportswoman: Women Have Long Fought Against the Assumption that they are Weaker than Men, and the Battle Isn't Over Yet." *Smithsonian Magazine*, (August 18). https://www .smithsonianmag.com/science-nature/rise-modern-sportswoman-180960174/

Marcal, Katrine. 2016. *Who Cooked Adam Smith's Dinner: A Story of Women and Economics*. Pegasus Books.

Mather, Victor. 2017. "Madison Square Garden is Seeking to Sell the Liberty." *New York Times*, (November 14), https://www.nytimes.com/2017/11/14/sports/ basketball/madison-square-garden-liberty.html

McCracken, Voros. 2001. "Pitching and Defense: How Much Control do Hurlers Have?" *Baseball Prospectus*, (January 23). https://www.baseballprospectus.com/ news/article/878/pitching-and-defense-how-much-control-do-hurlers-have/

Metcalfe, Jeff. 2019. "WNBA star Breanna Stewart to Miss Season after Achilles Injury in EuroLeague Championship." *AZCentral.com*, (April 16). https://www .azcentral.com/story/sports/wnba/mercury/2019/04/14/breanna-stewart-injury-have -major-impact-wnba-cba-talks/3470025002/

Moran, Eddie. 2019. "First Half Viewership Spike Has WNBA Optimistic About 2019 And Beyond." *Front Office Sports*, (August 2). https://frontofficesports.com/wnba -viewership-growth/

National Collegiate Athletic Association. 2021. "NCAA Sports Sponsorship and Participation Rates Database." https://www.ncaa.org/about/resources/research/ncaa -sports-sponsorship-and-participation-rates-database

National Federation of State High School Associations (NFHS). 2021. "Participation Statistics." https://members.nfhs.org/participation_statistics

Negley, Cassandra. 2020. "WNBA Average Viewership Grows 68 Percent During a Season Focused on Social Justice." *Yahoo! Sports*, (October 1). https://sports.yahoo.com/wnba-average-viewership-up-68-percent-national-tv-windows-marketing-growth-210452911.html

Nwulu, Mac. 2019. "MLS on ESPN Scores Viewership Increase for 2019 Regular Season." *ESPN.com*, (October 8). https://espnpressroom.com/us/press-releases/2019/10/mls-on-espn-scores-viewership-increase-for-2019-regular-season/

Ourand, J. 2016. "ESPN's New Deal Double Rights Fee." *Sports Business Journal*, (May 9). https://www.sportsbusinessdaily.com/Journal/Issues/2016/05/09/Media/ESPN-WNBA.aspx

Parkinson, Nick. 2020. "Forbes 2020: Fury, Wilder, Joshua Make Top 20 to Highlight Dominance of Heavyweight Boxing". *ESPN.com*, (June 22). https://www.espn.com/boxing/story/_/id/29333644/forbes-2020-fury-wilder-joshua-make-top-20-highlight-dominance-heavyweight-boxing

Peach, Jim. 2007. "College Athletics, Universities, and the NCAA." *The Social Science Journal*, 44: 11–22.

Porter, Catherine and Danila Serra. 2017. "Gender Differences in Choice of Major: The Importance of Female Role Models." December, Southern Methodist University, Department of Economics Departmental Working Papers 1705.

Pugh, William. 2020. "THE LONG RON Top 10 International Goal Scorers of All Time with Cristiano Ronaldo just Eight off Top Spot." *The Sun*, (September 9). https://www.thesun.co.uk/sport/12622460/top-international-goal-scorers-cristiano-ronaldo/

Rafael, Dan. 2015. "Floyd Mayweather beats Manny Pacquiao in Unanimous Decision." *ESPN.com*, (May 2). https://www.espn.com/boxing/story/_/id/12810858/floyd-mayweather-defeats-manny-pacquiao-unanimous-decision

Ranard, Chelsey. 2018. "The Challenges of Being a Female Sports Fan Despite Making Up a Large Percentage of Fans." *GirlTalkHQ*, (June 12). https://girltalkhq.com/the-challenges-of-being-a-female-sports-fan-despite-making-up-a-large-percentage-of-fans/

Raviprakash, Suhas, Izzy Wray, Paul Lee, and Kevin Westcott. 2020. "Women's Sports Gets Down to Business: On Track for Rising Monetization." *Deloitte Insights*, (December 7). https://www2.deloitte.com/us/en/insights/industry/technology/technology-media-and-telecom-predictions/2021/womens-sports-revenue.html

Ring, Jennifer. 2009. *Stolen Bases: Why American Girls Don't Play Baseball*. University of Illinois Press.

Schultz, Jaime. 2018. *Women's Sports: What Everyone Needs to Know*. Oxford University Press.

Shelton, Sandi Kahn. 2017. "Fierce Sexism Kept Female Swimmer Out of Olympics Until 100 Years Ago." *New Haven Register*, (July 27). https://www.nhregister.com/news/article/Fierce-sexism-kept-female-swimmers-out-of-11542472.php

Stevenson, Betsey and Hanna Zlotnik. 2018. "Representations of Men and Women in Introductory Economics Textbooks." *AEA Papers and Proceedings*, 108: 180–185.

Surdam, D. 2012. *The Rise of the National Basketball Association*. University of Illinois Press.

Toma, Mattie. 2017. "Missed Shots at the Free-Throw Line: Analyzing the Determinants of Choking Under Pressure." *Journal of Sports Economics*, 18(6): 539–559.

TooFab Staff. 2020. "Candace Parker Tells Steve Harvey WNBA Players Make '10–20 Times More' Overseas." *TooFab*, (February 3). https://toofab.com/2020/02/03/candace-parker-steve-harvey-wnba-pay-gap/

Treber, Jaret, Rachel Levy, and Victor Matheson. 2013. "Gender Differences in Competitive Balance in Intercollegiate Basketball." In Eva Marikova Leeds and Michael Leeds (eds), *Handbook on the Economics of Women in Sports*. Edward Elgar Publishing, pp. 251–268.

Veblen, Thorstein. 1899. *The Theory of the Leisure Class*: *An Economic Study in the Evolution of Institutions*. https://www.semanticscholar.org/paper/The-Theory-of-the-Leisure-Class-Veblen/4c50f78fc5cd078c3c8dee0b57f9ed0d3863ccea

Von Allmen, Peter. 2013. "Coaching Women and Women Coaching: Pay Differentials in the Title IX Era." In Eva Marikova Leeds and Michael Leeds (eds), *Handbook on the Economics of Women in Sports*. Edward Elgar Publishing, pp. 269–289.

Wealthsimple. 2018. "Skylar Diggins-Smith Wants to be Paid like a Man and Isn't Afraid to Say It." *Wealthsimple*, (August 21). https://www.wealthsimple.com/en-us/magazine/skylar-diggins-smith

Windhorst, Brian and Zach Lowe. 2017. "A Confidential Report Shows Nearly Half the NBA Lost Money Last Season. Now What?" *ESPN.com*, (September 19). https://www.espn.com/nba/story/_/id/20747413/a-confidential-report-shows-nearly-half-nba-lost-money-last-season-now-what

Wojnarowski, Adrian. 2017. "Stephen Curry's Supermax Deal Becomes Richest in NBA History." *ESPN.com*, (June 30). https://www.espn.com/nba/story/_/id/19779626/golden-state-warriors-star-stephen-curry-inks-super-max-contract-five-years-201-million

Women's Media Center. 2019. "The Status of Women in the U.S. Media 2019." https://womensmediacenter.com/reports/the-status-of-women-in-u-s-media-2019

Young, Jabari. 2020. "Major League Soccer has a 25-year Plan, but it Needs to Secure Huge Media Deals First." *CNBC.com*, (February 27). https://www.cnbc.com/2020/02/27/major-league-soccer-has-a-25-year-plan-but-it-needs-to-secure-huge-media-deals-first.html

Zimbalist, A. 2001. *Unpaid Professionals*. Princeton University Press.

9. Incorporating media into the sports economics curriculum

Jadrian Wooten

MOTIVATION

The use of media in the classroom has increased significantly over the past decade as hosting costs have decreased and the number of streaming services has increased. Early research on the use of media in the classroom focused on identifying clips in movies and then highlighting their connection to the curriculum. Today, much of the work on integrating media in the classroom takes one of two approaches. The broad approach to using media in the classroom is to integrate clips from a wide variety of sources, but to do so in short segments, typically less than three minutes long.

For example, in the hit television show *The Big Bang Theory*, Leonard stops by his neighbor's apartment after a Nebraska football game watch party. His neighbor claims the party went well because "their team" had won. Leonard is quick to point out how strange it is for people to say "we won" when they weren't actually part of the game. Basking in reflected glory (BIRG) is a common practice among sports fans whose emotions are tied with the performance of their team. Even though Leonard doesn't reference the concept by its academic term, it is a clear application of the concept. The entire clip is only 18 seconds long and can be embedded in a slide deck or streamed directly from the website Bazinganomics.com (Tierney et al. 2016).

Short clips can be used at the start of a lesson or as part of a review session before an exam. These clips can be embedded in course learning management systems and tied to a quiz or a discussion board. The versatility of media is their main attraction. It's up to the instructor to determine the best approach to using the clip relative to their teaching style; because the media clip is so short, it can often be used in a variety of ways.

The second use of media in the classroom takes a narrower approach. This stream of research identifies media to teach a specific topic. The media in question is often much longer, typically entire episodes of television shows or full-length films. If a section of the course were dedicated to teaching marginal revenue product, instructors may show the entirety of the film *Moneyball* rather than specific clips. Because the film is over 2 hours long, it requires faculty to be creative in how this is achieved. Instructors could break the film into multiple parts and show each part during class, assign the film for students to watch on their own time, or reserve a classroom for one night and require student attendance.

The goal of any media is to complement the concept being taught, but the integration process varies. Educators wanting a more engaging way to teach have a variety of ways to use media, either as a whole or in parts. Both approaches use media, but how the instructor will use media depends on several factors, including course design, teaching style, and time constraints.

SUPPORT FOR USING MEDIA

Media can be used as a component of a variety of active learning techniques that have garnered more attention over the past decade (Lang 2016; Agarwal and Bain 2019). The types of media available to educators, outlined below, can be as varied as film and television clips, music videos, podcasts, popular press books, or news articles (Wooten et al. 2021; Picault 2019). The general use of media is often associated with visual media, but each section below outlines techniques for incorporating different media sources as well.

Media can be used to enhance learning both in the classroom and as a component of out-of-class work. The key is recognizing its ability to enhance learning and classroom dynamics rather than as an additional component of an already designed course (Al-Bahrani et al. 2016). Presenting additional material to students doesn't necessarily imply additional learning will occur. Instructors focused on reducing students' cognitive overload can increase learning (Clark, Nguyen, and Sweller 2011). Reducing cognitive load doesn't necessarily mean that instructors need to reduce the workload associated with their class. Consideration for *how*, rather than *how much*, material is taught can reduce cognitive overload. Instructors can reduce cognitive overload by explicitly organizing lectures, building on students' prior knowledge, and identifying connections among topics throughout a lecture. Media allows an instructor to present a more complex topic in a different way that better resonates with students.

Another key insight from learning science that can be achieved with media comes from the novelty that media provides. Willingham (2009) provides a compelling justification for media use in the classroom when he asks, "Why do students remember everything that's on television and forget what we lecture?" Educational psychologists and researchers have suggested for decades that different forms of media can aid student learning of abstract concepts through verbal and visual forms (Salomon 1979) and create a learning environment that extends the possibilities for educators to introduce interactive learning to more traditional lectures (Bransford, Browning, and Cocking 1999).

CONCERNS WHEN USING MEDIA

Media should be used to enhance and supplement course content, not serve as a replacement for teaching. Think back to grade school when a teacher may have put on a movie instead of teaching for the day. Even if the movie was relevant to the course, if it wasn't integrated with the course content, the movie was more for entertainment purposes rather than education. When selecting media, it's important to ensure that its content helps instructors achieve course learning objectives.

Instructors are often nervous regarding copyright concerns when using media. Media producers emphasize their copyright power at the start of many of their programs, even if not entirely accurately about the legal ways their programs can be reproduced. The use of digital media during class often falls under the fair use exemption in the Federal Copyright Act under most circumstances, even when showing an entire film. The key distinction is the purpose of the showing, which protects educators who show media for educational purposes. Faculty concerned with copyright issues can often work with librarians to handle concerns.

Some media usage may require additional work on the part of faculty, but that burden has progressively decreased as more media is available online and classroom facilities are better equipped for displaying media. The most common concern is ensuring the audio-visual equipment is functional before playing any media. Beyond the additional technical work, instructors may need to explain relevant background information around the scene to ensure students focus on the content of the segment. For example, showing a clip from *The Daily Show* may benefit from a few minutes of explaining satire, especially if a significant portion of the class comprises international students. Instructors must also consider whether the media contains objectionable content and weigh the cost and benefits of using such media.

Most media sources include captioning or transcripts for students and should be provided to students regardless of whether they require academic accommodations. It requires some forethought to ensure captioning is turned on for movies or television shows, but for older scenes, captioning may need to be added. Providing links to the media sources in a course management system is encouraged so that students can review the material at another time, especially if the content is part of a formal assessment. Many universities have instructional designers who can help with captioning and hosting concerns.

WAYS TO USE MEDIA IN YOUR CLASSROOM

There are a variety of active learning methods for using media in the classroom, many of which have been written about in peer-reviewed research or synthesized in pedagogy books. Instructors looking for techniques specific to economics are encouraged to visit *The Journal of Economic Education, Journal for Economic Educators*, or *Journal of Economics Teaching*. For a broader approach to teaching, check out the work of James Lang in *Small Teaching* or his work with Flower Darby in *Small Teaching Online*.

Introducing a Concept or Generating Discussion

Introducing difficult or confusing concepts with media can put students at ease with the material or help transition to difficult concepts, even if it isn't connected to an assessment. A brief clip, such as that from *The Big Bang Theory* mentioned previously, could be used to introduce the lesson and doesn't require any graded component. If possible, instructors should embed the file into their slide deck for an easy transition between material. If an instructor spends most of their time without slides or uses PDF slides, it may be awkward to switch to an internet stream for such a short clip.

Difficult concepts benefit from media usage as well. For example, calculating the expected costs and benefits of fourth down conversions may be so mathematically advanced that it could overwhelm some students. Using a scene from *Young Sheldon* (discussed below) provides a brief introduction of a difficult concept so that students can acclimate themselves to the pending lesson. No assessment needs to be attached the clip if it's used as an introduction.

Controversial topics may benefit from media when instructors want to present both sides of the argument. For example, whether to pay college athletes has merits on both sides, but an instructor teaching the material may reveal their bias in the way they frame arguments. Allowing a media source, such as a podcast or film clip, to present the arguments may come across more neutral and won't inadvertently introduce instructor bias into the discussion. If media has incorrect information, which can happen, instructors can use it to start a discussion related to the problems in their analysis.

Prompting a Poll Question

One of the primary tools of learning science has been improving retrieval methods. Broadly speaking, there are two ways of improving learning through strategic design: spaced repetition and scaffolding. Using poll questions, often with the aid of a classroom response system is an effective way of asking students to retrieve prior knowledge (Calhoun and Mateer 2011; Wooten, Acchiardo, and Mateer 2020). Media can be used with summative assessments by showing a particular clip and asking students to apply previously learned content to the particular clip. By spacing the time between when the material is learned and when students need to retrieve the material, faculty can improve student learning (Chew and Cerbin 2020).

Scaffolding occurs when students are asked to build on prior knowledge. It's much easier to learn new material if students already have some knowledge about the material. By reviewing prior material, students benefit from spaced retrieval, but if that information is then used as an introduction to the next lesson, they also benefit from scaffolding. Combining these can be difficult with clips that are only a few minutes long since there may not be much to review, but instructors can still ask students to predict outcomes. The Carl Wieman Science Education Initiative (2017) has published a Clicker Resource Guide that outlines effective use of classroom response systems.

Segmenting Media

The above approaches are relatively straightforward when video segments are short (2–3 minutes) and can be easily played in class without the fear of students losing attention. There are clips, however, that contain a rich amount of content, and last longer. These media sources may benefit from segmentation, which takes longer clips and breaks them into shorter clips to account for limited attention spans and as a way to weave discussion questions between segments (Wooten 2020). This approach allows some of the benefits of spaced practice, albeit very closely spaced, coupled with creating cliffhangers to keep students engaged.

For longer video clips or podcasts, faculty identify natural break points and use software to clip the files into segments. This can be done using the latest version of PowerPoint for both Windows and Mac, but other software, such as Camtasia and iMovie, also have clipping capabilities. The less technical version of this approach would require a faculty member to simply pause the media source at predetermined intervals. This process turns a longer clip into a series of four to eight shorter clips that have assessment questions in between.

Problem Sets and Quizzes

The simplest way to assess student understanding of content is to assign media and ask students to summarize the results. Depending on the context and length of media, it could be used as a theme for a series of a questions. This approach, however, has limitations when the media is longer, particularly trade books or film. The assessment approach for these will depend on the structure of the course, the learning objectives, and the comfort level of the instructor.

One way to assess student understanding of longer media sources is through "read along" sheets that require students to answer questions scattered throughout the source. Students are assigned a set of questions that are similar across the class or they could be assigned unique sheets using a free cloud-based program known as Create Random Assignments (Wooten and Smith 2018). The questions could be shuffled or presented chronologically, and a student would answer questions as they progress through media.

Another way of assessing comprehension is with Monte Carlo Quizzes (Fernald 2004). Students are assigned various media sources each week and a set of possible questions that could be asked of each source. On quiz day, a die is rolled multiple times to determine the quiz topic for the day. Because the quiz outcome is random, students are encouraged to prepare for all possible questions and can then use their prepared responses for the quiz. Question types typically focus on summary, application, or critiques of the media source.

Writing Op-Eds

If writing is a major component of the course, students may benefit from a shift away from a traditional term paper. Hall and Podemska-Mikluch (2015) outline the use of op-ed articles to address the economic way of thinking and to do so in a way that is different from the traditional approach of requiring students to share their opinion through an online discussion board. While many argue that writing is too time-intensive on the grading aspect, there are a variety of ways to mitigate these concerns. Mahalingam (2013) argues that improvements in technology have made assessing writing easier, while Trautman et al. (2003) argue that peer writing can alleviate many of the issues.

Hall and Podemska-Mikluch argue that op-eds are an effective use of time because they require students to carefully consider their argument given space constraints. Students are allowed to write about topics of interest to them and this allows them to be active members of civil society. The op-eds are typically 550–750 words in length, which allows an instructor to provide more feedback compared with traditional term papers. Because the topics are usually policy based, students can present their research on topics as varied as paying college athletes, stadium subsidies, or ticket reselling. Students are encouraged to submit their articles to local newspapers at the end of the semester.

Designing a Course around Media

The above approaches are ways to add media into a classroom or into current assessments, but it focuses on instructors looking to make marginal changes.

An instructor may want to design an entire course that has media as the focal point (Vidal, Mungenast, and Vidal 2020). This approach takes the deliberate nature of film as the basis for engaging students with specific content. Given the vast amount of content available through ESPN's *30 for 30* (Al-Bahrani and Patel 2015), as well as movies such as *SonicsGate* and *Moneyball*, there are a sufficient number of sources such that an entire course could be designed without much searching.

Rather than applying media to various topics, the topics are selected based on the media available. Students watch some films on their own and have class discussion the following period. If the course is taught as an evening course, the film could be shown in the first half of class with a discussion to follow. The same assessment methods presented above could also be applied to a course centered on media as well.

POPULAR MEDIA READY TO USE

The following sections provide a brief look at resources that are available online and ready to implement in the classroom now. The options below are available at no cost to the instructor and can often be downloaded from the sites where the source is hosted. For visual media, captioning is often already included. Because these resources are available online, they continue to grow as new media are identified. Check out Economics Media Library (Wooten 2018) and The Economics Instructor's Toolbox (Picault 2021) for new additions.[1]

Television Shows

There are a variety of websites dedicated to hosting segments of television shows online, but there are also several academic papers that identify time stamps of relevant content available on popular streaming platforms. The benefit of using segments from television shows is that they are often short and do not take up a large portion of class time. Television scenes can be used effectively to introduce topics and as the basis for problem sets or polling questions. It would be difficult to create an entire class around television show segments, but longer clips could be segmented, and discussion added between scenes. The following are just a few of my favorite scenes for teaching sports economics.[2]

In a scene from *The Big Bang Theory* spinoff, *Young Sheldon*, the Cooper family sits around the television watching a Texas A&M football game.[3] Sheldon's dad is a football coach at the local high school and his brother plays for the team as well. A fourth down comes up and the family, sans Sheldon, comments how it's time to punt. Sheldon points out that always punting on fourth down doesn't make sense. He goes on to explain the basis of Romer (2006) that shows teams should consider the likelihood of success on fourth down relative to how often the opposing team scores from various parts of the field.

The hot hand fallacy and gambler's fallacy play a prominent role in decision making in sports, but also outside of the field of play. Even shows like *Modern Family*, which isn't primarily focused on sports can be used to teach sports economics (Wooten, Staub, and Reilly 2020). Cam coaches the local high school football team, and we see a progression of superstitions he's developed over the years.[4] Whether it's eating a particular meal for breakfast or stubbing his toe on the coffee table, Cam believes in the process. The behavioral aspect of addiction and superstitions can be seen in everything from a basketball player who appears to be on a hot streak to a gambler avoiding particular machines in a casino.

Adam Ruins Everything is a half-hour informational comedy television show that attempts to debunk common misperceptions surrounding a wide range of topics and includes a significant amount of content that can be used in the classroom (Wooten & Tierney 2019). There are multiple episodes that contain content relevant to the sports economics curriculum. In "Adam Ruins Games," the host discusses the economic impact (or lack thereof) from hosting the Olympics. In "Adam Ruins Football," he focuses on how the winners of playoff systems in American sports systems aren't actually indicative of the best team in their sport.[5]

The Simpsons has a vast number of scenes that can be used to teach economics (Hall 2005, 2014; Luccasen and Thomas 2010), particularly sports economics. In "MoneyBART," Lisa uses her knowledge of statistics to coach the little league team to a winning record, à la *Moneyball*. Bart is upset and accuses Lisa of taking the fun out of the game. In "Homer Loves Flanders," Homer waits in line eight days to buy tickets for a concert, only to lose out to a scalper who buys them all before he gets his chance. This scene is engaging for a discussion of ticket pricing strategies and whether it's in the team's best interest to sell tickets at lower prices to ensure sell outs.[6]

Film and Documentaries

The use of film and documentaries to teach topics in sports economics is significantly deeper than references in television shows. The pre-eminent sports documentary series, *ESPN 30 for 30*, contains a wide variety of relevant scenes to teach economics (Al-Bahrani and Patel, 2015 and Chapter 3 of this book), but a few episodes are more relevant to the standard sports economics curriculum. The third episode in the series, *Small Potatoes: Who Killed the USFL*, looks at the formation of the United States Football League (USFL) as a rival to the National Football League. The league initially competed as a spring football league and was able to sign three straight Heisman winners. The 12-team league played in front of respectable crowds and had generally favorable television ratings until overexpansion doomed the league.

The 30th episode of the series, *Pony Excess*, looks at the cartel behavior of the NCAA and how a small private school in the Dallas suburbs would end up receiving the NCAA's "death penalty." This episode is an appealing addition to the debate on paying college athletes and the incentive structure of the NCAA. The popularity of the initial series resulted in ESPN producing 157 different episodes around various sports issues and famous stories. Other popular ESPN documentary series, such as *Outside the Lines*, can also be used in the classroom.[7] There is likely a documentary about a regionally specific topic, either from ESPN or independent producers, which would match student interest and can be integrated into the course.[8]

The most popular sports film for teaching economics is likely *Moneyball*, the story of the Oakland A's quest to use statistical analysis to win baseball games. Economic educators have endorsed the film for teaching economics (Mateer, O'Roark, and Holder 2016) and have created projects and simulators for teaching with the film or book (Wooten and White 2018). The most common use of the overall concept is in valuing the contribution of players and employees based on the value of their productivity.[9]

Another feature-film that can be used when teaching the labor component of sports economics is *Battle of the Sexes*, which looks at the historic 1973 tennis match between Billie Jean King and Bobby Riggs. The "Press Release" scene looks at the pay discrepancy between men's and women's sports.[10] The tournament promoter argues that men are paid more because they are stronger and faster and must be paid more from an opportunity cost standpoint. King (played by Emma Stone) argues instead that players should be paid based on their marginal revenue product.

News Sources

Newspapers and television news stations regularly devote a significant portion of their coverage to regional sports teams. Regional coverage could include key topics related to the sports curriculum, such as player pay, government subsidies for stadiums, or relocation concerns.[11] These segments may be short interviews with team executives or interviews with researchers who focus on sports-related issues.[12] Longer publications, such as those in *The Atlantic*, *Sports Illustrated*, or *The Economist* could also be assigned as part of weekly readings.

The Retro Report is a series of short documentaries produced by *The New York Times* over a variety of historical events.[13] In "Rebel Without a Clause," journalists investigate the impact of Curt Flood's 1972 Supreme Court case against Major League Baseball, which would eventually lead to the end of the reserve clause and the beginning of free agency. In "Picking a Winner: The 1998 N.F.L. Draft," reporters look at the difficulty in selecting the first pick of the 1998 Draft, which focused on the choice of Peyton Manning or Ryan Leaf. Leaf would go on to be considered one of the biggest busts in NFL history, while Manning would play for 18 seasons, win two Super Bowls, and was inducted into the NFL's Hall of Fame in 2021.

Podcasts

Podcasts bridge the gap between traditional journalism and storytelling found in television and film. They have also been used as a major component of teaching economics because of their engaging storylines (Moryl 2013). The range of podcasts available span the political spectrum, but also vary considerably by depth of content. AudioEcon[14] is a website dedicated to categorizing major podcasts by economic topic and includes a few podcasts specifically dedicated to sports economics (Moryl 2014).

EconTalk[15] is a podcast series hosted by Russ Roberts that focuses on interviews with a single guest, often economists, on various topics (Hall 2012). Because the focus tends to be based on the guest's research experience, there are particular episodes that are relevant to sports economics. Roger Noll was a guest in 2012 and Michael Lewis joined as a guest in 2007 to discuss *Moneyball*. Sports-related topics from various guests include the hot hand fallacy with Ben Cohen and sports subsidies with Skip Sauer.

Freakonomics[16] may be the most famous podcast series and blog site within the pop culture realm of economics. On the podcast side of their enterprise, they discuss sports-related topics as varied as the impact of beer sales on attendance (Episode 91) and sports gambling (Episode 388). Freakonomics Radio also created a special series known as "The Hidden Side of Sports" which looks more closely at how sports developed such a commanding presence in our lives. Several of these episodes feature discussions with Victor Matheson, co-editor of this book on teaching sports economics.

Trade Books

The last way to incorporate popular media into the classroom is through traditional print media. While *Moneyball* is often closely linked with sports economics, the print version of the story had a heavier focus on the player stories than on sabermetrics. Since the release of *Freakonomics*, the market for popular press books has grown tremendously and three additional books were published in the series.[17] In *Freakonomics*, Levitt and Dubner (2006) use sports as an example of incentive problems when summarizing corruption in sumo wrestling matches.[18] Levitt and Dubner (2014) investigate the behavioral decision and incentives of taking penalty kicks in the first chapter of *Think Like a Freak.*[19]

A few popular press books written in the same style as *Freakonomics*, but focused more on sports, include *Scorecasting, Soccernomics,* and *Stumbling on Wins.* In *Scorecasting,* Moskowitz and Wertheim (2011) look at various behavioral issues in sports economics including fourth down conversions, the hot hand fallacy, and statistical discrimination in the hiring of coaches. In *Soccernomics,* Kuper and Szymanski (2018) mix business, economics, and psychology to investigate topics in soccer at various levels of the sport. In *Stumbling on Wins,* Berri and Schmidt (2010) take a *Moneyball*-like approach to various sports including basketball and football. The authors evaluate the behavior of coaches and general managers to see if their decisions are supported by the data.

Other strong contenders for sports-themed economics books that can be used in the classroom include *15 Sports Myths and Why They're Wrong, Field of Schemes, United States of Soccer, The Q Factor, AstroBall,* and *The Numbers Game.* One benefit of using popular press books in the classroom, as opposed to journal articles, is their simplification regarding much of the empirical process. The books are written for a wide audience, which mirror sports economics classrooms. Depending on the prerequisites for the course, the student composition may be varied enough that reading an academic article may be overwhelming. The last benefit is one of cost concerns. Traditional textbooks can be prohibitively expensive, but many trade publications sell for under $20.

FINAL THOUGHTS

The availability of resources and the ways in which media can be used in the classroom can be daunting at first. The multitude of ways media can be used, and used effectively to increase learning, means that a faculty member only needs to identify the media source they are most comfortable using. Just because one method works well in one class, or with one instructor, doesn't mean it's a panacea that works in every other classroom. The methods of learning science (scaffolding, spaced repetition, retrieval exercises, reducing cognitive load) can be applied to any course, but the ways to do those things vary.

If an instructor doesn't like reading, it may not be a good idea to assign popular press books in class, no matter how closely it aligns with the content of the course. Engaged instructors who are using the tools correctly will have a bigger impact on student learning than a disengaged instructor who understands the research. It's relatively easy to be engaging on the first day of the course (Acchiardo and Mateer 2014) but using media in the classroom can be a method of staying engaged throughout the entire term.

NOTES

1. Economics Media Library can be accessed at www.EconMediaLibrary.com and The Economics Instructor's Toolbox at www.theecontoolbox.com.
2. Other scenes that almost made this section include a scene in *Brooklyn 99* where Captain Holt shares that his favorite movie is *Moneyball* because the statistical analysis is so beautiful and a scene in *Parks and Recreation* where NBA players are hired at 75% of their original salary by a local entertainment conglomerate because the NBA players are currently on strike and have nothing else to do (Wooten and Staub 2019).
3. This scene can be found on the Economics Media Library (http://EconMediaLibrary .com).
4. This scene can be found on Economics of Modern Family (http://ModernFamilyEcon .com).
5. He opens with the episode with the same observation as Leonard from *The Big Bang Theory* by questioning why sports fans are so attached to their team's performance.
6. Both scenes can be found on Economics Media Library (http://EconMediaLibrary .com).
7. The Economics Media Library contains an older segment from the show focused on racism in association football (soccer).
8. *SonicsGate* which chronicles the history of the Seattle SuperSonics and their relocation to Oklahoma City, was a popular addition to a sports economics course taught at Washington State University.
9. Scenes from *Moneyball* can be found on the Teaching Economics with Moneyball (https://www.moneyballsimulator.info/).
10. This scene can be found on the Economics Media Library (http://EconMediaLibrary .com).
11. The Economics Media Library (http://EconMediaLibrary.com) includes a few segments of news clips airing interviews of team executives threatening to leave cities if they don't receive subsidies for a new stadium.
12. Reason TV and John Stossel have both interviewed prominent economists for segments on their shows about topics surrounding sports economics.
13. All of the documentaries are available at https://retroreport.org/ and sports has its own unique filter.
14. https://audioecon.com/
15. https://www.econtalk.org/
16. freakonomics.com/sports/
17. *Freakonomics* has also been adapted to a full-length movie.
18. The work is based on Duggan and Levitt (2002).
19. The work is based on Chiappori, Levitt, and Groseclose (2002).

REFERENCES

Acchiardo, C., & Mateer, G. (2014). First Impressions: Why the First Day Matters. *Perspectives on Economic Education Research*, *9*(2), 1–9.

Agarwal, P., & Bain, P. (2019). *Powerful Teaching: Unleash the Science of Learning.* Hoboken, NJ: John Wiley & Sons.

Al-Bahrani, A., & Patel, D. (2015). Using *ESPN 30 for 30* to Teach Economics. *Southern Economic Journal*, *81*(3), 829–842.

Al-Bahrani, A., Holder, K., Patel, D., & Wooten, J. (2016). Art of Econ: Incorporating the Arts through Active Learning Assignments in Principles Courses. *Journal of Economics and Finance Education, 15*(2), 1–17.

Berri, D., & Schmidt, M. (2010). *Stumbling on Wins: Two Economists Expose the Pitfalls on the Road to Victory in Professional Sports.* Upper Saddle River: Financial Times Press.

Bransford, J., Brown, A., & Cocking, R. (Eds.) (1999). *How People Learn: Brain, Mind, Experience, and School.* Washington, DC: National Academy Press.

Calhoun, J., & Mateer, D. (2011). Incorporating Media and Response Systems in the Economics Classroom. In G. Hoyt and K. McGoldrick (Eds.), *International Handbook on Teaching and Learning Economics.* Cheltenham, UK and Northampton, MA, USA: Edward Elgar Publishing.

Carl Wieman Science Education Initiative. (2017). *Clicker Resource Guide: An Instructors Guide to the Effective Use of Personal Response Systems (Clickers) in Teaching.* Vancouver: University of British Columbia.

Chew, S., & Cerbin, W. (2020). The Cognitive Challenges of Effective Teaching. *The Journal of Economic Education*, *52*(1), 17–40.

Chiappori, P., Levitt, S., & Groseclose, T. (2002). Testing Mixed-Strategy Equilibria When Players are Heterogeneous: The Case of Penalty Kicks in Soccer. *American Economic Review*, *92*(4), 1138–1151.

Clark, R., Nguyen, F., & Sweller, J. (2011). *Efficiency in Learning: Evidence-Based Guidelines to Manage Cognitive Load.* Hoboken, NJ: John Wiley & Sons.

Duggan, M., & Levitt, S. (2002). Winning Isn't Everything: Corruption in Sumo Wrestling. *American Economic Review*, *92*(5), 1594–1605.

Fernald, P. (2004). The Monte Carlo Quiz: Encouraging Punctual Completion and Deep Processing of Assigned Readings. *College Teaching*, *52*(3), 95–99.

Hall, J. (2005). Homer Economicus: Using the Simpsons to Teach Economics. *Journal of Private Enterprise*, *20*(2), 165–76.

Hall, J. (2012). Incorporating EconTalk Podcasts into the Principles Classroom. *Journal of Private Enterprise*, *28*(1), 113–118.

Hall, J. (Ed.). (2014). *Homer Economicus: The Simpsons and Economics.* Palo Alto, CA: Stanford University Press.

Hall, J., & Podemska-Mikluch, M. (2015). Teaching the Economic Way of Thinking Through Op-Eds. *International Review of Economics Education*, *19*, 13–21.

Kuper, S., & Szymanski, S. (2018). *Soccernomics: Why England Loses, Why Germany and Brazil Win, and Why the US, Japan, Australia, Turkey – and Even Iraq – are Destined to Become the Kings of the World's Most Popular Sport.* London: Hachette UK.

Lang, J. (2016). *Small Teaching: Everyday Lessons from the Science of Learning.* Hoboken, NJ: John Wiley & Sons.

Levitt, S., & Dubner, S. (2006). *Freakonomics: A Rogue Economist Explores the Hidden Side of Everything.* New York: William Morrow.

Levitt, S., & Dubner, S. (2014). *Think Like a Freak: How to Think Smarter about Almost Everything.* New York: William Morrow.

Luccasen, R., & Thomas, M. (2010). Simpsonomics: Teaching Economics Using Episodes of *The Simpsons. The Journal of Economic Education, 41*(2), 136–149.

Mahalingam, B. (2013). Revival of Essay Writing in Economics. *International Journal of Pluralism and Economics Education, 4*(2), 183–191.

Mateer, G., O'Roark, B., & Holder, K. (2016). The 10 Greatest Films for Teaching Economics. *The American Economist, 61*(2), 204–216.

Moryl, R. (2013). T-shirts, Moonshine, and Autopsies: Using Podcasts to Engage Undergraduate Microeconomics Students. *International Review of Economics Education, 13,* 67–74.

Moryl, R. (2014). Podcasts as a Tool for Teaching Economics. *The Journal of Economic Education, 45*(3), 284–285.

Moskowitz, T., & Wertheim, L. (2011). *Scorecasting: The Hidden Influences Behind How Sports are Played and Games are Won.* New York: Crown Archetype.

Picault, J. (2019). The Economics Instructor's Toolbox. *International Review of Economics Education, 30,* 100154.

Picault, J. (2021). Looking for Innovative Pedagogy? An Online Economics Instructor's Toolbox. *The Journal of Economic Education, 52*(2), 174.

Romer, D. (2006). Do Firms Maximize? Evidence from Professional Football. *Journal of Political Economy, 114*(2), 340–365.

Salomon, G. (1979). Media and Symbol Systems as Related to Cognition and Learning. *Journal of Educational Psychology, 71*(2), 131–148.

Tierney, J., Mateer, G., Smith, B., Wooten, J., & Geerling, W. (2016). Bazinganomics: Economics of *The Big Bang Theory. The Journal of Economic Education, 47*(2), 192.

Trautman, N., Carlsen, W., Eick, C., Gardner, F., Kenyon, L., Moscovici, H., Moore, J., Thompson, M., & West, S. (2003). Online Peer Review: Learning Science as It's Practiced. *Journal of College Science Teaching, 32*(7): 443–447.

Vidal, D., Mungenast, K., & Vidal, J. (2020). Economics Through Film: Thinking Like an Economist. *International Review of Economics Education, 35,* 100186.

Willingham, D. (2009). Why *Don't Students Like School?: A Cognitive Scientist Answers Questions About How the Mind Works and What it Means for the Classroom.* Hoboken, NJ: John Wiley & Sons.

Wooten, J. (2018). Economics Media Library. *The Journal of Economic Education, 49*(4), 364–365.

Wooten, J. (2020). Integrating Discussion and Digital Media to Increase Classroom Interaction. *International Review of Economics Education, 33,* 100174.

Wooten, J., & Smith, B. (2018). Create Random Assignments: A Cloud-Based Tool to Help Implement Alternative Teaching Materials. *The Journal of Economic Education, 49*(3), 297.

Wooten, J., & Staub, K. (2019). Teaching Economics Using NBC's *Parks and Recreation. The Journal of Economic Education, 50*(1), 87–88.

Wooten, J., & Tierney, J. (2019). Adam Ruins Everything: Except Economics. *Journal of Economics and Finance Education, 18*(1), 34–53.

Wooten, J., & White, D. (2018). An In-Class Experiment to Teach Marginal Revenue Product Using the Baseball Labor Market and Moneyball. *Journal of Economics Teaching, 3*(1), 115–133.

Wooten, J., Acchiardo, C., & Mateer, D. (2020). Economics is a Kahoot! *The Journal of Economic Education, 51*(3–4), 380.

Wooten, J., Staub, K., & Reilly, S. (2020). Economics Within ABC's Modern Family. *The Journal of Economic Education, 51*(2), 210.

Wooten, J., Al-Bahrani, A., Holder, K., & Patel, D. (2021). The Role of Relevancy in Economics Education: A Survey. *Journal for Economic Educators, 21*(1), 11–34.

PART III

Classroom activities for sports economics – moving away from chalk and talk

10. The jigsaw reading

Victor A. Matheson

HOW TO DO A JIGSAW READING

Journal articles provide an excellent source of material for students to use both to learn economic principles and to develop critical reading skills. The "Jigsaw Reading" is an active learning activity that can be adopted in any classroom as a method to expose students to journal articles. The jigsaw reading combines several important aspects of learning, including reading comprehension, writing, oral presentation, and small-group work, into a single in-class assignment.

The format of the jigsaw reading is simple. First, the professor selects four to six articles of interest for the class being taught. After a very brief introduction to each article, each student either selects one of the articles or is assigned to one of the articles by the professor. Care must be taken that as close to an equal number of students as possible are assigned to each article. The students in class are then assigned to groups with one person from each different paper in each group. In the more than likely event that the groups do not work out evenly, it is best to assign two people from the same paper to a single group rather than have some groups missing a particular paper.

Next, the students work on the homework portion of the assignment. Each student reads their selected article, writes a two to three-page summary of the article, and prepares a short (five to ten minute) presentation of their article.

Finally, the in-class portion of the assignment takes place. On a previously announced day, students assemble in their assigned group and then take turns presenting their paper to the other members of their group. Each presentation should take five to ten minutes with a bit of time reserved for questions from the other members of the group. In groups where there are two presenters from a single paper, care should be taken that each presenter gets a chance to discuss some portion of their paper. In order to encourage each group member to pay attention during the times they are not presenting, it is worthwhile to require them to take notes on every other paper, to be turned in with the written summary of their own paper at the end of the group exercise. The entire exercise should take between 25 and 50 minutes depending on the number of papers chosen.

While the presentations are going on, the professor may wander around the class from group to group in order to listen in on the presentations. In addition, the professor should watch the clock and announce every five to ten minutes or so that groups should be moving on to the next presenter if they have not done so already.

When all is said and done, each student will have read one journal article, written a summary of that article, given a short oral presentation of that article, and learned about three to five other articles from their classmates' presentations.

ADVANTAGES OF THE JIGSAW READING

The jigsaw reading has several specific positive aspects that make it an effective active learning tool. First, it is effective in any size classroom from four to 100 (although the administrative aspects of assigning papers and assigning students to small groups become more difficult in larger classes). While active discussion and student presentations to the whole class are difficult or impractical in bigger classrooms, small group work like the jigsaw reading is equally effective in large classes as in small classes. In fact, the jigsaw reading may actually work to establish a sense of community in larger classrooms. Research shows that students tend to feel less responsibility towards their fellow students and the professor in impersonal classrooms (Gleason, 1986). In addition, students who feel anonymous in class are less motivated to learn and less likely to do the required work (Brock, 1976). As several students in the survey group noted, if students are simply expected to read an article which is then discussed in class, some "students may tend to ride the coat-tails of others."

This technique allows all students to make an oral presentation to a group with a minimum use of class-time. The in-class portion easily fits within a one-hour block of time. A common complaint with many active learning techniques is the large amount of time that they take away from other classroom activities (such as lecturing). The common response of practitioners of active learning is that the tradeoff of less class time is balanced by improved student learning (Davis, 1993, p. 154). The jigsaw reading, however, adds an active learning component with almost no loss in classroom time when compared with presenting the same material in lecture format, and actually increases classroom time when compared with presenting material through student presentations to the whole class.

Another attractive feature of the jigsaw reading is that it is effective in any level of class from principles to advanced graduate level and in any field. The only difference is the papers selected. For example, in Sports Economics, which at my institution is a lower-level elective for economic majors only, I have frequently used this assignment to introduce the topic of discrimination in sports. I use Lawrence Kahn, "The Effects of Race on Professional Football Players' Compensation," *Industrial and Labor Relations Review* (1992), Clark Nardnelli and Curtis Simon, "Customer Racial Discrimination in the Market for Memorabilia: The Case of Baseball," *Quarterly Journal of Economics* (1990), Mark Kanazawa and Jonas Funk, "Racial Discrimination in Professional Basketball: Evidence from Neilsen Ratings,' *Economic Inquiry* (2001), Janice Fanning Madden, "Differences in Success of NFL Coaches by Race, 1990-2002: Evidence of Last Hire, First Fire," *Journal of Sports Economics* (2004), and Joseph Price and Justin Wolfers, "Racial Discrimination Among NBA Referees," The Quarterly Journal of Economics (2010) as the five papers in the assignment. This assignment has a clear unifying theme while giving students exposure to multiple sports (football, baseball, and basketball), multiple types of discrimination (employer, employee, and customer discrimination), and multiple ways to test for discrimination. However, a collection of papers can be found on essentially any topic.

Next, students may be more attentive to a peer teacher in a small group than a professor in a large classroom. For one thing, since each student must make a presentation, there is a sense of empathy for the student presenters that is not present for a professor's presentation. As the groups are small, there is no place for inattentive students to hide. Students may feel more comfortable asking questions and challenging the conclusions of a peer than the professor. Students may also discount the editorial comments of a professor more easily than those of a fellow student (e.g. sport economics professors always say that about stadium subsidies, etc.) (Moffet, 1968, p. 193).

Furthermore, requiring each student to teach others about the important aspects of their assigned paper likely increases the student's own understanding of the paper. It is a widely accepted belief in educational psychology that "the process of teaching in itself gives a deeper insight into the subject matter" (Whitman, 1988). In preparing for teaching, the teacher must review and organize the material, a process by which the teacher "may need to seek out its basic structure and, in so doing, may gain a better understanding of it" (Gartner et al., 1971). At the very least, the fear of appearing unprepared in front of a group of peers gives a strong incentive for adequate preparation. Roughly two-thirds of the students from the survey group reported that the group presentation caused them to take more time reading and understanding their article than simply writing a summary would have done.

Another advantage of the jigsaw reading is that it does not necessarily require direct supervision by a faculty member. While the activity is slightly more effective with a professor present, it is a useful tool to use in lieu of a lecture when the instructor has a planned absence. This assignment thus eliminates the hassle of finding a substitute instructor or of rescheduling the missed class period. The assignment also works well as a break in-between lectures for classes that meet for extended time periods of three or four hours.

One final advantage of the jigsaw reading is that it is fully effective in a remote, online, or distance learning setting. One simply sets up a shareable Google doc as a signup sheet and either has students in each group set up their own time for a virtual meeting or does the jigsaw presentations during a regularly scheduled online meeting time using a feature such as the Zoom breakout rooms for the individual groups.

DISADVANTAGES OF THE JIGSAW READING

It is unfair to present the benefits of the jigsaw reading without presenting its shortcomings as well. First, if students do not fully understand the paper they are presenting, they will spread incorrect information to their group members. While wandering the class from group to group (or popping into breakout rooms on Zoom) in order to listen in on the presentations can help to partially solve this problem, monitoring all of the information being presented is difficult for the professor, especially in large classes. The selection of papers that are easily accessible to the class is also an important issue in this regard. Papers at the upper limit of the students' ability to read and comprehend are probably inappropriate for this assignment.

Several students surveyed about this project have reported that the oral presentations tend to be somewhat vague and unstructured. Though nearly all students agreed that they learned something from each of the other articles, many felt they would have learned significantly more had they read the article themselves. Of course, assigning all of the articles to each student significantly increases the workload upon the students.

High attendance is also crucial for success. If large numbers of students are absent on the day of the assignment, it will be necessary to rearrange the groups, and it will be difficult to create groups each with a single presenter for each topic. In order to create groups that each have all four or five papers represented, it may be necessary for some groups to have more than one presenter for each paper. Assigning some portion of the points on the assignment to the in-class presentation gives an incentive to encourage attendance on the day of the project. Again, the presentation day should be announced well in advance.

Finally, from personal experience, this learning technique tends to diminish in effectiveness the more times it is used for a single class. It tends to be difficult to test students on the content of the material in the papers because, if the professor asks a test question on the specific content of a particular paper, the students who actually read the paper rather than just hearing an oral presentation on the paper have a large, unfair advantage in answering the question.

Thus, if the jigsaw reading is used several times in the semester, the students may begin to feel that they will not be held responsible for the material presented by the other members of their group. Therefore, concentration in the group presentation portion of the assignment begins to fall. For this reason, I tend to not use this assignment more than once in a single course.

VARIATIONS ON THE JIGSAW READING

Several variations on the standard jigsaw reading could be made to accommodate the special circumstances of specific classes. First, in classes where research papers are a significant component, upon completion of their papers students could be assigned to small groups to make short presentations of their papers to their group members. While this variation has the disadvantage that students don't get to learn about every other paper in the class (as in the standard jigsaw reading), the students still benefit from being required to organize a short presentation and get to hear about the papers of a few of their peers. These small group presentations have an advantage over presentations to the entire class of being more time effective and of being less intimidating to the student presenter.

A second variation involves presentations of group papers or projects. "Project groups" of four or five students are assigned to research a specific topic or complete a project. On the day that projects are due, rather than have each project group as a whole present their results to the entire class, four or five new "presentation groups" are formed with one member from each project group. Each student then presents the results of their project group to the presentation group to which they are assigned.

A third variation works well when the instructor has several shorter articles (fewer than five pages) to present. If the articles are short enough, the class can be broken into groups with each group receiving each of the articles. Each group member reads one of the articles and presents it to the other group members. This is the same as the standard jigsaw reading except that the reading is actually done during the class period rather than ahead of time.

A final variation would allow students to select their own journal article on a specific topic rather than choose an article from a designated list.

Aju Fenn, my co-editor for this book, uses a similar project, but provides the students with a handout detailing "How to Read a Journal Article in Five Minutes," which gives students tips about how to maximize their understanding of a quantitative journal article without getting bogged down. While Professor Fenn's suggestions are probably better utilized for students (or faculty!) reading multiple articles (for example, as preparation for writing a literature review) than for a deeper dive into a single article, his handout is provided as an Appendix to this chapter.

CONCLUSIONS

"Research on students' academic success and intellectual development has demonstrated the effectiveness of modes of instruction that emphasize active learning and collaborative activities and engage students in intellectual discovery" (Davis, 1993, p. xix). The jigsaw reading provides any professor, regardless of teaching ability and irrespective of course content and class size, with an effective tool with which to promote active and effective learning.

ACKNOWLEDGMENTS

The author would like to thank the members of the Preparing Future Faculty Program at the University of Minnesota, including Dr. Carolyn Evans and Dr. Mary Everly, for their helpful instruction in active teaching methods.

REFERENCES

Brock, Stephen C. 1976. *Practitioners' Views on Teaching the Large Introductory College Course. Manhattan*. Kansas: Center for Faculty Evaluation and Development in Higher Education, Kansas State University.

Davis, Barbara Gross. 1993. *Tools for Teaching*. San Francisco: Jossey-Bass Publishers.

Gartner, Alan, Mary Kohler, and Frank Riessman. 1971. *Children Teach Children: Learning by Teaching*. New York: Harper and Row.

Gleason, Maryellen. 1986. Better Communication in Large Courses. *College Teaching*, 34(1), 20–24.

Moffet, James. 1968. *Teaching the Universe of Discourse*. Boston: Houghton-Mifflin.

Whitman, Neal A. 1988. *Peer Teaching: To Teach is to Learn Twice*. ASHE-ERIC Higher Education Report Series Number 4. Washington, DC: Association for the Study of Higher Education.

APPENDIX 10A

How to Read an Economics Journal Article in 5 Minutes

1. When I am new to an area of the literature, I just copy and paste article citations followed by the abstracts into a single document. Then I read that summary document to get an idea of what has been done.
2. Read the abstract if there is one. From the abstract you should be able to identify the main research question (i.e. What is the impact of factors A, B and C on Y?), the dataset used and the main results of the study.
3. Next skim the introduction, to see if there are any sub-research questions that the paper poses. There will usually be a paragraph towards the end of the introduction which will spell out all the research questions.
4. Skip the literature review and look for the regression model. This model will have dependent and independent variables well specified. Connect these variables to the ones in the research question.
5. Skim the regression results for the findings. Which variables impact Y? Are their signs in the expected direction? (For example does own price of potatoes have a negative sign? Does income have a positive or a negative sign?)
6. Finally read the conclusions to complete your picture of the research question and the findings of the paper. Sometimes, I begin by reading the conclusion. If it is clear enough then, I can skip steps 1 to 5.

A Closer Look

7. As you settle on your research question you may want to know more about the other studies done. Read the references to find other articles that your library database search may have missed.
8. You may be interested in gathering data. Read the data section and look at the references to see if you can gather the same data.
9. You may be interested in the methodology employed. Read the data and methods section of appropriate articles.

11. Starting point bias and final offer arbitration: a classroom experiment

Victor A. Matheson

INTRODUCTION

In this classroom experiment, the ability of people to place reasonable dollar values on player value is tested, and an economic anomaly known as "starting point bias" or the "anchoring effect" is exposed (Furnham and Boo, 2011). The science of economics depends critically on the assumption that people are able to place specific values routinely and rationally on goods that do not have a well-defined market price, either because the market doesn't exist, or in the case of baseball players, the products are highly differentiated. Of course, valuing players is one of the most important jobs of team managers. In Major League Baseball, players with between three and six years of experience who are without a contract are eligible for salary arbitration. In this process, the player and the team each submit a salary demand/offer to an independent arbitrator who will then determine the player's salary for the upcoming season.

In regular arbitration, there would always be the incentive for the team to knowingly provide a "low-ball" offer in order to influence the arbitrator to come up with a low value while the player has the incentive to inflate his value for the same reason. The purpose of this paper is to provide a simple classroom experiment that can be used by sports economics teachers to demonstrate how easily people can be misled when asked to estimate a dollar value of something without a clear market price. The experiment can be easily altered for use in a law and economics class that studies tort awards or in an environmental and natural resource economics class or any other course in which contingent evaluation is taught. It is also obviously a natural fit for a behavioral or experimental economics class. The next section presents the methodology of the experiment. This is followed by empirical results from this experiment that I have collected over the years to show the sort of results one might expect in their own classroom. The paper closes with conclusions and suggestions for further classroom discussion.

METHODOLOGY

In this exercise, students are given a hypothetical situation where they are asked to place a dollar value on a non-market good. Every student is randomly given one of two handouts and specifically instructed to complete the handout without discussing their answers with other students. These handouts are included in Appendices 11.1 and 11.2 at the back of this chapter.

Essentially the handout asks the students to act as jurors in a personal injury case where a 50-year-old construction worker was injured on the job due to the negligence of his employer and has lost his leg as a result. (Playing the Dropkick Murphy's "Shipping Up to Boston" while the students fill out the survey would make for an appropriate background soundtrack!) The students are asked to write down how much the worker should be awarded as damages. There are also some demographic pieces on the form, but these are not essential for the experiment and are included, at least in part, as red herrings to distract the students from how they might be being manipulated. Do not answer any student questions about how they should determine the worker's tort award other than to emphasize that the students should put a dollar amount for the award.

The trick here is that the two handouts are identical with one exception. One group of students was first asked on the handout whether the worker deserved to be compensated more or less than $10,000 and then asked how much more or less. Another group of students was first asked whether the worker deserved to be compensated more or less than $10,000,000 and then asked how much more or less. It is crucial that the students only be exposed to one of the two awards.

I also used to include a third random handout with no suggested award as a control group, but the results were as expected and simply served to complicate the experiment without improving the learning outcome. I have also tried variations of this experiment with a more sports-specific set-up, but none have resulted in such clear results as this well-calibrated scenario. Obviously, other scenarios can be posed as long as the basic idea of suggesting different values to different groups is maintained. In addition, the observed differences between the two groups is likely to be maximized when a typical unbiased response lies in-between the two suggested starting points and the difference between the two starting points is large.

When students are finished, collect the surveys. Tabulation of the student responses can either be done on the spot or outside the classroom by the instructor with results presented in a subsequent class. The experiment has a greater impact on the students if feedback is provided immediately, and a computerized classroom with a spreadsheet or statistical package will greatly speed the process.

In my classes (which average roughly 25 students), I read off the award amount from each handout one by one and then write the award amount in one of two columns on the board representing the responses from the "$10,000 suggestion" students and the "$10,000,000 suggestion" students (without, of course, labeling the columns or describing what method I am using to distribute answers to either column). When I have finished reading out and recording all of the surveys, I then calculate either the mean or the median of each column. (Calculating the median is clearly quicker to do in your head and also reduces the impact of any potential outliers on the measure of central tendency.) The difference between the figures in the two columns will invariably be large and obvious (as I show in the next section). I then ask the students how I decided to place each individual award amount in either column. Students generally say, "Male vs. female" or "Republican vs. Democrat" or any of the other demographic identifiers included on each survey (which empirically have no statistically significant impact on awards). Occasionally a bright student will get an idea about what they have been given as a starting point, but since the students don't know that half of the class has been given a different starting point than themselves, this is pretty rare. Then I make the "big reveal" about the differences between the two surveys. The whole process generally takes less than 10 minutes.

WHAT RESULTS CAN YOU EXPECT?

W.C. Fields famously once said, "Never work with animals or children," because you can't anticipate what you are going to get. The same problem applies to live classroom experiments. This experiment, however, is as close to a sure thing as is possible.

Table 11.1 shows the summary data from 545 surveys I have given in 20 separate economic courses, primarily in sports economics but also occasionally in environmental economics or public finance, over the past 15 years or so.

On average, the group of students who were suggested the $10,000,000 figure returned mean awards 7.5 times higher and median awards 16.7 times higher than those who had the $10,000 figure suggested to them. Of course, the figures in Table 11.1 represent the results for the entire 545 surveys in the sample. So, how does this experiment work in classes of 30 or fewer? Table 11.2 shows the ratio of the mean and median awards for the $10,000,000 and $10,000 groups for the 20 classes in the sample. The average class size is just over 27 students.

For an average observed class, the average ratio of the means of the two groups exceeds 10 and the average ratio of medians exceeds 20. In smaller

Table 11.1   *Results of starting point bias experiment*

	$10,000 suggested	$10,000,000 suggested
Mean	$934,790	$6,983,714
Median	$300,000	$5,000,000
Minimum	$8,000	$150,000
Maximum	$20,000,000	$180,000,000
Standard deviation	$2,218,196	$13,308,711
Observations	$n = 273$	$n = 272$

Note: A hypothesis test that the means of the $10,000 and $10,000,000 group are the same can be rejected at the 99.999% significance level

Table 11.2   *Typical classroom results*

	Ratio for means by class	Ratio for median by class
Mean	13.65	24.96
Median	10.31	22.22
Minimum	1.33	6.32
Maximum	44.35	60.00
Standard deviation	11.90	17.98
Observations	$n = 20$	$n = 20$

classes it is possible that a small handful of responses can skew the class means, leading to less dramatic results, but the mean awards of the $10,000,000 group has always exceeded the mean awards of the other group by at least 33% in my trials, and the lowest ratio of median awards has never been below a factor of six. A factor of six, at the very worst, is still big enough to have some "wow" factor, and more typical results are even more impressive to the students.

DISCUSSION

So, what does this have to do with sports economics? If people (including arbitrators) are easily influenced by a starting point or have a natural tendency to want to accommodate both sides, players and teams have the incentive to ask for salaries that are far away from what they actually feel is a fair value. For example, if when a player says $5 million and the team says $3 million, the arbitrator simply splits the difference and chooses $4 million, a player wishing to maximize his salary wants to ask for an even larger amount and the team wants to offer even less in order to get the arbitrator's average award to move in their respective directions. Baseball solved this problem through the introduction of "final offer arbitration." In final offer arbitration the team and the player still submit their offers, but the arbitrator must choose one offer or the other and cannot split the difference. This prevents the runaway offers that would be likely to occur in the presence of regular arbitration given the sort of results shown in this experiment, as offers that are too far from a reasonable salary are more likely to be rejected in favor of the other side's offer.

Sometimes the professor may wish to discuss other aspects of the experiment or the arbitration process. One reason the students are so easily manipulated in this experiment is that they were given no additional information, such as the average wage of construction workers or the work-life expectancy of people in these jobs. A typical court case would include expert witnesses to inform the jurors about these things. Similarly, MLB arbitrators are likely to have more experience in evaluating player salaries and are provided with information regarding the salaries of other players with potentially similar playing statistics. See Chapter 14 in this book for another classroom experiment on arbitration where the students are assigned roles as club owners, players, or arbitrators, and owners and players argue their cases to a panel of three arbitrators (Brown, 2022).

REFERENCES

Brown, Amber (2022). "Arbitration in the Classroom: A Classroom Experiment to Model MLB's Salary Arbitration." In Aju J. Fenn and Victor A. Matheson (eds.), *Teaching Sports Economics and Using Sports to Teach Economics*. Edward Elgar Publishing.

Furnham, Adrian and Hua Chu Boo (2011). "A literature review of the anchoring effect." *The Journal of Socio-Economics*, 40(1), 35–42.

APPENDIX 11.1 TEST CASE IN FORENSIC ECONOMICS

You are being asked to participate in a research experiment regarding jury awards in lawsuits. Please read the description of the case below and answer the questions that follow. *It is critical that you not discuss your answers with any fellow students nor should you look at their survey form until after you have completed the questions and turned in your sheet.* The results of the experiment will be made available to you via the Internet within the next several weeks. Thank you for participating in this project.

Suppose you have been asked to serve on a jury on a matter dealing with personal injury. In the case before you, a 50-year-old construction worker was injured on the job due to the negligence of his employer. As a result, this man had his right leg amputated at the knee. Due to this disability, he cannot return to the construction trade and has few other skills with which he could pursue alternative employment.

The negligence of the employer has been firmly established and health insurance covered all of the related medical expenses. Therefore, your job is to determine how to compensate this worker for the loss of his livelihood and the reduction in his quality of life.

Should the plaintiff in this case be compensated more or less than $10,000? How much more or less than $10,000 should the plaintiff be compensated? (Write down the total dollar amount you think the plaintiff should receive.)

What is your gender?
    Male   Female
What is your year in school?
    First-year   Sophomore   Junior   Senior
Counting a high school AP economics course as 1 semester and not counting any classes you are taking this semester, how many economics courses have you had? (Circle one. If more than 4 sems., write number.)
    0 sem.   1 sem.   2 sem.   3 sem.   4 sem.   More_____
What is your hometown? (Write down your city and state/province if you are from U.S. or Canada and your city and country if you are an international student.)

_____

What best describes your political leanings?
Strong Democrat Leaning Democrat Leaning Republican Strong Republican

APPENDIX 11.2 TEST CASE IN FORENSIC ECONOMICS

You are being asked to participate in a research experiment regarding jury awards in lawsuits. Please read the description of the case below and answer the questions that follow. *It is critical that you not discuss your answers with any fellow students nor should you look at their survey form until after you have completed the questions and turned in your sheet.* The results of the experiment will be made available to you via the Internet within the next several weeks. Thank you for participating in this project.

Suppose you have been asked to serve on a jury on a matter dealing with personal injury. In the case before you, a 50-year-old construction worker was injured on the job due to the negligence of his employer. As a result, this man had his right leg amputated at the knee. Due to this disability, he cannot return to the construction trade and has few other skills with which he could pursue alternative employment.

The negligence of the employer has been firmly established and health insurance covered all of the related medical expenses. Therefore, your job is to determine how to compensate this worker for the loss of his livelihood and the reduction in his quality of life.

Should the plaintiff in this case be compensated more or less than $10,000,000? How much more or less than $10,000,000 should the plaintiff be compensated? (Write down the total dollar amount you think the plaintiff should receive.)

What is your gender?
    Male   Female
What is your year in school?
    First-year   Sophomore   Junior   Senior
Counting a high school AP economics course as 1 semester and not counting any classes you are taking this semester, how many economics courses have you had? (Circle one. If more than 4 sems., write number.)
    0 sem.   1 sem.   2 sem.   3 sem.   4 sem.   More ____
What is your hometown? (Write down your city and state/province if you are from U.S. or Canada and your city and country if you are an international student.)

    _____

What best describes your political leanings?
Strong Democrat Leaning Democrat Leaning Republican Strong Republican

12. Randomness and the hot hand fallacy

Joshua Congdon-Hohman and Victor A. Matheson

THE HOT HAND FALLACY IN SPORTS

When Larry Bird, Michael Jordan, or Steph Curry have hit three difficult basketball shots in a row, you might hear the commentator say that he's "on fire."
When a baseball player has home runs in two straight games, you might hear
that the player is swinging a "hot bat." There is a widely held belief in sports
that performance can be streaky and that players' successes in consecutive
attempts or games must reflect a temporary improvement in their abilities,
possibly due to higher levels of concentration and confidence. In the literature,
this is often referred to as a "hot hand," and surveys have found a strong belief
in these elevated performance periods among players, coaches, and fans in
many sports, but most pronounced in basketball.

The question is whether these periods of temporarily elevated skill really
exist or are simply a reflection of patterns we would expect to find when
randomly drawing from an independent and identical distribution of outcomes
based on each player's fixed abilities. Psychologists first examined this
phenomenon in the context of how people make decisions based on limited
information and the shortcuts we use to process difficult-to-interpret patterns.
The idea that mistakes are made in interpreting patterns in small samples of
randomly generated observations goes back into the 1940s (see Wagenaar,
1972, for a review of early studies) and popularized by the work of Tversky
and Kahneman (1971). Specifically, researchers found that subjects (including
trained statisticians) would misjudge the likelihood of random events based on
a small sample of data, even when presented with the true distribution of the
random events.

To test these common and errant heuristics people use to deal with the
non-representativeness of small samples outside of a laboratory setting,
Gilovich, Vallone, and Tversky (1985) examined patterns in basketball shooting and statistically tested the "hot hand" belief. Using a limited sample of
NBA players, the authors found no statistical evidence that the likelihood of

making a shot or free throw changed based on the success or failure of the previous shot. Similarly, they found that the patterns in the shot makes and misses were statistically indistinguishable from the patterns that would be predicted with a constant likelihood of making each basket. The authors came to the same conclusion using collegiate players in an experimental shooting setting without defenders. Though challenged on various grounds,[1] the findings of Gilovich, Vallone, and Tversky have largely held up to further examination in other basketball settings, including Adams (1992), Koehler and Conley (2003), Rao (2009), Avugos, Bar-Eli, Ritov, and Sher (2013), and Lantis and Nesson (2021). The conclusions of this research have led to the broadly held conclusion that the "hot hand" in basketball is considered a fallacy among statisticians, though still a widely held belief among competitors, fans and commentators.

The results from tests of the "hot hand" theory have been more varying outside of basketball shooting. In baseball, Albright (1993) finds that hitting streaks generally match what would be expected under probability theory, while Green and Zwiebel (2018) find evidence of "hot" streaks when looking at a large number of individual performance categories. In golf, Livingston (2012) and Cotton, McIntyre, Nordstrom, and Price (2019) find no evidence of a "hot hand" in aggregate performance data for amateur and professional golfers, although there are some occasions of individual golfers performing better or worse than strict probability theory would suggest. There have been studies that find some evidence of hot hand performances in individual sports such as tennis (Klaassen and Magnus, 2001), horse-shoeing (Smith, 2003), and bowling (Dorsey-Palmateer and Smith, 2004).

AN IN-CLASS EXPERIMENT IN RANDOMNESS

The hot-hand fallacy can be shown in a variety of simple in-class experiments. Rodney Fort provides another variation on this activity in his chapter on "Economical Sports Economics Classroom Activities" in Chapter 17 of this book (Fort, 2022). In this version of the experiment, first ask students to get out a blank sheet of paper and a coin. In this age of digital currency, you will likely have to bring a penny for every person in class since no one carries old-fashioned money anymore. Tell the students that they will be creating two columns of figures. One will be a list of Heads and Tails generated by flipping a coin. The other will be random column of Heads and Tails that the students will generate by hand.

Next, have the students write by hand a column of 25 (what they feel as) random Hs or Ts. They can create this column in either the first or the second column on their paper, but the students should not indicate anywhere on their paper which of the two columns is the one generated by hand. It is important

Table 12.1   *Probability of various streak lengths*

Longest streak	Probability (%)
1	0.0
2	0.7
3	14.5
4	29.7
5	25.0
6	14.8
7	7.8
8	3.8
9	1.8
10 or more	1.8

that this column is generated before the students create a truly random column using a coin.

Finally, have the student fill the other column with 25 Hs or Ts generated by flipping their coin. Again, the students should not indicate anywhere on the paper which column was generated by flipping the coin. When both columns are finished, the students should write in their own notes, not to turn in, which column was created by hand and which was done with the coin. The students will then put their name on their paper and turn it in to the professor. The professor will then tell each student which column was generated by hand and which was generated by coin. As the professor reveals his or her guesses, a running tally of correct guesses should be kept.

The way to tell which column is which is by taking advantage of the fact that most people's concept of "randomness" doesn't allow for long streaks to exist. In reality, however, streaks are a very real part of randomness. For example, in a sample of 25 random coin flips, the probabilities of the longest streak being of a certain length are shown in Table 12.1.

On the other hand, it is rare for people trying to create a random list of heads and tails by hand to put more than three or four heads or tails in row. So, simply by selecting the column with the longest streak of heads or tails, the professor will correctly choose the column that was generated by the true randomness of the coin roughly 75% of the time.[2] Note that it can be somewhat time-consuming to actually count out the length of streaks on each sheet, so it may be a better use of class time to do the experiment at the end of one class period, collect the papers and create a guess for each student on the professor's own time, and then reveal the guesses at the beginning of the next period.

CONCLUSION

Most sports economics students are reluctant to believe that the hot hand does not exist in sports. This in-class experiment demonstrates that pure random chance is likely to generate streaks much longer than a typical student would normally consider "random" and would instead attribute to streakiness. In fact, we should expect hot and cold streaks to happen all of the time even if a player's underlying chance of getting a hit, making a basket, or completing a pass hasn't changed. Indeed, this experiment roughly replicates the actual playing statistics for a high scoring NBA player such as James Harden who, in the 2018–2019 season, took about 25 shots a game and made about half of them. We should expect Harden, simply by random chance, to have a stretch where he either makes or misses at least six shots in a row from the floor roughly every third game he plays. It's not that he is streaky; it's that streaks happen as a part of randomness. Humans, however, don't easily see randomness in streaks and are more likely to try to impose a pattern on randomness that doesn't really exist.

NOTES

1. While researchers (Wardrop, 1995, and Arkes, 2013, for example) have questioned the ability to identify true "hot hand" effects with the small samples and statistical methods used by Gilovich, Vallone, and Tversky (1985), some researchers believe they have found evidence supporting the hot hand theory in basketball and reject it being a "fallacy." Aharoni and Sarig (2012) found an improvement in shooting percentages following a made basket once adjusting for defensive responses by the opponent. Miller and Sanjurjo (2018) concludes that current evidence actually points to the existence of the hot hand once the appropriate statistical, small sample bias is adjusted for. In both studies, however, the magnitude of any hot hand effect is extremely small, on the order of just a few percentage points, even if it may be possible to show a statistically significant effect given enough data.
2. Roughly half of the time the coin will generate a streak of five or more. Because the students will rarely include their own streak of five or more when doing the column by hand, the professor will win nearly all of those. The other half of the time, the coin and the students will be creating longest streaks of roughly even length. By random chance the professor will win half of those. In total, that equates to a roughly 75%-win percentage for the professor. This figure roughly approximates my own win percentage over a large number of trials of this experiment.

REFERENCES

Adams, Robert M. 1992. "The 'hot hand' revisited: Successful basketball shooting as a function of intershot interval." *Perceptual and Motor Skills* 74(3): 934.
Aharoni, Gil, and Oded H. Sarig. 2012. "Hot hands and equilibrium." *Applied Economics* 44(18): 2309–2320.

Albright, S. Christian. 1993. "A statistical analysis of hitting streaks in baseball." *Journal of the American Statistical Association* 88(3): 1175–1183.

Arkes, Jeremy. 2013. "Misses in 'hot hand' research." *Journal of Sports Economics* 14(4): 401–410.

Avugos, Simcha, Michael Bar-Eli, Ilana Ritov, and Eran Sher. 2013. "The elusive reality of efficacy–performance cycles in basketball shooting: An analysis of players' performance under invariant conditions." *International Journal of Sport and Exercise Psychology* 11(2): 184–202.

Cotton, Christopher S., Frank McIntyre, Ardyn Nordstrom, and Joseph Price. 2019. "Correcting for bias in hot hand analysis: An application to youth golf." *Journal of Economic Psychology* 75: Article 102091.

Dorsey-Palmateer, Reid, and Gary Smith. 2004. "Bowlers' hot hands." *The American Statistician* 58(1): 38–45.

Fort, Rodney. 2022. "Economical Sports Economics Classroom Activities." In Victor A. Matheson and Aju J. Fenn (eds.), *Teaching Sports Economics and Using Sports to Teach Economics*. Edward Elgar Publishing.

Gilovich, Thomas, Robert Vallone, and Amos Tversky. 1985. "The hot hand in basketball: On the misperception of random sequences." *Cognitive Psychology* 17(3): 295–314.

Green, Brett, and Jeffrey Zwiebel. 2018. "The hot-hand fallacy: Cognitive mistakes or equilibrium adjustments? Evidence from major league baseball." *Management Science* 64(11): 5315–5348.

Klaassen, Franc J.G.M., and Jan R. Magnus. 2001. "Are points in tennis independent and identically distributed? Evidence from a dynamic binary panel data model." *Journal of the American Statistical Association* 96(454): 500–509.

Koehler, Jonathan J., and Caryn A. Conley. 2003. "The 'hot hand' myth in professional basketball." *Journal of Sport and Exercise Psychology* 25(2): 253–259.

Lantis, Robert M., and Erik T. Nesson. 2021. "Hot shots: An analysis of the 'hot hand' in NBA field goal and free throw shooting." *Journal of Sports Economics* 22(6): 639–677.

Livingston, Jeffrey A. 2012. "The hot hand and the cold hand in professional golf." *Journal of Economic Behavior & Organization* 81(1): 172–184.

Miller, Joshua B., and Adam Sanjurjo. 2018. "Surprised by the hot hand fallacy? A truth in the law of small numbers." *Econometrica* 86(6): 2019–2047.

Rao, Justin M. 2009. "Experts' perceptions of autocorrelation: The hot hand fallacy among professional basketball players." Working Paper. University of California, San Diego.

Smith, Gary. 2003. "Horseshoe pitchers' hot hands." *Psychonomic Bulletin & Review* 10(3): 753–758.

Tversky, Amos, and Daniel Kahneman. 1971. "Belief in the law of small numbers." *Psychological Bulletin* 76(2): 105–110.

Wagenaar, Willem A. 1972 "Generation of random sequences by human subjects: A critical survey of literature." *Psychological Bulletin* 77(1): 65–72.

Wardrop, Robert L. 1995. "Simpson's paradox and the hot hand in basketball." *The American Statistician* 49(1): 24–28.

13. This class is a Kahoot! Using Kahoot! to test student knowledge in class

Jadrian Wooten

WHAT IS A KAHOOT!?

Kahoot! is a game-based online learning platform that is available at no cost for educators. Kahoot! provides upgrade options and university site licenses for a nominal monthly fee, but most features are available to educators at no additional charge. The basic Kahoot! is a multiple choice quiz that can be used as a review tool or just a general break from the traditional "chalk and talk" lecture. Administrators can alter the amount of time at the question-level and the relative value of each question. Questions in the basic account can include images, YouTube videos, and even support math notation.

Kahoot! quizzes can also be used for summative or formative assessment. Instead of assigning paper-based quizzes, Kahoot! games can be accessed by students on any internet-enabled device. Students can access the game by downloading an application or through a web browser. Kahoot! encourages social learning by requiring students to look up more frequently from their devices in order to read questions and see answer options. Questions and answers are displayed through an overhead projector, while the students' device only shows shapes and colors corresponding to answer choices. This design limits academic misconduct from students logging in at home when they should be in class.

Instructors who are familiar with classroom response systems (clickers, Top Hat, Poll Everywhere) will find Kahoot! very similar. The benefit of using Kahoot! relative to other systems is that students find it engaging, there is no cost to instructors or students, there is no account setup required by students, and it is based on a gaming philosophy. Each classroom response system has some functionality that makes it unique, and it's up to the instructor to determine which approach supports their learning objectives and teaching philosophy.

Kahoot! users can share quizzes with other users through their online account. This has resulted in a public good scenario where educators create a variety of high-quality Kahoot! games and share them with other interested educators (Wooten, Acchiardo, & Mateer, 2020). Shared Kahoot! games can be copied to local accounts, so the original quiz remains with the creator and any changes made by the other user are restricted to their own copy. The sharing feature also allows educators to share the Kahoot! with students who may want to use the game as part of a review strategy. This may be superior to other online study methods, such as Quizlet, since the games are created by educators rather than other students. Kahoot! games that are used as an assessment should probably not be shared with students if the instructor intends to use the same Kahoot! in other semesters since the link could be shared with future students as well.

WHY KAHOOT!?

The appeal of using Kahoot! over other response systems is the social aspect. With countdown timers and a player leaderboard, the activity replicates the engagement of trivia games that are played in pubs around the United States, but the questions are focused on the material taught in class. Because the platform can be used on a laptop, cell phone, or tablet, students do not need to purchase an additional device (like a clicker) or an additional subscription (like Top Hat or Poll Everywhere) to participate.

A lack of motivation among students has been shown to result in reduced learning outcomes and increased negative classroom environments (Liu, Bridgeman, & Adler, 2012). Student response systems have a positive impact on classroom environment, student and teacher perceptions, and learning performance (Caldwell, 2007). A growing body of research has focused specifically on Kahoot!'s impact on both learning and classroom engagement. Many of the gamification elements of Kahoot! are correlated with increased student engagement relative to a traditional lecture (Wang, Zhu, & Sætre, 2016) and relative to traditional paper-based assessments (Wang & Lieberoth, 2016).

Much of the research on using Kahoot! has found positive learning gains, but there are researchers who find little to no impact on learning (Wang & Tahir, 2020). The research space has also shown improvements in areas that many instructors may not have considered before using Kahoot!, including improved class attendance, fewer late arrivals, and an increase in the number of students accessing course material (Fotaris, Mastoras, Leinfellner, & Rosunally, 2016). Kahoot! was used as part of a quasi-experiment in which some students were taught using a traditional paper-based approach while others were taught with a variety of game-based response systems, including Kahoot! (Filologiczna, 2016). There was no significant difference in pre-test scores, but the game-based course performed significantly better on a post-test relative to the paper-based classroom (90% vs. 75%). While many studies focus on K-12 education, researchers have found positive learning gains with university students at Purdue University (Bawa, 2019) and LaSalle University (Kinder & Kurz, 2018) as well as university students in Greece (Tsihouridis, Vavougios, & Ioannidis, 2017) and Portugal (Esteves, Pereira, Veiga, Vasco, & Veiga, 2017).

There are researchers, however, that have found no apparent gains in learning from using Kahoot! compared with a traditional paper-based assessment (Wang & Lieberoth, 2016) or compared with other online platforms that are not game-based (Göksün & Gürsoy, 2019). While the learning gains may not be consistently positive, researchers don't find harm from using Kahoot! games. If there are no gains in learning, but students enjoy the experience, that may be a worthwhile investment on the part of faculty, particularly those in teaching roles or appointments that rely heavily on student evaluations.

Some critics argue the countdown timer and visible leaderboard may overwhelm anxious students, but Turan and Meral (2018) found that relative to non-game based assessments, Kahoot! decreased test anxiety levels while increasing engagement. Other researchers have found that Kahoot! allows quiet, perhaps more reserved, students an opportunity to participate in a way that they may not otherwise do in a traditional classroom setting (Licorish, Owen, Daniel, & George, 2018).

HOW DO I START USING KAHOOT! IN MY CLASSROOM?

Creating a Kahoot! is relatively self-explanatory in the system, but Wooten, Acchiardo, and Mateer (2020) provide a guide on their website.[1] Instructors who may be apprehensive about technology will likely find the system straightforward. Instructors create a university-affiliated account on the Kahoot! website,[2] and can choose whether to upgrade their accounts to unlock additional features for their quizzes. The main advantage of upgraded accounts comes in the form of question types available. The basic (free) version allows instructors to only ask multiple choice or "images as answer" questions. Upgraded accounts can ask multi-select questions, puzzles, polls, sliding scale, image reveal, open-ended questions, or create word clouds.

The basic membership for higher education accounts limits game sizes to no more than 50 students at a time. Each additional upgrade level increases player limits. It's important to sign up for the higher education account because personal use Kahoot! games are limited to 10 players.

To create a new Kahoot! game, account holders click the "Create" button and are presented with the first question template for the quiz. From here, instructors add a question prompt and answer options, adjust the time and point value for that particular question, and add an image or video if they want. Kahoot! supports question banks, so questions can be added from other Kahoot! games an instructor has previously created. If questions are stored in a spreadsheet, those can be uploaded as well. Instructors can decide whether their newly created Kahoot! is publicly available and what type of music is played during the game.

When it's time to play a Kahoot!, instructors navigate to their account and select the appropriate Kahoot! from their list of available quizzes. Instructors have the option of playing the game in class or assigning it to students to play on their own. Before starting the game, instructors have the option of adjusting a variety of game-level settings including whether to allow students to play individually or as teams. Instructors can assign random (friendly) names to students or allow students to enter their own name.[3] Instructors can change the lobby music, randomize the order of questions and answers, or enable two-step join, which is mentioned in more detail below. After the settings are determined, instructors start the game, which opens a lobby for students to join. Students join by navigating their devices to "Kahoot.it" or by opening the Kahoot! application. Each game has a unique game PIN, and a waiting room shows players who have joined.

The results of each Kahoot! session can be downloaded to a spreadsheet, which allows instructors to identify problematic questions. This spreadsheet, if formatted properly, may also be used to upload scores to a course management system if it is used as part of a formal assessment. Spreadsheets can be downloaded immediately after the game, but are also stored in a separate portion of an instructor's account. Students are allowed to leave feedback at the conclusion of the game; however, if this is used as a formal assessment in the course, many of them may not recommend your Kahoot! to their friends.

ASKING THE RIGHT QUESTIONS

Multiple-choice question writing can be just as effective as open-ended questions, so long as they are designed in a particular way. The Carl Wieman Science Education Initiative (CWSEI) (2017) has a list of question types that they have found to be the most effective:[4]

1. Quiz on the reading assigned in preparation for the class
2. Test recall of lecture point
3. Do a calculation or choose next step in a complex calculation
4. Survey students to determine background or opinions
5. Elicit/reveal pre-existing thinking
6. Test conceptual understanding
7. Apply ideas in new context/explore implications
8. Predict results of lecture demo, experiment, or simulation, video, etc.

9. Draw on knowledge from everyday life
10. Relate different representations (graphical, mathematical, ...)

Researchers have found that questions framed on the second half of the list have the largest direct impact on learning and they are also the types of questions that students report as the most valuable. The CWSEI has prepared an instructor guide for the effective use of classroom response systems, and while much of their work has focused on writing questions for more traditional classroom response systems, the same approach can be applied to Kahoot! games as well.

KAHOOT! LIMITATIONS

Like with any other system, recognizing limitations ahead of time can help instructors adjust their classroom instructions and assessment decisions. The most common issue is the adverse impact of a countdown timer and awarding points based on how quickly questions are answered. Students may answer questions without much consideration because they are aware their overall score improves if they answer quickly. If Kahoot! is part of a formal assessment, this can be mitigated by reminding students that it is primarily a quiz, and a game at a secondary level.

While Kahoot! has its own scoring system, the conversion to course scoring should be based on accuracy, like any traditional quiz points would be assigned. Bonus points could be awarded to students with the highest scores, which really only goes to students who answer questions correctly. Incorrect answers, regardless of how fast they are selected, don't result in any points. Because Kahoot! sessions are typically played with the entire class at one time, it is not possible to adjust the timing element for individual students. This could pose potential issues for students who require academic accommodations. Concerned instructors should work with their campus Disability Resource office to ensure compliance.

Other limitations can be more easily mitigated. There can be a significant amount of noise associated with the game because of the built-in music, but also because students are engaged with the activity. This could be mitigated by an instructor's presence. Students without a device would not be able to participate, but many universities offer laptop and tablet rentals through their library or IT departments. This can also be mitigated if quiz dates are announced in advance. Finally, being ranked on performance may not appeal to some students. This has not been a concern when the formal grade for the quiz is associated with accuracy; however, there may be a self-selection issue.

There are limitations on the administrative side as well, namely the character limit on questions and answers. Questions are limited to 120 characters and responses are limited to 75 characters. This requires a faculty member to be skilled at condensing questions. There is always the risk of losing internet connection or playing in a room with bandwidth capacity issues. Capacity concerns would need to be addressed with campus tech support, but internet disruptions are often intermittent and therefore hard to troubleshoot.

A final issue deals with authentication and academic misconduct. Players join the game using a code displayed on an overhead screen, but players don't technically need to be in the room to join the game. A student could send the game code to another student who is skipping class, and that other student can still participate. The student outside of class wouldn't be able to see the questions and answers on their device but could still submit random guesses. Kahoot! has mitigated this somewhat with an option to enable a two-step joining process, where students enter a second code that changes every six seconds. Unfortunately, because the game can be played on a laptop, tablet, or smartphone, a student could always login to multiple devices and submit answers on behalf of other students who are not in the room. This can be mitigated by instructors or teaching assistants who walk around the room as the game is being played or by taking attendance.

As with any other assessment, students could cheat off others in the class. After the time expires, students who answered correctly will receive a green screen while students who answered incorrectly will see a red screen. If a student is completing the Kahoot! on their phone, this can be hidden under their desk or may not be as visible to others around them. Students completing the Kahoot! on a laptop, however, will inevitably have their results seen by students sitting behind them. Attentive students may recognize that a student in front of them consistently answers questions correctly and may withhold their answers until seeing what the student in front of them selects. Because of the timing component, the copying student cannot earn a higher Kahoot! score than the original student, but if Kahoot! is used for assessments, they will earn credit for work they didn't complete. As such, I often recommend students complete Kahoot! games on a phone or tablet that can be laid flat on a desk.

FINAL THOUGHTS

Kahoot! games have been an easy way to rejuvenate a classroom that has a heavy lecture component or one that just needs a new spark. The setup, administration, and execution of the game is relatively easy compared with other systems. While it is rare a student enjoys a paper-based quiz, students actively note that Kahoot! quizzes are fun. The same multiple-choice questions, but delivered with red triangles, blue diamonds, yellow circles, and green squares is enough for many to find quizzes engaging. The same quiz could be done with classroom remotes, but batteries die unexpectedly, and students regularly leave their remotes at home. Cell phones, to many faculty's chagrin, aren't often left at home and rarely die unexpectedly. By no means are Kahoot! games perfect, nor are they without their limitations. The games are not only engaging for students, but faculty have also found them engaging and a nice change of pace from the traditional "chalk and talk" of yesteryear.

NOTES

1. www.EconKahoots.com
2. www.Kahoot.com
3. Inappropriate names can be manually removed by the instructor before the game starts.
4. https://cwsei.ubc.ca/

REFERENCES

Bawa, P. (2019). Using Kahoot to Inspire. *Journal of Educational Technology Systems*, *47*(3), 373–390.

Caldwell, J. (2007). Clickers in the Large Classroom: Current Research and Best-Practice Tips. *CBE-life Sciences Education, 6*(1), 9–20.

Carl Wieman Science Education Initiative. (2017). *Clicker Resource Guide: An Instructors Guide to the Effective Use of Personal Response Systems (Clickers) in Teaching.* Vancouver: University of British Columbia.

Esteves, M., Pereira, A., Veiga, N., Vasco, R., & Veiga, A. (2017). The Use of New Learning Technologies in Higher Education Classroom: A Case Study. *International Conference on Interactive Collaborative Learning* (pp. 499–506). Springer.

Filologiczna, W. (2016). Effects of Modern Technologies on Teaching English Vocabulary to Primary School Learners. *CER Comparative European Research*, 155–157.

Fotaris, P., Mastoras, T., Leinfellner, R., & Rosunally, Y. (2016). Climbing up the Leaderboard: An Empirical Study of Applying Gamification Techniques to a Computer Programming Class. *Electronic Journal of e-Learning, 14*(2), 94–110.

Göksün, D., & Gürsoy, G. (2019). Comparing Success and Engagement in Gamified Learning Experiences via Kahoot and Quizizz. *Computers & Education, 135*, 15–29.

Kinder, F., & Kurz, J. (2018). Gaming Strategies in Nursing Education. *Teaching and Learning in Nursing, 13*(4), 212–214.

Licorish, S., Owen, H., Daniel, B., & George, J. (2018). Students' Perception of Kahoot!'s Influence on Teaching and Learning. *Research and Practice in Technology Enhanced Learning, 13*(9), 1–23.

Liu, O., Bridgeman, B., & Adler, R. (2012). Measuring Learning Outcomes in Higher Education: Motivation Matters. *Educational Researcher, 41*(9), 352–362.

Tsihouridis, C., Vavougios, D., & Ioannidis, G. (2017). Assessing the Learning Process Playing with Kahoot – A Study with Upper Secondary School Pupils Learning Electrical Circuits. *International Conference on Interactive Collaborative Learning* (pp. 602–612). Springer.

Turan, Z., & Meral, E. (2018). Game-Based Versus to Non-Game-Based: The Impact of Student Response Systems on Students' Achievements, Engagements and Test Anxieties. *Informatics in Education – An International Journal, 17*(1), 105–116.

Wang, A., & Lieberoth, A. (2016). The Effect of Points and Audio on Concentration, Engagement, Enjoyment, Learning, Motivation, and Classroom Dynamics Using Kahoot!. *European Conference on Games Based Learning, 20.*

Wang, A., & Tahir, R. (2020). The Effect of Using Kahoot! for Learning – A Literature Review. *Computers & Education, 149,* 1–22.

Wang, A., Zhu, M., & Sætre, R. (2016). The Effect of Digitizing and Gamifying Quizzing in Classrooms. *European Conference on Games Based Learning.* Academic Conferences International Limited.

Wooten, J., Acchiardo, C.-J., & Mateer, G. (2020). Economics is a Kahoot! *The Journal of Economic Education, 51*(3–4), 380.

14. Arbitration in the classroom: a classroom experiment to model MLB's salary arbitration

Amber Brown

INTRODUCTION

This experiment recreates Major League Baseball's Final Offer Salary Arbitration (FOA) process in the classroom. By participating in the experiment, students will gain an understanding of how FOA works and the implications for salaries in Major League Baseball (MLB). They make their case for the player's appropriate salary based on his contributions to team wins and salaries of players with comparable statistics. They see first-hand how risk preferences influence the outcomes of the hearings. The shortcomings of arbitration, specifically the omission of market size and the revenue potential of the team in determining player value, as well as newly emerging strategies are discussed. The goal of this experiment is to demystify the arbitration process and clearly demonstrate its implications for MLB salaries.

LEARNING OBJECTIVES

*   Understand MLB final offer salary arbitration procedures and rules.
*   Investigate the criteria arbitrators use to determine player salaries.
*   Understand the role risk aversion plays in the arbitration process.
*   Recognize spillover effects of former settlements on current salary decisions.
*   Identify determinants of marginal product of labor and marginal revenue product.
*   Analyze the value of various statistics in determining the contribution of a player to wins.
*   Compare MLB and NHL arbitration processes.
*   Understand the file-and-trial strategy.

- Determine when it is preferable to sign a player under the reserve system to a long-term contract.

ARBITRATION PROCEDURES

Players drafted in Major League Baseball (MLB) play their first six years under the reserve clause. They cannot negotiate with clubs other than the club which drafted them. Clubs are allowed to, but not required to, pay them the league minimum. After a player has approximately three years of major league service, he may negotiate for a new contract, and if no agreement can be reached, then the player may request salary arbitration.

In final offer salary arbitration, players and clubs exchange salary figures through the Players' Association and the MLB Labor Relations Department. A hearing is set for some time during the first three weeks of February. Hearings are normally held in Arizona or Florida in a neutral site such as a hotel conference room. Players and clubs can continue to negotiate in an attempt to settle until the time of the hearing. If they are still unsuccessful, then they attend the binding arbitration hearing at the scheduled time.

During the hearing, the player and club both have an hour to argue their case and a half-hour for rebuttal and summation. Both sides argue their case based on the salaries of other players in the league with comparable statistics. Players with three to five years of service time make comparisons with other players within one year of their service time. Players are not required to attend but normally do so. Owners and players may have their agents, general managers (GMs), or specialized staff present to argue their case. Arbitrators decide within 24 hours, choosing *either* the player *or* club salary. Their decision is final and binding. No opinions are given by the arbitrators and the record of their votes is not released to the Association and the Labor Relations Department until the following March.

The timetable for arbitration (2021) is as follows:[1]

Filing date for arbitration if negotiations are unsuccessful:

Exchange of salary figures: Friday, January 15
Arbitration hearings: February 1 – February 20

Arbitrators are instructed to consider the following evidence:

- the quality of the Player's contribution to his Club during the past season (including, but not limited to, his overall performance, special qualities of leadership and public appeal)
- the length and consistency of his career contribution
- the record of the Player's past compensation

- comparative baseball salaries
- the existence of any physical or mental defects on the part of the Player, and
- the recent performance record of the Club including, but not limited to, its league standing and attendance as an indication of public acceptance

Only publicly available statistics shall be admissible. For purposes of this provision, publicly available statistics shall include data available through subscription-only websites.

Evidence which is not permissible includes:

- the financial position of the Player and the Club
- press comments, testimonials, or similar material
- offers made by either Player or Club prior to arbitration
- the cost to the parties of their representatives, attorneys, etc.
- salaries in other sports or occupations
- any of the provisions of the Competitive Balance Tax

A BRIEF HISTORY OF FOA

Until 1976, there was no free agency, and all players were under the reserve system. Players were only allowed to negotiate with their current team, and if they did not find the terms offered by their current team acceptable, their only option was to leave professional baseball. Curt Flood sued MLB in1973 (*Flood v. Kuhn*) over the legality of the reserve system. The case went to the Supreme Court and, although Flood lost by a close 5–3 decision, it had a significant impact on public opinion as fans increasingly sided with players wishing to be free to negotiate with any team. Owners agreed to salary arbitration (beginning in 1974) in order to avoid free agency. Dave McNally and Andy Messersmith played without contracts and were declared free agents by arbitrator Peter Seitz after the 1975 season due to a provision in the rules. (Mr. Seitz was eventually fired by the owners after he also declared Catfish Hunter a free agent.) Marvin Miller, then head of the Players' union, negotiated free agency with the owners to begin in 1976. Players are under the reserve clause and only able to negotiate as a free agent after their sixth year. However, players with three to six years of service, and those who are in the top 22% of second-year players in terms of service time, are eligible for salary arbitration. Final Offer Arbitration differs from traditional arbitration in that arbitrators can chose only the owner's bid or player's request, but no other number. This method was first introduced by Carl Stevens in 1966 in order to encourage both sides to bargain more earnestly before choosing arbitration. If arbitrators could choose any value, each side had an incentive to ask for a more extreme number since the arbitrator, wanting to appear fair and thus continue working as an arbitrator, often chose a salary halfway between. Neither side had much of an incentive to negotiate a salary before arbitration, so it is said these final offer arbitration rules had a "chilling" effect on negotiations (Warren, 1990). With FOA, choosing an excessively high or low bid greatly increases the chances that the other party will win the hearing. For a quick classroom experiment on how excessively high or low starting points can influence awards, see Victor Matheson's examination of this topic in Chapter 11 in this book (Matheson, 2022).

Arbitrators predominantly choose the submitted salary which is closest to their estimated value of the player. Thus, the arbitrators' estimated value will lie between the midpoint of the submitted salaries and the winning request/offer. For example, in the following case,

owner's offer	midpoint	player's request
$4 million	$5 million	$6 million

an arbitrator will likely vote in favor of the player if they determine the player is worth $5,000,100. Likewise, if they decide the player's worth is $4,999,000, they will likely decide on behalf of the owner.[2] When submitting offers, owners and players weigh the increase in the probability of being chosen against the decrease in salary or profits of a more conservative figure.

THE EXPERIMENT

This experiment has been performed in classes of approximately 40–50 students within a 50-minute time frame. It is adaptable to classes of all sizes.

All students are given the risk assessment quiz (Appendix 14.A). They are asked to quickly fill it out and put it aside. The discussion of risk is postponed until after the experiment.

Note: It is also possible to leave out the risk assessment portion of the experiment entirely.

Initially, two or more panels of three arbitrators each are designated. For a class of 40, three panels are usually sufficient. The panels will hear several cases throughout the class period. Arbitrators are given instructions along with a list of permissible and impermissible evidence (Appendix 14.B).

Each of the remaining students is designated either as a player or an owner. Every participant is given the list of statistics for current MLB pitchers with six years or less of major league service (MLS) (Appendix 14.C). Players and owners receive the statistics for a fictitious player who is arbitration eligible and currently earning the league minimum salary, $563,500 in 2020. (Appendix 14.D). Everyone also receives definitions of the given statistics (Appendix 14.E).

This experiment starts with the filing of salary figures. That is, it is assumed negotiations have been unsuccessful thus far. Owners and players are asked to submit their salary figures to the arbitrators on a folded slip of paper. It is important to emphasize to players and owners that they should *not* collaborate when determining the figure or let each other see the figures until they have both been submitted. Next, players and owners have a chance to present their cases to the arbitrators. The player will begin and present for up to 3 minutes, then the club will have up to 3 minutes to present their case. The player will have a 1-minute rebuttal, and the owner will also have a 1-minute rebuttal. It should be stressed that the presentations are not discussions, and those not presenting are not allowed to interrupt. Creativity is encouraged and the parties are allowed to ad lib to present the full portrayal of the player, including their personality, public appeal, etc. They may also use statistics not provided if they choose. Arbitrators decide between the owner's bid and player's request, away from earshot of the owners and players, and the following information is written on the white board:

	Player	Team/Owner	Player's request	Owner's offer	Winner
For example	Al Bino	Philadelphia	$14 million	$11 million	Owner

If a backlog of cases occurs, players and owners who have completed their cases can form new arbitration panels.

When players and owners are done negotiating contracts, students are asked to go back to their risk assessment test and score themselves as either risk-averse (mostly A answers), risk-neutral (mostly C answers), or risk-loving (mostly B answers). They then add this information on the board alongside their name with either A (risk-averse), N (risk-neutral), or L (risk-loving). For example:

	Player	Team/Owner	Player's request	Owner's offer	Winner
For example	Al Bino(L)	Philadelphia(N)	$14 million	$11 million	Owner

QUESTIONS AND IDEAS FOR DISCUSSION OR HOMEWORK

Compare the Number of Cases Won by Players with the Number Won by Clubs. How does this Ratio Compare to Actual MLB Cases?

From 1974 to 2020, there have been 250 arbitration cases won by players and 324 cases won by management. Management has won 57% of the time.[3] Faurot (2001) rejects the hypothesis that management wins 50% of the time. Fortunately, classroom outcomes mostly coincide with the MLB data. The owners win in the majority of cases. The next questions give possible explanations for this outcome.

How does the Preference for Risk of Owners and Players Influence the Outcome of Arbitration?

- A *risk-averse* player would accept a lower salary to avoid the uncertainty of arbitration and a risk-averse owner would accept lower profits to avoid a given amount of uncertainty.
- *Risk-neutral* players and owners care only about the expected salary or profits and are not influenced by the amount of uncertainty.
- *Risk-loving* players and owners would take on extra risks for the possibility of a higher payoff.

The risk of arbitration for the player is getting a lower salary than the negotiated one. The risk for the owner is paying more through arbitration than through negotiation. Using data from 1986–1991, Burgess and Marburger (1993) found that salaries determined through arbitration hearings differed significantly from negotiated salaries, and that arbitration awards won by players were higher and those won by management were lower than the negotiated settlements.[4]

Note that all players and owners were required to go to arbitration for this experiment. In actuality, the vast majority of arbitration-eligible players negotiate a contract and avoid arbitration. Risk-averse players who are willing to accept lower salaries to avoid the uncertainty of arbitration will likely find an acceptable offer from risk-averse or risk-neutral owners. Likewise, risk-averse owners will successfully negotiate with risk-averse or risk-neutral players. Hanany (2007) found that if at least one side is risk-averse, then there is a negotiated salary that both would prefer to arbitration. From their empirical analysis, they concluded that players are most likely to be risk averse. Risk-loving players will not be able to find an acceptable negotiated salary and will go to arbitration.

Risk-neutral players and owners suffer no costs from uncertainty and would be indifferent between negotiation and arbitration if the expected salary were the same and there were no costs of arbitration, but arbitration is not costless. The trend has become to replace GMs and player agents with specialized teams of arbitration specialists. In addition to the financial and travel costs, hearings can involve high emotional costs as well. Listening to your employer point out your shortcomings and explain why you are not worthy of the salary you request is a brutal way to spend four hours and can be demoralizing.[5] Players and owners would compare the financial, travel and emotional costs, including costs of uncertainty, as compared with the salary savings (owners) or increases (players).

Even though owners tend to win the majority of arbitration cases, they are not in favor of the arbitration process. During collective bargaining negotiations in the 1994–95 players strike, owners were willing to shorten the number of years required for free agency from six to four in exchange for abolishing salary arbitration (Calcaterra, 2019). Arbitration tends to push up salaries. Just the threat of arbitration can cause owners to negotiate more generously and, once figures have been filed, owners might offer higher figures than without arbitration in order to appear fair to the arbitrators. Arbitrators chose the player's request or owner's offer which is closest to their estimated value of the player. Thus, owners, fearing a large jump in salary, may offer a salary higher than their estimate of the player's value in order to be over the midpoint.

Given that everyone was required to go to arbitration, the relative risk preferences of the arbitrated cases can be compared with the expected outcomes. Did the relatively more risk-averse party prevail at the hearing? If not, what might be the reason?

What Statistics were the Most Useful in Arguing Your Case?

During arbitration hearings, players' salaries are compared with the salaries of other players within one service year. In the experiment, players and owners are given a limited number of statistics for current day pitchers. It should be noted that only one year of the player's career stats are used in the experiment, although a player with three or more years of experience would obviously use more than just their last year of statistics. Presentations usually center on which of these stats were most important and which stats are important that were left out. Just as not every arbitrator is a "baseball" person, not every student in class will be a baseball fan. Presenting advanced statistics may be a better indicator of the player's worth, but if they are not easily understandable to the arbitrators, they will not help the presenter's case. Astute students, however, will make the case that popular pitching statistics reflect the play of the team more than just the play of the pitcher. Proponents of sabermetrics have long claimed that a great deal of what is perceived as being pitching is in fact defense, and single season win-loss records have almost no value as an indicator of a pitcher's contribution to a team (Laurila, 2012).[6]

What Data Determine how Much the Player is Worth? Of these Data, which are Impermissible in the Hearing?

A player's worth depends on their ability to bring in revenues for the team. Of course, this will depend on how much the player increases win percent (marginal product of labor) and how much the increased win percent increases revenues (marginal revenue product, MRP). The arbitration process emphasizes the marginal product of labor of a player over the potential increase in revenues.

A player's contribution to win percent is generally assumed to be dependent on the statistics mentioned above. How much the win percent contribution adds to revenue depends on, amongst other things, the size of the market in which he plays. This information is inadmissible during a hearing. The justification for the omission is that the player should not be penalized for playing in a small market given that it was not his choice where to play during the draft. On the other hand, a small market team may be forced to pay the value of the player to a large market even though they do not have the fans or revenue potential to earn that money back.

Other inadmissible evidence which may have been presented might be the popularity of the player in the press or testimonials about the personality of the player. Students who inadvertently used this evidence can make their arguments for why it is important in determining the value of a player. For example, a player may be attracting fans even if he is not adding to his team's win percentage.

How did Arbitrated Salaries Compare with Previous Salaries?

The monopsony power of the owners is instrumental in keeping the salary below the MRP under the reserve system. Each player was earning the league minimum ($563,500) before arbitration. Using both the data from the experiment and from actual arbitration cases, students can easily see the substantial jumps in salary after arbitration. Salaries of players who become arbitration eligible increase significantly. Jose Berrios of the Twins had a salary increase of over 500% ($620,000 to $4,025,000).[7] It is unlikely that his productivity increased by 500%, so if arbitrated salaries are at least somewhat reflective of the player's MRP, it must be the case that he was paid way below his MRP. Given that the players have no ability to market their services on a free market, clubs can pay them less than their marginal revenue product without the fear of them signing with another team. The salaries of first-year free agents increase substantially, which is also a stark illustration of the exploitation of the players under the reserve system.

How do You Expect the File-and-Trial Strategies to Affect the Arbitrated Salaries?

A strategy adopted by an increasing number of teams is the file-and-trial policy. Clubs adopting this policy refuse to negotiate further with the player once they have officially exchanged salary figures. By creating this very credible threat of arbitration, players and their agents wishing to avoid arbitration will have an incentive to submit a more conservative figure of their estimated worth and not one aggressively high that they can negotiate downwards from. Not surprisingly, agents and players are not in favor of the strategy. Spreads between the owner and player submitted salaries are less under this strategy. Students can discuss whether they would expect an increase or decrease in the number of arbitrated cases and whether they would expect this to increase or decrease the amount of arbitration awards.[8]

Did Previous Settlements Written on the Board Affect any of Your Decisions?

Students write up arbitration hearing results as they are settled. Arbitrators, owners, and players are all aware of previous settlements. Most participants will admit to having been influenced by the previous settlements, illustrating a spillover effect.

In actual MLB arbitration, clubs and the players union like to avoid scheduling cases with a potentially large award granted to the other side scheduled on the first day, in order to avoid any undesirable spillover effects.

Why would an Owner Offer a Long-term Contract to a Player under the Reserve Clause? Why would a Player Accept One?

Aaron Nola signed a four-year contract with the Philadelphia Phillies for $45 million in 2020. In doing so, he will forgo three years of arbitration. The contract goes through his remaining three years of arbitration and one year of free agency, with a club option for the second year of his free agency. He gave up potentially signing a large contract two years earlier as a free agent. Nola stated, "It just felt right for me at this time."[9]

Evan Longoria signed a six-year deal after playing only six games with the Tampa Bay Rays. When he signed, he claimed, "For me, the security of a long-term contract and knowing that now I'm pretty much set for life, it's just very assuring to me."[10]

These are two examples of players who may have potentially made more by going through arbitration and free agency but chose signing contracts early and the security of guaranteed money over several years. This would be indicative of risk-averse behavior to take less in order to avoid uncertainty.

A team offering such a contract must believe the money offered is less than the minimum they could offer the player during their arbitration-eligible years and the first years of their free agency. The team incurs the risk that the player will stay healthy and productive, and therefore should receive a discounted salary.

How does NHL Salary Arbitration Differ from MLB Arbitration?

Salary arbitration in the National Hockey League (NHL) differs from FOA in several ways:

- Players must be restricted free agents with a given combination of experience and age.
- Either the player or club may request salary arbitration.
- Arbitrators can view the evidence from both sides at least 48 hours before the hearing and can request more evidence or witnesses. In MLB, arbitrators know nothing of the player before he walks through the door.
- Arbitrators can choose any amount, not only the player's or owner's submission.
- If a player requested (a one-year contract) arbitration and is awarded $3.5 million or more, the club can decline, and he becomes an unrestricted free agent.
- If a player requested (a two-year contract) arbitration and is awarded $3.5 million or more, the club can decline, pay the player the salary for the first year and then he becomes an unrestricted free agent in the second.
- If the club requested arbitration, the arbitrator's decision is binding.
- Arbitrated salaries fall between restricted and unrestricted free agent salaries.[11]

CONCLUSION

This experiment is fun and allows for a lot of interaction with fellow students. This encourages students to try hard in making the best case for the appropriate salary. They gain an appreciation not only of the difficulty of comparing statistics of different players but also of the tension that exists in hearings between owners and players. Participating in mock hearings allows for a better understanding of the process and a more memorable experience than would a traditional presentation.

NOTES

1. Major League Baseball Collective Bargaining Agreement 2017–2021 (Major League Baseball Players Association, 2020).
2. This need not be the case, especially if an arbitrator is reluctant to award a record amount.
3. Brown (2015) and Arbitration Tracker for 2020. MLB Trade Rumors. (n.d.) https://www.mlbtraderumors.com/arbtracker2020
4. Burgess and Marburger (1993).
5. The following two articles provide great insights into the emotional costs of an arbitration hearing: C. Harlan (2010), "Washington Nationals Pitchers Sean Burnett, Brian Bruney Lose Out in Arbitration." *Washington Post* (February 21); and B.J. Rains (2013), "Players Reflect on Arbitration Hearings: Kyle Lohse." *MLB Trade Rumors* (February 19).
6. Bill (1987).
7. Baseball Reference. https://www.baseball-reference.com/players/b/berrijo01.shtml #all_br-salaries
8. Reiter (2014).
9. T. Zolecki (2019), "New 4-year deal 'felt right' for Nola." MLB.com (February 13). https://www.mlb.com/news/aaron-nola-phillies-contract-extension-c303874434
10. Associated Press (2008).
11. National Hockey League Players Association (2013), "NHL Collective Bargaining Agreement 2012–2022." *Collective Bargaining Agreement.*

REFERENCES

Associated Press. (2008). *Longoria's Deal with Rays Could Be Worth up to $44 Million.* ESPN.com (April 18). Retrieved November 10, 2014, from https://www.espn.com/mlb/news/story?id=3353025

Brown, Maury. (2015). "Who's Winning The MLB Salary Arbitration Game? Here's Data From 1974 to 2015." (February 23). Retrieved August 26, 2020, from https://www.forbes.com/sites/maurybrown/2015/02/23/whos-winning-the-mlb-salary-arbitration-game-heres-data-from-1974-to-2015/

Burgess, Paul L., and Daniel R. Marburger. (1993). "Do Negotiated and Arbitrated Salaries Differ under Final-Offer Arbitration?" *Cornell University, ILR Review* 46(3): 548–559.

Calcaterra, Craig. (2019). "Baseball strike in 1994–95 began 25 years ago." *NBC Sports.com* (August 12). Retrieved August 26, 2020 from https://mlb.nbcsports.com/2019/08/12/baseball-strike-in-1994-95-began-25-years-ago/

Faurot, D. J. (2001). "Equilibrium Explanation of Bargaining and Arbitration in Major League Baseball." *Journal of Sports Economics* 2(1): 22–34.

Hanany, E., D. M. Kilgour, and Y. Gerchak. (2007). "Final-Offer Arbitration and Risk Aversion in Bargaining." *Management Science* 53(11): 1785–1792.

Harlan, Chico. (2010). "Washington Nationals Pitchers Sean Burnett, Brian Bruney Lose Out in Arbitration." *Washington Post* (February 21).

James, Bill. (1987). *The Bill James Baseball Abstract, 1988*. New York: Ballantine.

Laurila, David. (2012). *The BP Wayback Machine: Roger Abrams. Baseball Prospectus*. Baseball Prospectus (January 19). Retrieved November 10, 2014 from https://www2016.baseballprospectus.com/news/article/15876/the-bp-wayback-machine-roger-abrams/

Major League Baseball Players Association. (2020). "Basic Collective Bargaining Agreement 2017–2021." *Major League Baseball*. Retrieved August 20, 2020 from https://www.mlbplayers.com/cba

Matheson, A. Victor. (2022). "Starting Point Bias and Final Offer Arbitration: A Classroom Experiment." In Victor A. Matheson and Aju J. Fenn (Eds), *Teaching Sports Economics and Using Sports to Teach Economics*. Edward Elgar Publishing.

National Hockey League Players Association. (2013). "NHL Collective Bargaining Agreement 2012–2022." *Collective Bargaining Agreement*. Retrieved November 10, 2014, from http://www.nhlpa.com/inside-nhlpa/collective-bargaining-agreement.

Rains, B. J. (2013) "Players Reflect on Arbitration Hearings: Kyle Lohse." *MLB Trade Rumors* (February 19). Retrieved November 10, 2014 from http://www.mlbtraderumors.com/2013/02/arbitration-rewind-kyle-lohse-beats-minnesota-in-2005-and-2006.html.

Reiter, Ben. (2014). "Inside the Strategy That's Turning Arbitration Upside down." *SI.com. Sports Illustrated* (February 7). Retrieved November 10, 2014 from https://www.si.com/mlb/2014/02/07/arbitration-file-go-craig-kimbrel-darwin-barney

Warren, James. (1990). "College Prof Spawns Baseball Arbitration." *Chicago Tribune* (March 4). Retrieved November 10, 2014 from http://articles.chicagotribune.com/1990-03-04/sports/9001190091_1_stephen-goldberg-arbitration-labor-law

Zolecki, Todd. (2019). "New 4-year deal 'felt right' for Nola." MLB.com (February 13). Retrieved August 26, 2020, from https://www.mlb.com/news/aaron-nola-phillies-contract-extension-c303874434

APPENDIX 14.A: RISK ASSESSMENT QUIZ

1. Suppose you could bet $5 on a coin flip. If the coin lands on heads, you win $5 and if it lands on tails, you lose your bet. Would you take the bet?
   a) no
   b) yes
   c) don't care

2. Suppose you have a winning lottery ticket of $1,000. You can collect your winnings or trade it in on another ticket that has a 50% chance of being a $2,000 winner. Would you
   a) keep your ticket?
   b) trade it in on the other ticket?
   c) don't care – either way

3. Suppose you can bet $1,000 on either wheel A or B, each with 100 numbers. On wheel A, if you land on 1–50 you will win another $1,000 and if you land on numbers 51–100 you will lose your $1,000. For wheel B, if you land on 1–10 you will win another $9,000 and if you land on 11–100, you will lose your $1,000. Would you choose
   a) Wheel A?
   b) Wheel B?
   c) don't care – either one is fine

APPENDIX 14.B: INSTRUCTIONS FOR ARBITRATION EXPERIMENT

If You are a Player

Your goal is to get the best salary that you can. Currently you are earning the league minimum of $563,500 and are going to an arbitration hearing. Determine your requested salary based on the contracts of comparable players within one service year of you. Write your requested salary on a slip of paper and hand it to the arbitrators. Do not let the club owner see your amount before it is announced by the arbitrators. During the hearing you will have up to 3 minutes to present your case. The owner will have up to 3 minutes to present their case, then you will each have another minute for rebuttal and summary. You many only speak during your assigned time. You may not argue directly with the owner. Note the permissible and impermissible evidence below.

If You are a Club Owner

Your goal is to pay the lowest salary and maximize your profits. Currently you are paying the player the league minimum of $563,500 and are going to an arbitration hearing. Determine the offered salary based on the contracts of comparable players within one service year of the player. Write your salary offered on a slip of paper and hand it to the arbitrators. Do not let the player see your amount before it is announced by the arbitrators. During the hearing you will have up to 3 minutes to present your case. The player will have up to 3 minutes to present their case, then you will each have another minute for rebuttal and summary. You many only speak during your assigned time. You may not argue directly with the player. Note the permissible and impermissible evidence below.

If You are an Arbitrator

During the hearing, the player will present first for up to 3 minutes, arguing for their requested salary. Then the owner will have up to 3 minutes to present their case, then each will have another minute for rebuttal and summary. You will only listen to their cases and not ask questions unless it is for the purposes of clarification.

Afterwards you will make your determination of which salary figure you find more appropriate. The party which wins at least two out of three arbitrator votes will win the hearing. Do not let either the player or the owner know how you voted or your reasons for your vote.

Impermissible and Permissible Evidence

Permissible evidence:
- the quality of the Player's contribution to his Club during the past season (including but not limited to his overall performance, special qualities of leadership and public appeal);
- the length and consistency of his career contribution;
- the record of the Player's past compensation;
- comparative baseball salaries;
- the existence of any physical or mental defects on the part of the Player, and;
- the recent performance record of the Club including but not limited to its League standing and attendance as an indication of public acceptance.

Impermissible evidence:
- the financial position of the Player and the Club;
- press comments, testimonials, or similar material;
- offers made by either Player or Club prior to arbitration;
- the cost to the parties of their representatives, attorneys, etc.;
- salaries in other sports or occupations;
- any of the provisions of the Competitive Balance Tax.

APPENDIX 14.C: MAJOR LEAGUE BASEBALL DATA FOR 2019

Name	Team	Years	Salary	W	L	ERA	GS	IP	H	ER	BB	SO	WHIP
Alex Wood	CIN	5.123	$9,650,000	1	3	5.8	7	35.2	41	23	9	30	1.402
Gerrit Cole	HOU	5.111	$13,500,000	20	5	2.5	33	212.1	142	59	48	326	0.895
Zach Wheeler	NYM	5.098	$5,975,000	11	8	3.96	31	195.1	196	86	50	195	1.259
Michael Wacha	STL	5.062	$6,350,000	6	7	4.76	24	126.2	143	67	55	104	1.563
Sonny Gray	CIN	5.061	$7,500,000	11	8	2.87	31	175.1	122	56	68	205	1.084
Trevor Bauer	CLE	4.158	$13,000,000	11	13	4.48	34	213	184	106	82	253	1.249
James Paxton	NYY	4.151	$8,575,000	15	6	3.82	29	150.2	138	64	55	186	1.281
Kevin Gausman	ATL	4.151	$9,350,000	3	9	5.72	17	102.1	113	65	32	114	1.417
Marcus Stroman	NYM	4.148	$7,400,000	10	13	3.22	32	184.1	183	66	58	159	1.307
Jacob deGrom	NYM	4.139	$9,000,000	11	8	2.43	32	204	154	55	44	255	0.971
Kyle Hendricks	CHC	4.081	$7,405,000	11	10	3.46	30	177	168	68	32	150	1.13
Anthony DeSclafani	CIN	4.062	$2,125,000	9	9	3.89	31	166.2	151	72	49	167	1.2
Robbie Ray	ARI	4.007	$6,050,000	12	8	4.34	33	174.1	150	84	84	235	1.342
Mike Foltynewicz	ATL	3.163	$5,475,000	8	6	4.54	21	117	109	59	37	105	1.248
Noah Syndegaard	NYM	3.149	$6,000,000	10	8	4.28	32	197.2	194	94	50	202	1.234
Eduardo Rodríguez	BOS	3.13	$4,300,000	19	6	3.81	34	203.1	195	86	75	213	1.328
Steven Matz	NYM	3.099	$2,625,000	11	10	4.21	30	160.1	163	75	52	153	1.341
Vincent Velasquez	PHI	3.086	$2,249,000	7	8	4.91	23	117.1	120	64	43	130	1.389
Jon Gray	COL	3.062	$2,925,000	11	8	3.84	25	150	147	64	56	150	1.353
Jose Urena	MIA	3.04	$3,200,000	4	10	5.21	13	84.2	99	49	26	62	1.476

APPENDIX 14.D: ARBITRATION ELIGIBLE "PLAYERS"

Name	Team	Years	W	L	ERA	GS	IP	H	ER	BB	SO	WHIP
Orin Julius	BOS	2	10	6	3.66	25	140	155	57	60	210	1.536
Bugs Zappa	CHW	3	7	7	3.69	31	195	166	80	69	189	1.205
Walter Mellon	CLE	4	8	7	4.77	28	83	104	44	59	114	1.964
Gene E. Yuss	DET	5	4	10	5.87	22	112	108	73	86	178	1.732
Richard P. Cox	DET	2	12	6	2.40	27	150	84	40	42	194	0.840
Robin Banks	FLA	3	6	5	3.72	20	155	177	64	70	173	1.594
Jumbo Winks	HOU	4	10	7	1.96	32	197	165	43	56	196	1.122
Dwayne Pipe	KC	3	6	6	2.91	28	170	156	55	49	204	1.206
Chuck Waggon	LAD	4	8	5	2.90	31	189	171	61	41	154	1.122
Victor E. Lane	MIN	5	6	6	3.10	25	177	153	61	75	162	1.288
Cam Payne	MIN	3	5	10	2.71	24	136	119	41	42	176	1.184
Parker Carr	NY	4	15	6	3.64	23	126	175	51	58	135	1.849
Stan Still	NYM	4	4	8	2.47	21	120	180	33	78	234	2.150
Frankie Frank	OAK	5	7	7	3.06	31	109	152	37	72	237	2.055
Bill Loney	PHI	3	10	8	3.47	35	96	95	37	41	164	1.417
Gene Poole	PIT	5	9	8	2.44	27	166	133	45	89	236	1.337
Jim Shorts	SD	4	8	5	2.24	23	165	79	41	81	238	0.970
Zack Ramento	SEA	4	12	5	4.34	25	87	85	42	83	150	1.931
Dilbert Pickles	SF	4	4	9	2.39	29	132	126	35	44	130	1.288
Frank Enstein	TB	3	5	7	3.30	24	180	124	66	78	103	1.122

APPENDIX 14.E

Statistic		A higher value is…
W	number of wins	better
L	number of losses	worse
GS	games started	better
IP	innings pitched	better
H	hits	worse
ER	earned runs	worse
BB	base on balls	worse
SO	strike outs	better
WHIP	walks+hits per inning pitched	worse
ERA	earned run average	worse

15. Measuring productivity in Major League Baseball

Stacey Brook

INTRODUCTION

As long as I have been teaching Sports Economics, students have been interested in sports player production. This interest dramatically increased with the publication of *Moneyball* by Lewis (2003). Economists also have been interested in sports player production. Starting with Scully (1974) for Major League Baseball (MLB) and Scott, Long and Sompii (1985) for the National Basketball Association (NBA), sports league production functions have been employed to estimate player productivity. The primary motivation was to test the relationship between a player's salary and their marginal revenue product.

Blass (1992) continues this inquiry by estimating a MLB batter player production model (which he calls Runs Created) to evaluate the human capital model of investment. The Blass Runs Created model is: Runs Scored = f(Singles, Doubles, Triples, Home Runs, Non-intentional Walks, Hit Batsman, Stolen Bases, Grounded into Double Plays plus Caught Stealing, Sacrifice Flies, Outs). In Chapter 9 of *The Wages of Wins* (Berri et al. 2006, 2007), this Runs Created model is used to estimate MLB batter consistency. The activities presented in this chapter are computationally intensive and give students an introduction to how Excel is used by analysts in the real world. Therefore, the computational details are presented in appendices. An instructor may choose to demonstrate the calculations first before asking students to do these computations on their own.

For this sports economics classroom exercise, there are two types of activities one can choose: Activity 1 is for students with a knowledge of regression and advanced computational skills. Activity 2 involves basic Excel computations. Activity 1 asks students to calculate MLB batters' production based on their regression estimates of the MLB team production model. Activity 2 gives the students the marginal effects of the MLB team production function (Blass's Runs Created Model) and asks students to first calculate MLB batters' production based on the given regression estimates of the MLB team production model. Next, students are then told to calculate batters' consistency. Each activity should take close to one 50-minute class period. This can be done by the instructor or done by students with laptops or in a computer lab.

ACTIVITY 1

Before we can estimate a MLB batter's production, we first need to estimate a MLB team production function. This is because the MLB team production function provides the marginal effects of the variables used to calculate the player's production. So the first step is to estimate the Runs Created Model at the team level. The Microsoft Excel details are contained in Appendix 15.A under the heading MLB Team Production. Next given the estimates from the Runs Created Model, students can quickly calculate the batter's estimated production. These details are also contained in Appendix 15.A under the heading MLB Batter's Production. Once the batters' production estimates are generated instructors may ask students what conclusions they can draw about players and their value to a team.

ACTIVITY 2

This activity is meant for students with some knowledge of Excel. Students are given the team production estimates from the previous activity. They are then told to calculate individual batters' production. Next, students are asked to rank batters and to grade them based on their ranks. These computational details are given in Appendix 15.B under the headings Top 20 MLB Batters 2009–2019 and MLB Batter Grades. Finally, students are asked to measure MLB Batters' consistency. These details are given in Appendix 15.B under the heading MLB Batter Consistency.

CONCLUSIONS

Using MLB team and player data allows one to evaluate the marginal effect of various batter statistics aggregated to the team level, and to relate them to the ability of MLB teams to score runs. One assumption we made along the way was that sports team productivity is linear (which is an excellent way to get students to think about this issue). If sports team productivity is linear, then the Blass Runs Created model can be used to evaluate individual players' contributions to team performance. Once those contributions (such as aggregate runs created) are estimated, a number of additional questions can be answered, from who is most productive to the degree of consistency in production among MLB batters. This is by no means an exhaustive list, but it does allow students the opportunity to use real world data to perform data analytics.

REFERENCES

Berri, David J., Martin B. Schmidt, and Stacey L. Brook. 2006. *The Wages of Wins: Taking Measure of the Many Myths in Modern Sport.* Stanford, CA: Stanford University Press.

Berri, David J., Martin B. Schmidt, and Stacey L. Brook. 2007. *The Wages of Wins: Taking Measure of the Many Myths in Modern Sports – Updated.* Stanford, CA: Stanford Business Books.

Blass, Asher A. 1992. "Does the Baseball Labor Market Contradict the Human Capital Model of Investment?" *The Review of Economics and Statistics*, 74: 261–268.

Lehman, Sean. 2021. Lehman's Baseball Archive. http://www.seanlahman.com/baseball-archive/statistics/. Copyright 1996–2021: http://creativecommons.org/licenses/by-sa/3.0/.

Lewis, Michael. 2003. *Moneyball: The Art of Winning an Unfair Game.* New York: W.W. Norton & Company.

Scott, Frank Jr., James Long, and Ken Sompii. 1985. "Salary vs. Marginal Revenue Product under Monopsony and Competition: The Case of Professional Basketball" *Atlantic Economic Journal*, 13(3): 50–59.

Scully, Gerald W. 1974. "Pay and Performance in Major League Baseball." *American Economic Review*, 64(6): 917–930.

APPENDIX 15.A

Classroom Activity 1: A Step-by-Step Guide

In order to estimate the Blass (1992) Runs Created model for the 2009 to 2019 MLB seasons, the classrooms/students need to have a computer[1] with internet access and Microsoft Excel – including the Microsoft Excel Analysis ToolPak add-in if you are running the regression using Microsoft Excel. To get the Analysis ToolPak add-in: choose File|Options; then choose Add-ins and under the Inactive Application Add-ins, choose Analysis ToolPak and then choose OK.

MLB team production

1. I use Lehman's Baseball Archive (Lehman, 2021). Download the following .zip file at: https://github.com/chadwickbureau/baseballdatabank/archive/master.zip, and save it to your computer desktop (or other folder), then unzip (extract) the file. Under the folder core, you will use the following two .csv files: Teams.csv and Batting.csv.

2. Open the Teams.cvs file (opens in Microsoft Excel) and add two worksheets, Team Data and Player Data. Copy the first row (variable names) of the Teams.csv file to the Team Data worksheet and the first row (variable names) of the Batting.csv file to the Player Data worksheet. Copy rows 2597 to row 2926 from the Teams.csv file to the Team Data worksheet and copy rows 91480 to row 107430 from the Batting.csv file to the Player Data worksheet. Save the Excel spreadsheet as an .xlsx file. Insert[2] three columns to the right of column Q and cut *BB* (column X), *SO* (column Y), and *CS* (column AA), and paste them to the three newly added columns.

3. We will need to add[3] the following variables by creating columns in the Team Data worksheet: *Singles* (in column U), *Outs* (in column Y), *NBB* (in column Z) and *GIDPCS* (in column AA). Additionally, two variables need to be renamed[4] when using Microsoft Excel's Add-in to run the Runs Created regression. Change the variable 2B to *Double* and the variable 3B to *Triple*.

4. All but two variables are in (or can be calculated) in the Team Data worksheet. For the two additional variables, add two more columns in the Team Data worksheet and label them *IBB* (in column AE) and (in column AF) *GIDP*.

5. Now we need to calculate the team level number of intentional walks (*IBB*). To do this insert the following formula in cell AE2: =SUMIFS(PlayerData!$R:$R,PlayerData!$B:$B,'2009-2019'!$A2,PlayerData!$D:$D,'2009-2019'!$C:$C); and calculate the team level number of

grounded in double plays (*GIDP*) by inserting the following formula in cell AF2: =SUMIFS(PlayerData!$V:$V,PlayerData!$B:$B,'2009-2019' !$A2,PlayerData!$D:$D,'2009-2019'!$C:$C). Copy and paste[5] down to the end of the 2019 season (row 331).

6. Now we need to calculate the following: *Singles* = *H* (Hits) – *Double* (Doubles) – *Triple* (Triples) – *HR* (Home Runs), which in Excel =Q2-V2-W2-X2; *Outs* = *AB* (At Bats) – *H* (Hits), which in Excel =P2–Q2; Non-intentional walks (*NBB*) = *BB* (Walks) – *IBB* (intentional walks), which in Excel =R2–AE2; and GIDPCS = GIDP (*Grounded Into Double Play*) + CS (*Caught Stealing*), which in Excel =AF2+T2.

7. To run the MLB Runs Created regression[6] in Microsoft Excel, choose Data|Data Analysis, then choose Regression and click OK. In the box that appears for the (dependent variable) or Input Y Range: O1:O331; and for the (independent variables) or Input X Range: U1:AD331. Checkmark Labels and choose OK. The regression results appear in a new worksheet (by default).

8. Alternatively, you can use STATA and open the .do file in STATA and choose Tools|Execute or CTRL D. The Blass model will run and the regression results appear in the STATA main window.

Notice the coefficient for each variable is of the correct theoretical sign and statistically significant at conventional levels.

MLB batter production
Now that the MLB Team Production coefficients are estimated, we can quickly calculate the batter's estimated production. Here are the steps to make the calculations using the MLBBlassRunsCreatedPlayerData2009-2019.xlsx Microsoft Excel file.

1. Insert two columns in column A and column B. Name them Runs Created and Aggregate Runs Created. Copy and paste the coefficients (or link from the Excel regression results worksheet) to the Player Data worksheet. (I put the variable names in cells AA2:AA11 and the corresponding coefficients in cells AB2:AB11).

2. An individual batter's production is the sum (since sports team production is linear) of the marginal effect on a co-variate times the amount of that co-variate the player accumulated during the season. Thus, for Doubles this equals the coefficient on Doubles (cell AB3) times the number of doubles the player accumulated in the season for that team (cell M2) for the first player in this worksheet. Insert the following formula in cell A2: =AB$2*(K2-L2-M2-N2)+AB$3*L2+AB$4*M2+AB$5*N2+AB$6*(I2-

K2)+AB$7*(R2-T2)+AB$8*(X2+Q2)+AB$9*P2+AB$10*U2+AB$1
1*W2. Copy and paste to the end of the data in this worksheet.

3. Some players have played for multiple teams, and since we are evaluating all players over the course of a season, we need to sum the total season production for players on multiple teams during a given season. This is simply done by entering the following formula in cell B2: =IF(E3>1,"",IF(E2=1,A2,SUMIFS (A:A,D:D,D2,C:C,C2))). Then copy and paste to the end of the worksheet.

NOTES

1. If the classroom has access to STATA, the .do file can be downloaded: https://depauledu-my.sharepoint.com/:f:/g/personal/sbrook_depaul_edu/EiYLUoLd0GpHgCaxy1sj5FYBIRJ-asZOL7jBIWx5mQ2oew?e=tV9gXh
2. Re-arranging these columns is not necessary if you are using STATA.
3. If you are using STATA, these variables are generated in the STATA .do file.
4. The Double variable is renamed (*Doub*) in the STATA .do file.
5. Or double click on the square on the bottom right of the cell.
6. This regression (using robust standard errors) is already in the STATA .do file.

APPENDIX 15.B

Activity 2: A Step-by-Step Guide

MLB batter production

Using the given MLB Team Production coefficients, we can quickly calculate the batter's estimated production. Here are the steps to make the calculations using the MLBBlassRunsCreatedPlayerData2009-2019.xlsx Microsoft Excel file.

1. Insert two columns in column A and column B. Name them Runs Created and Aggregate Runs Created. Copy and paste the given team production coefficients. I put the variable names in cells AA2:AA11 and the corresponding coefficients in cells AB2:AB11.
2. An individual batter's production is the sum (since sports team production is linear) of the marginal effect on a co-variate times the amount of that co-variate the player accumulated during the season. Thus, for Doubles this equals the coefficient on Doubles (cell AB3) times the number of doubles the player accumulated in the season for that team (cell M2) for the first player in this worksheet. Insert the following formula in cell A2: =AB$2*(K2-L2-M2-N2)+AB$3*L2+AB$4*M2+AB$5*N2+AB$6*(I2-K2)+AB$7*(R2-T2)+AB$8*(X2+Q2)+AB$9*P2+AB$10*U2+AB$11*W2. Copy and paste to the end of the data in this worksheet.
3. Some players have played for multiple teams, and since we are evaluating all players over the course of a season, we need to sum up the total season production for players on multiple teams during a given season. This is simple done by entering the following formula in cell B2: =IF(E3>1,"",IF(E2=1,A2,SUMIFS (A:A,D:D,D2,C:C,C2))). Then copy and paste to the end of the worksheet.

Top 20 MLB batters 2009–2019

Once batters' estimated production numbers are known, usually at this point, many students are interested in which player was the best in terms of an individual season production. Here are the steps to make the calculations using the MLBBlassRunsCreatedPlayerData2009-2019.xlsx Microsoft Excel file.

I created a new worksheet and calculated the Top 20 batters as follows:

1. In cell A2, type 1, highlight rows A2 to A21, then Fill|Series|Linear.
2. Label cell B1 =PlayerData!C1; cell C1 =PlayerData!D1; cell D1 =PlayerData!F1; and cell E1 =PlayerData!B1.

3. Insert the following formulas: in cell B2
    =VLOOKUP($E2,PlayerData!$B$2:$Z$15952,2,FALSE); in cell C2
    =VLOOKUP($E2,PlayerData!$B$2:$Z$15952,3,FALSE); in cell D2
    =VLOOKUP($E2,PlayerData!$B$2:$Z$15952,5,FALSE) and in cell E2
    =LARGE(PlayerData!B:B,A2). Copy cells B2 to E2 down to cells B21
    to E21.

MLB batter "grades"

Berri, Schmidt and Brook (2006) use the Blass Runs Created model to estimate the consistency of MLB hitters. In order to measure consistency, the authors "graded" each MLB player for each season as follows: all players that are in the top 20% of batters in a given season are graded as "A" players, then the next highest 20% of batters in a given season are graded as "B" players, etc. In the book, the authors eliminate all batters with fewer than 100 at bats; no such elimination takes place in the steps below, but that is easily enough achieved by sorting the players in Excel. First, we must grade all the players for each season.

Here are the steps to make the grade calculations.

1. Create a new Excel worksheet called PlayerSorted and Copy|Paste Values the following variables: playerID, yearID, teamID and Aggregate Runs Created to columns C, D, E & F, respectively. Sort by yearID and then Aggregate Runs Created.
2. In cell G1, type Season; in cell G2 type 2009, highlight rows G2 to G12, then Fill|Series|Linear.
3. In cell H2, type =COUNTIF(D:D,G2) and copy and paste to cell H12. This gives the number of players by season.
4. In column A, type 1 in cell A2 and in cell A3 insert: =IF(D3=D2,A2+1,1); double click on the lower right plus sign (or copy down). This gives the yearly rank for each player for each season.
5. In column B, in cell B1 type, Grade, and in cell B2 type =IF(A2/ VLOOKUP(D2,$G$2:$H$12,2,FALSE)<=0.2,1,IF(A2/ VLOOKUP(D2,$G$2:$H$12,2,FALSE)<=0.4,2,IF(A2/ VLOOKUP(D2,$G$2:$H$12,2,FALSE)<=0.6,3,IF(A2/ VLOOKUP(D2,$G$2:$H$12,2,FALSE)<=0.8,4,5)))) Then copy down to the end of the player data (double click the black lower right plus in cell B2 makes this easy). These are the player's season grades.

Now all the players have a grade and we can formally investigate the degree of consistency (by grade) that MLB batters have from one season to another.

MLB batter consistency

Berri, Schmidt and Brook (2006) use the Blass Runs Created model to estimate the consistency of MLB hitters. The authors then take each player's production and compare season to season grades to determine the number of players that are consistently graded from one season to the next. Admittedly, this is a rather ad hoc measure of consistency, but it is one easily calculated in Excel.

Here are the steps to make the consistency calculations.

1. In a new worksheet, highlight columns B to F in the Players Graded work-sheet and copy and paste values to columns A to E in this new worksheet. Sort by playerID and then yearID.
2. I typed the following headers: Grade in cell G1; Player in cell H1; Season in cell I1; Team in cell J1 and Agg. Runs Created in cell K1.
3. In cell G2 type =IF($B2=$B3,IF($C2+1=$C3,A3,"")," ") and copy to cell K2, then copy down to the end of the player dataset.
4. In cell M1, type Consistency and in cell M2 type =IF(G2="","", IF(A2=G2,1,0)); in cell N1, type Near Consistency and in cell N2 type =IF(G2="","",IF(A2+1=G2,1,0)); in cell O2 type =IF(G2="","", IF(A2-1=G2,1,0)). Then copy and paste down to the end of the dataset.
5. Finally, we can calculate the number of players that were consistent from one season to the next, the number of players that moved up one grade and the number of players that moved down one grade (we could do more, but I think this is enough). To do this, in cell R2 through cell R6, type 1 to 5. In cell S2 type =COUNTIFS(M:M,1,$G:$G,$R2) and copy over to cell U2 and then copy those three cells down to cells S6 to U6.

16. Teaching marginal revenue product using *Moneyball*

Dustin White and Jadrian Wooten

TEACHING WITH *MONEYBALL*

The popularity of Michael Lewis's *Moneyball* segued into a feature film of the same title starring Brad Pitt as Billy Beane.[1] Not only is this one of the top-rated movies for teaching economics (Mateer, O'Roark, & Holder, 2016), the subject is also one of the pre-eminent sports economics examples, and it is familiar to many students before enrolling in class. The film was nominated for six Academy Awards, including Best Picture and has been referenced in popular television shows such as *The Simpsons* and *Brooklyn 99*.

The use of media in the classroom has increased in prominence over the past two decades due in part to the ability to better integrate video clips in the economics classroom (Picault, 2019; Hoyt & McGoldrick, 2019). Online resources have made it easier to identify television and film clips (Wooten, 2018) or to use popular press books (Wooten & Smith, 2018). (Check out Chapter 9 in this volume for a discussion on incorporating popular media into the sports economics curriculum.) Baseball and *Moneyball* have been used to teach courses in statistics (Wang, 2007), human resource management (McHugh, 2009), and economics (Wooten & White, 2018). Baseball is generally popular among undergraduates from the United States, Korea, Japan, and Central America, to the extent that references using *Moneyball* as a tool for economic analysis may enhance student learning by addressing an area of common student interest.

We summarize a project that uses *Moneyball* techniques to teach marginal revenue product. This approach has been used in principles of microeconomics, labor economics, and sports economics courses. Each course has a modified version of the project to account for prerequisite knowledge of statistics or econometrics. This project could also be altered to cover topics in statistics, econometrics, or managerial economics. In addition to the written project, we have developed an online simulator that allows instructors to simulate a baseball season and postseason by using the *Moneyball* technique. All resources described below, and an online simulator, are available at no cost to students or faculty.

MARGINAL REVENUE PRODUCT

Moneyball is an excellent context for teaching marginal revenue product (MRP) because it is conceptually similar to the process covered in many textbooks. In the film, Peter Brand states that he sees systematic misunderstandings by baseball teams of the most valuable traits for baseball players to possess. This generates an opportunity for the Oakland Athletics (a small market team with low revenue relative to teams from larger markets) to sign specific groups of players that are undervalued by other teams to less expensive contracts than an efficient market would allow.

The film version of *Moneyball* emphasizes the fact that the Oakland Athletics value getting on base more than other franchises, showing Billy Beane (the General Manager) constantly reminding players that it is more important to get on base than to sacrifice bunt or steal bases or do anything else that might be popular among baseball players but does not lead to efficient scoring outcomes. This is initially a source of conflict among the coaching staff and can be used to introduce principle–agent problems as well.

Marginal revenue product is often taught in a two-step approach, and the project takes the same two-step approach. The value of a worker (baseball player) to a firm (team) is based on the additional revenue they produce. This component is based on the worker's productivity (marginal product) and on the value of the product being produced (marginal revenue). Any changes to those two items will change the value of the worker to the firm. If a worker is more productive, like a baseball player generating more runs, their marginal revenue product increases. If the price of the product being sold, like tickets to a baseball game, increases then the value of workers increases as well.

In competitive markets, workers are paid the marginal revenue product of the last worker hired. This assumption does not hold outside of the economics classroom, especially in baseball labor markets. Often, students are taught that workers will be paid based on their marginal revenue product. If a worker is being underpaid at one firm, but can generate more money at another firm, they will leave and work for the higher paying firm. This type of analysis is presented in the baseball labor market as a player leaving their team to seek other opportunities through free agency, to be paid closer to their marginal revenue product.

THE PROJECT

The project does not require intimate knowledge of baseball or even econo-metrics, but some familiarity with aspects of the game can help students move through the project without feeling lost in the details of the game. Students collect data from the most recent, complete season in Major League Baseball, manipulate the data through a variety of calculations, create a series of scat-terplots using the data, and then analyze the results of trendlines to make predictions on player value. After completing the project, students will be able to articulate the intuition behind marginal product and marginal revenue, describe the process of calculating marginal revenue product, and be able to describe the relationship between two variables (actual salary and predicted salary) based on a correlation coefficient.

Students collect data from a variety of secondary sources and organize their data in a spreadsheet (either Excel or Google Sheets). All calculations and graphs are contained in this single file.[2] Students must be mindful of how data are presented online, how that information is transferred to their spreadsheet, and how attention to detail is important given their small sample size. Once the initial data set is created, students calculate ticket revenue using attendance and ticket price data, and then create an index of performance based on the work of Hakes and Sauer (2006). This index is used for estimating marginal revenue for teams and players.

Students estimate marginal revenue by using trendline equations comparing the performance index and ticket revenue for the previous season. The slope of the trendline represents the change in a team's revenue following a 1-point increase in the performance index. An improvement in team performance usually results in increased revenue for the team through additional ticket sales. The project starts with an analysis at the team (firm) level first, then moves on to valuing a roster of free agents. The same performance index is calculated at a player level, but modifications are made to extract the concept of marginal product. All available free agents are compared against a baseline player nicknamed the "Mendoza Player."[3] To identify a particular player's impact, students measure the player's performance index relative to a Mendoza player.

The written project ends after students combine their analysis of marginal revenue and marginal product to estimate the marginal revenue product that a particular player brings to a team over a Mendoza Player. Because the marginal revenue calculation looks at team level performance, the marginal product calculation for the players should consider that the firm (the team) is looking to hire only that one additional player and not a team full of those players. The marginal product estimation is divided by ten to look at the approximate impact a single player has on the overall performance of a team.

Combining these two calculations, students estimate the value of the player's performance on a generic team's ticket revenue.

All marginal revenue product estimations are scaled upward by the league minimum salary to allow the calculated value to represent an estimated salary to encapsulate the idea that workers will be paid a wage equal to their marginal revenue product. Students compare this estimation with the player's actual upcoming salary to determine if a player is under- or overvalued relative to their actual salary. Discussion usually follows the project on why a player may not be paid exactly their estimated marginal revenue product and what other areas of revenue a firm may be trying to increase besides ticket revenue. This is also a good opportunity to circle back to the notion that workers are actually paid below their marginal revenue product, which enables a firm to earn profit. If all workers were paid their marginal revenue product, the firm wouldn't earn any additional profit.

The analysis portion of the course typically brings a higher level of discussion than a traditional approach to teaching marginal revenue product because students are quick to identify a variety of different factors that are unaccounted for in the estimation. This can segue into a discussion of the assumptions in the traditional economic approach to estimating marginal revenue product or as motivation for the importance of an econometrics course.

THE SIMULATOR

An extension of the project occurs after its conclusion when students assume the role of general manager and must draft a team of free agents to compete against other teams in the class. The simulator is available to download or can be run completely online through a web application.[4] Instructors use this program to help students apply the knowledge gained in their exploration of marginal revenue product from the written project.

Students are organized into two to ten teams, and take turns drafting free agents in order to field nine players in a simulated season subject to a salary cap. The draft is completed in a snake-order and students select players for their team from a list of available free agents. Once a team reaches their salary cap, any remaining roster spots will be allocated toward a Mendoza Player. Each free agent may only be selected by a single team, but the Mendoza Player can be assigned to multiple teams.

After team rosters are complete, the program simulates a season based on the teams' relative on-base percentage and slugging average. The program allows for some randomness so that the best teams aren't guaranteed to win, but better teams are more likely to win. Once the regular season is complete, a playoff series is arranged where teams face off during the "post season."

Instructors click through each round of the playoffs and a final champion is determined.

The authors typically award bonus points to the teams that perform the best in this activity, as it is closely related to a deep understanding of MRP and its implications in selecting players for their team. The simulation can take upwards of 45 minutes depending on the size of the class and the number of teams, in addition to the quality of student preparation. The longest portion of the simulation involves students selecting their players. It may be helpful for instructors to institute a 20-second "draft clock" for each team so that it progresses more quickly. Pauses are built into the simulator to allow an instructor time to stop and discuss the simulation process or to invite questions and predictions about the outcome.

ONLINE RESOURCES

All of the project instructions and pedagogy recommendations are available in the appendix of Wooten and White (2018) as well as available online at www .MoneyballSimulator.info. The resources include the original article published in the *Journal of Economics Teaching*, sample rubrics, student checklists for their paper, and additional resources that can be used to integrate *Moneyball* into the classroom including scenes from the film and teaching guides for other topics.

CONCLUSIONS

This project has been a valuable addition, not only to our sports economics courses, but also to our principles of microeconomics and labor economics course. For many of our students, this has been the only data-driven project they were required to complete entirely on their own. Students experience each step of the research process, from data collection, to analysis, to application. It has been an effective assignment to engage students at a variety of levels and the simulator provides an added joy of watching students compete over a project that they have spent a considerable amount of time working on.

ACKNOWLEDGMENTS

The authors thank Darren Grant (Sam Houston State University) for providing the basis for the initial project concept as a way to introduce a research component into his undergraduate courses.

NOTES

1.	Stefani and Albert (2011) provide a brief introduction to *Moneyball* as a film review.
2.	Ben Smith has developed a Google app that allows instructors to create collaboration spaces for students, but retain file ownership of the work. If the project is completed as a group project, consider checking out the Google App: https://bensresearch.com/software/#group
3.	Mario Mendoza was popular in baseball lore as the minimum threshold to play in professional baseball.
4.	The simulator file can be downloaded for Windows, Mac, or Linux.

REFERENCES

Hakes, J., & Sauer, R. (2006). An Economic Evaluation of the *Moneyball* Hypothesis. *Journal of Economic Perspectives, 20*(3), 173–185.

Hoyt, G., & McGoldrick, K. (2019). 50 Years of Economic Instruction in *The Journal of Economic Education. The Journal of Economic Education, 50*(2), 168–195.

Mateer, G., O'Roark, B., & Holder, K. (2016). The 10 Greatest Films for Teaching Economics. *The American Economist, 61*(2), 204–216.

McHugh, P. P. (2009). "Batter up, Student on Deck": The Utility of *Moneyball* in Management Education. *Journal of Management Education, 33*(2), 219–238.

Picault, J. (2019). The Economics Instructor's Toolbox. *International Review of Economics Education, 30*, 100154.

Stefani, R., & Albert, J. (2011). *Moneyball*: Brad Pitt, the Statistician and the Movie. *Significance, 8*(4), 185–186.

Wang, S. C. (2007). Teaching Statistical Thinking Using the Baseball Hall of Fame. *CHANCE, 20*(1), 25–31.

Wooten, J. (2018). Economics Media Library. *The Journal of Economic Education, 49*(4), 364–365.

Wooten, J., & Smith, B. O. (2018). Create Random Assignments: A Cloud-Based Tool to Help Implement Alternative Teaching Materials. *The Journal of Economic Education, 49*(3), 297.

Wooten, J., & White, D. R. (2018). An In-Class Experiment to Teach Marginal Revenue Product Using the Baseball Labor Market and *Moneyball. Journal of Economics Teaching, 3*(1), 115–133.

17. Economical sports economics classroom activities

Rodney Fort

INTRODUCTION

In this brief chapter, three "economical" sports economics teaching activities are detailed that take less than one standard 50-minute class session to run. The author has used them all in classes ranging from 50 to over 100 students many times. It is assumed here that the reader already agrees that in-class activities are useful for teaching sports economics concepts.

So, why use "economical" activities? In a lecture class primarily designed to impart a body of knowledge to many students, the opportunity costs of spending an entire lecture or more on activities are just too high (in the author's humble estimation). In terms of lost material coverage, extensive demonstrations are too expensive. Life is full of tradeoffs, and so is teaching.

The reader can rest assured that this opinion is not some inherent bias against longer activities. The author does use longer activities in smaller, problem-solving classes. In his Business Optimization in Sports, the entire class is driven by activities that also are designed to extend student spreadsheet abilities. The final project in that class is a semester-long activity, produced originally by my colleague, Stefan Szymanski, where students attempt to figure out the equilibrium talent spending in a Nash League.

The author did not invent any of the "economical" activities covered below and has only third-hand attributions. Hopefully, the reader will not mistake ignorance for insult. The "Arms Race in College Sports" activity is an application of Martin Shubik's "dollar bill game". "Overbidding for Media Rights" is adapted from a well-known winner's curse demonstration. "Griffey's Home Run Streak" adapts a coin toss demonstration of random streaks by my colleague, Wayne Joerding.

These three economical teaching activities can easily be used at the relevant point of only a portion of a single class session. Any of these activities usually takes about 20–30 minutes. Each activity also has the virtue of being as spontaneous as you wish since there is no student preparation required. Finally, there are almost no resources required to administer the activities. On two of them, you can augment your lunch money if your Department Chair and Dean allow (mine never did).

THE ARMS RACE IN COLLEGE SPORTS

This is an old activity credited to Martin Shubik. It is an auction activity designed to demonstrate situations of escalation that are (small scale) "ruinous" to at least one participant, and usually to both finalists. Students can then think whether or not this escalation logic applies to actual sports situations. The activity is useful for any ruinous escalation situation, but it seems best suited to an arms race (Shubik's original use) in sports. All arms races have expenditure increases, but not all expenditure increases are the result of an arms race!

Shubik's game gets straight to the essence of any escalation dilemma – it can be so expensive to come in second in some situations that individual rationality leads to collective ruin. It also very carefully defines what constitutes an arms race situation and demonstrates that ruin must be the consequence in the absence of tacit collusion, or outright cooperation.

However, students should not come away from the escalation activity lesson thinking advertising is always a dilemma or that every case of rising expenditure is an arms race. The "arms race" is too readily applied to situations where it would not be expected to hold. It would be gratifying to get a room full of reporters together and have them participate in this activity, repeatedly, or at least as long as it takes to wean them from the "everything is an arms race" refuge to which they seem to turn. The escalation activity makes it abundantly clear that (1) the horrible outcomes are a function of the information setting and (2) there must be inefficiency and the demise of at least one participant. Otherwise, the situation is not an arms race.

Anyway, here is the escalation activity cast as an Arms Race in College Sports demonstration. Resource requirement: A $5 bill and a bit of rehearsal beforehand. The author found it second nature after the very first use, long ago. Do not worry, it will not actually cost you anything to run the activity. The steps:

- Announce the sale of the fiver, but in order for the students to do as well as possible, there can be no talking, only concentration on what you are saying.
- Dramatic effect: Tape the fiver to the podium.
- Announce the sale of the fiver to the highest bidder and that you will also collect from the second highest bidder. No need to try to hide the "second highest bidder" part, but neither should you dwell on it or pause for very long.

- Begin the bidding at 25¢ for the fiver. Lots of hand will go up. It does not matter which, but point explicitly at the one you think raised their hand first. Keep pointing at that person and move on.
- Raise the bid to 50¢ for the fiver. Again, lots of hands will go up. Keep pointing at the previous 25¢ bidder and choose one of the many raised hands *on the other side of the classroom* for the new highest bidder at 50¢. It is important to "work opposite ends of the room, to reduce the chance for side discussion. Keep pointing at the current second highest and highest bidders and move on.
- Raise the bid to 75¢ for the fiver. Keep pointing at the previous 50¢ bidder, who is about to be second highest, and point at the new highest bidder at 75¢. Again, it helps to work opposite sides of the room. As always through the bidding, keep pointing at the current highest and second highest bidders and move on.
- Continue raising the bid in 25¢ increments. Eventually, the activity gets to the point where you are pointing at one student that has bid $4.50 and another student that has bid $4.75. Be sure you are still pointing at both of these last two students. Their names and bids may be crucial in the next step.
- Raise the bid to $5 for the fiver. Usually, the bidding pauses. If the bidding continues on past $5, it is not a big deal. Just continue on to whatever the second highest and highest bids end up being when eventually the bidding does pause. For example, this might occur at $5 and $5.25, or at $5.25 and $5.50.

Eventually, the bidding pauses. Suppose this happens at the typical point, where the high bid is $5, and the second highest is $4.75. It is time for the great reveal where two lessons are taught. First, you will enlighten the highest and second highest bidders about their predicament. Second, you will engage the class in understanding what really drives an arms race.

Use the white board and write down the name and bid of the highest and second highest bidders. Suppose Jason has bid $4.75, and Aliyah has bid $5. But Jason will bid no further, so the bidding pauses. This simple matrix demonstrates their situations to both the bidders and to the class.

Bidder	Current bid	If bidding stops	If bid another 25¢
Jason	$4.75	−$4.75	−25¢
Aliyah	$5.00	−$0	TBD

The following discussion starts the great reveal. Be especially gentle with the final two bidders since being an object lesson for their classmates may be embarrassing. Dialogue usually goes like this:

Me:	Jason, you do not wish to continue bidding?
Jason:	No, I'm finished bidding.
Me:	I just want to make sure you understand your situation. Everybody heard me say at the beginning that I was going to sell to the highest bidder and collect from the second highest bidder, right? (I motion to the class.)
Class:	Heads nod in the affirmative.
Me:	Jason, if you stop now, Aliyah gets the fiver for $5 as the highest bidder. But you will owe me $4.75 because I also am collecting from the second highest bidder, that is, you. If you increase your bid and Aliyah quits, you win the fiver for $5.25 and only lose 25¢. So, if you stop you owe me $4.75. If you bid again and Aliyah quits you only owe me 25¢. Do you see your situation? (A little matrix on the whiteboard shows bidders, current bid, position if bidding stops, position if bidding increases.)
Jason:	Yes.
Me:	Jason, do you want to bid $5.25 for my fiver?
Jason:	Yes.

I have never had anybody look forward and work back and quit at this point. It is alright if they do, since the point is still made; in retrospect, Jason would rather not be in the position of just handing you $4.75 without even the consolation of having won the bid. In any event, somebody is going to stop as second highest bidder eventually. And the explanation is always the same, "bankruptcy" versus a smaller loss. At this point, I go ahead and update the matrix on the white board:

Bidder	Current bid	If bidding stops	If bid another 25¢
Jason	$5.25	−25¢	TBD
Aliyah	$5.00	−$5.00	TBD

The dialogue continues:

Me:	Aliyah, you don't wish to continue bidding?
Aliyah:	No, I'm finished bidding.
Me:	Aliyah, I just want to be sure that you understand your situation. You are now the second highest bidder. If you stop bidding Jason gets the fiver for $5.25 as the highest bidder. But you will owe me $5 as the second highest bidder. If you bid $5.50 and Jason stops, you become the highest bidder and get the fiver for $5.50. So, if you stop now, you owe me $5. If you bid again and

	Jason stops, you will owe me 50¢. (Go ahead and put 50¢ in the bottom right box or the matrix.) Do you see your situation?
Aliyah:	Yes.
Me:	Aliyah, do you want to bid $5.50 for my fiver?
Aliyah:	Yes.

At this point in the activity, I do not subject the two bidders to any more explanation. I just go back and forth:

Me:	Jason, $5.75?
Jason:	Yes.
Me:	Aliyah, $6?
Aliyah:	Yes.
Me:	Jason, $6.25?
Jason:	Yes.

Eventually, one of them quits, and stays quit even after one last explanation of their predicament, which can also be summarized in the matrix on the white board. The activity ends. Circle their final positions on the whiteboard.

Moving on to the activity debrief, the students just witnessed both the required setting and the decision making that goes on during an arms race. The author relates that this activity has been used to explain the demise of the country formerly known as the Soviet Union after its nuclear arms race with the US. The main learning result is in *the situation* required, rather than the outcome. Coming in second must be truly tragic, and eventually at least one bidder faces "ruin", and typically both do. "Ruin" is that both end up bidding more than the prize.

It is obvious to the class that coming in second in a nuclear arms race is to be avoided. But it is time to relate their activity to a college sports example. There are numerous cool quotes out there that "college sports" suffers from an arms race (try the Drake Group, or the Knight Commission on Intercollegiate Athletics, or just Google it). But what does the activity suggest about these claims?

First, how tragic is it to "come in second"? Data available at the *USA Today NCAA Finances* annual report easily pop up the top 10 revenue FBS or D-I basketball programs. Nine of the top 10 "came in second". However, and far from tragic, the actual second place revenue typically is not far from coming in first. Even coming in tenth is nowhere near ruinous. Further, when has coming in second led to the demise of, say, an FBS program? Again, data may help, such as a display of the programs that decided at some point not to participate at the FBS level. There have been programs that stopped, but none disappeared because of "bidding to bankruptcy".

Discussion can be motivated by putting this to the students as a "what if it was you" proposition. This especially perks up the sport management students since this is a real management question. If college sports suffer an arms race, as is so well publicized, then why do university administrators continue to vie to enter the top ranks of college sports and throw themselves into that arms race? Again, a little data helps. There were 116 FBS programs in 2000. As of 2020, there are 130. Why would 14 university administrations jump willingly into the hungry jaws of an arms race? After all, everybody knows that the only way to win an arms race is to never enter one in the first place. Both Jason and Aliyah would have minimized their losses of they had recognized the arms race for what it was and just never raised their hands.

The punch line is that an arms race is a very particular explanation of a very particular situation. Coming in second must be truly tragic and, eventually, ruin must occur. If the second-place proposition is not tragic, and if we never actually observe ruin, then serious doubt is cast over the arms race claims about college sports.

OVERBIDDING FOR MEDIA RIGHTS

The origins of this activity are unknown to the author (sincerest apologies to the originator). The activity is based on the winner's curse result of overbidding for an asset. Students can then compare whether that logic is operative in sports situations. The activity is especially insightful on bidding for media rights for broadcast or streaming. This can also lead to a discussion of seemingly irrational outcomes, like the proper setting for media rights "bubbles".

Here's the winner's curse activity, cast in terms of Overbidding for Media Rights. The resource requirement is a sturdy Ziploc bag with coins of all varieties; students need to be able to see the contents. No paper money. Around $25 in change works well. It will not actually cost you anything to run the activity. In addition, there must be a means of recording names and bids. Paper reports work fine if the class is not too large. A pre-set Google Form works better since it can do all the bid collection for you, and it also sorts and creates the relevant display quickly and easily.

- Begin by holding the bag up for all to see. Announce that you are selling the bag of money to the highest bidder. If you have run the previous escalation activity prior to this, pause and make eye contact around the room. Then remind them, just the highest bidder.
- Alert the students that they need to report their name and bid. They should already have the Google Form notification. If you use paper records, let them know they need a portion of a sheet of paper, making it easy for them to share. "Name" and "Bid Amount" are all they need to provide.

- Familiarize the students with the asset. Walk around a big room so that everybody can see the bag. Ask a student to hold the bag, describe the contents, and guess its weight. The student may need some prompting. Just coins? All varieties? Mostly copper or silver? Does it weigh more or less than a 5 lb. bag of sugar?
- Students then record their bids. Try to keep chatting to a minimum; you may want to inform them that there should be no talking. Have them fill out the Google Form. You will be glad you set it up to report a spreadsheet. Alternatively, they can just write the information on a piece of paper.
- Close the bidding. If you have a Teaching Assistant (TA), it should not take even a couple of minutes to obtain the Google Forms spreadsheet and sort the bids from highest to lowest and calculate the average and median (the distribution will be skewed right). If not, it will not take you much longer. If paper reports are used, just have the students pass their bids to the aisle and collect them all. Sort through them to find the highest and lowest bids.
- Project the spreadsheet result from the podium. Students can see all bids, and easily identify the highest and lowest bids. If you use paper reports, just hold up the highest and lowest reports and announce the highest. Invariably, the winner will owe you money. After all, it is the winner's curse. Even if the bid is below the content of the bag, the lesson is still made, just not as dramatically.
- Reveal the amount in the bag, and inform the highest and second-highest bidder the amounts that they owe.

During the debrief, remind them of the history of the winner's curse, say for offshore drilling rights, and especially the information requirements – weak information about the expected value of the asset, inexperienced bidders, and competitive bidding. Walk them through these requirements as it relates to the activity itself, so they see that the winner's curse setting requirements were met for the bag of money exercise.

Discussion can be motivated by a few basic observations. Does the winner's curse setting look like what goes on in the bidding for sports media rights? Admittedly, there is competitive bidding, but does anybody know more about the true expected value of the rights than the major media providers participating in the bidding? Not likely. Are they inexperienced at this type of bidding? Certainly not, they have been doing it since sports went on the air in the 1950s. A reasonable conclusion is that just because a bid seems an outlandish sum, does not mean that it is. Remind them that even outcomes that were commonly believed to be overpayment "mistakes" paid off. The author's favorite is the entry of FOX into NFL bidding, but almost certainly there will be a growing list of examples as streaming becomes more popular.

As with the previous Arms Race in College sports activity, the punchline is that the winner's curse is a very particular explanation based on a very particular situation. There must be uncertainty over the expected value of the bag, typically inexperienced bidders (or inexperience with a process that might eventually be learned over time), and competitive bidding. If the above conditions do not describe sports media rights bidding, then there is no winner's curse. You might want to preview that they will see this same type of wrong application by observers of the player market, especially for rookies and free agents.

GRIFFEY'S HOME RUN STREAK

Finally, the author's all-time favorite, the simultaneous coin toss activity, learned from Wayne Joerding. The beauty of this activity is its simplicity in application and the fact that everything that occurs is due to random chance. Students can then apply this lesson to observed streaks in sports and wonder how much of a streak is just due to luck. Things that might appear to be the result of careful human design, can be just dumb luck (good or bad). Things that are completely random can look wonderful (for good streaks) and awful (for bad streaks). But streaks have a random component. The activity is also a simple demonstration of the fundamental problem with trying to make causal sense as an external observer.

Here is the activity in the form of "Griffey's Home Run (HR) Streak". There is both a larger class size and smaller class size approach. Resource requirement: your favorite heads/tails device. The author uses an old commemorative coin, but any coin will do. Students all need the same coin, ask the class to share if their neighbor has no coin. Or students can use their digital device to generate a random number using something like "FlipSimu" (https://flipsimu.com). Smaller classes will need a piece of paper for each student to record their streak results.

Larger Class Size

* Announce that it is time to determine the class champion in consecutive game HRs. The MLB record is eight games, shared by Ken Griffey, Jr. (630 career HRs), Dale Long (132 career HRs), and Don Mattingly (222 career HRs).
* Announce that they are a batter going to the plate, looking for a curveball or fastball. If they guess right, they hit a home run in that game. If not, they are done for the activity. And to make it a literal guess, they decide by tossing a coin. Heads = looking for fastball, Tails = looking for a curveball.

- Announce that you are the pitcher. And you have arrived at a strategy of choosing which pitch to throw by tossing a coin as well, the epitome of "mixing up your pitches". Heads = fastball, Tails = curveball. If a student hitter's coin toss matches your pitcher's coin toss, the result is a HR for that hitter in the first "game". Their streak is the number of consecutive hitter coin tosses that match our pitcher coin tosses.
- In each round representing one game, flip your coin as the pitcher. They all flip their coins as hitters. The hitters who match have a consecutive game HR "streak" of one. Repeat until the last remaining successful hitter finally ends their streak. As would be expected, there will be plenty of three-game streaks, fewer four-game streaks, and the longest hitter streak is usually from six to eight consecutive games.
- Congratulate the students with longer streaks for their obvious prowess at the plate. The best of them have matched the all-timers.

Smaller Class Size

- Announce that it is time to determine the class champion in consecutive game HRs. The MLB record is eight by Ken Griffey, Jr. (630 career HRs), Dale Long (132 career HRs), and Don Mattingly (222 career HRs).
- Announce that they will pair up and take turns being the pitcher and then the hitter.
- For their hitter turn, they are going to the plate looking for a curveball or fastball. If they guess right, they hit a home run in that game. If not, they are done for the activity. And to make it a literal guess, they decide by tossing a coin. Heads = looking for a fastball, Tails = looking for a curveball.
- For their pitcher turn, they have arrived at a strategy of choosing which pitch to throw by tossing a coin as well, the epitome of "mixing up your pitches". Heads = fastball, Tails = curveball. If the hitter toss matches the pitcher toss, the hitter is rewarded with an HR in that game. Their streak then is their consecutive game HR streak.
- Have the class pair up, one hitter and one pitcher. Have each pair toss their coins 25 times and record the longest HR streak. Then the two can reverse roles and do the same thing, remember to record the longest HR streak.
- Collect the results. Tally how many had their longest streak at two games, three games, four games, and so on.
- For a slight twist on this activity, check out Joshua Congdon-Hohman and Victor Matheson's version of this experiment in Chapter 12 of this book.

Debrief

What just happened? Remind them that everything was purely random. They have discovered that streaks occur at random. In the tail of the streak distribution, a long streak is still random. Remind them that it is human nature to want cause and effect. When we cannot find it, we hypothesize about it. And that is the most basic issue in statistical analysis – detecting an actual pattern out of randomness.

Discussion can be encouraged with a question. Since they just saw random streaks upwards of eight, how can they be confident that the historical consecutive game HR streak of eight reveals extraordinary skill or just dumb luck at guessing? You can Google "MLB consecutive game HR streaks". Information was found at The Baseball Almanac (https://www.baseball-almanac.com/recbooks/rb_hr5.shtml). This allowed the construction of the following table.

Consecutive game HR streak	Number of MLB players
2	34
3	7
4	4
5	4
6	2
7	3
8	3

Are the three players with the eight-game streak "better hitters" than those with seven-game streaks, or were they just luckier? And so, on until you get to the observation that 34 players had two-game streaks. I have also used this with another historic MLB streak, what many call the record that will never be broken, Joe DiMaggio's 56-game streak. If you create a similar table (or a histogram), it will show that DiMaggio's performance is so unlikely that it probably was only partly lucky.

The punchline takeaway is that streaks occur even in a completely random process. While it is human nature to ascribe causality, sometimes results are just blind luck. The danger of ascribing causality is the possibility of wasting scarce talent resources, spent on players who were luckier last year than observably good over a period of time.

CONCLUSION

Some lessons may be translated to students more effectively with activities than by lecturing. And even if the lessons are conveyed equally either way, activities are fun, so where is the harm in that? Of course, the answer is that any added value to students comes at a cost of time that could be spent conveying more material. This tradeoff is especially prevalent in larger lecture classes.

Three "economical" sports economics classroom activities are provided in this contribution. Shubik's escalation activity is informative in its setting for actual arms races and for assessing claims about an arms race in college sports. The winner's curse game is informative in its setting and for assessing whether or not there is such an outcome, as claimed, in bidding for sports media rights. Finally, a simple coin toss activity can impart the lessons that luck matters and that statistically assessing a process from the outside requires taking this into account.

Each of these "economical" sports economics classroom activities takes much less than an entire class period and are "tried and true" for their respective lessons, as can be vouched for by the author. They also are a good starting point if you have never used classroom activities since they have zero resource expense and can be used completely spontaneously without requiring a lot of student training.

Index

Printed and bound by CPI Group (UK) Ltd, Croydon, CR0 4YY

16/04/2025